INVENTING ANCIENT CULTURE

Inventing Ancient Culture discusses aspects of antiquity which we have tended to ignore. It asks the reader how far we have reinvented antiquity, by applying modern concepts and understandings to its study. Furthermore, it challenges the common notion that perceptions of the self, of modern societal and institutional structures, originated in the Enlightenment. Rather, the authors and contributors argue, there are many continuities and marked similarities between the classical and the modern world.

Mark Golden and Peter Toohey have assembled a lively cast of contributors who analyse and argue about classical culture, its understandings of philosophy, friendship, the human body, sexuality and historiography. To what extent have cultural systems changed or remained the same since antiquity? Are our understandings of marriage, of friendship or of romantic love really that different from those in the ancient world? *Inventing Ancient Culture* presents a wide array of positions on such questions, both from an empirical and from a theoretical angle. Usefully illustrated, it will act as an exciting introduction to new approaches in Classical Studies for both beginning and more experienced students.

Mark Golden is Professor of Classics at the University of Winnipeg. He is the author of *Children and Childhood in Classical Athens* (1990). **Peter Toohey** is Associate Professor in Classics and Ancient History at the University of New England, New South Wales. He is the author of *Reading Epic* (1992) and *Epic Lessons* (1996).

INVENTING ANCIENT CULTURE

Historicism, periodization, and the ancient world

*Edited by Mark Golden
and Peter Toohey*

London and New York

First published 1997
by Routledge
11 New Fetter Lane, London EC4P 4EE
29 West 35th Street, New York, NY 10001

Typeset in Garamond by
Ponting–Green Publishing Services, Chesham,
Buckinghamshire

Printed and bound in Great Britain by
Biddles Ltd, Guildford and King's Lynn

British Library Cataloguing in Publication Data
A catalogue record for this book is available from the
British Library

Library of Congress Cataloging in Publication Data
Inventing ancient culture: historicism, periodization and the
ancient world / edited by Mark Golden and Peter Toohey
p.   cm.
Includes bibliographical references and index.
1. Greece–Civilisation–To 146 B.C.   2. Rome–Civilisation.
3. Greece–History–To 146 B.C.–Periodization.
4. Rome–History–Periodization.   5. Social change.
6. Social evolution.   7. Social structure.
I. Golden, Mark, 1948– .   II. Toohey, Peter, 1951– .
DE59.I58   1996
938–dc20   96–14853
CIP

ISBN 0–415–09959–5 (hbk)
ISBN 0–415–09960–9 (pbk)

For
✝ Katie Rose Becker-Golden, Max Becker-Golden,
Kathleen Toohey, and Matthew Toohey

CONTENTS

CONTENTS

ILLUSTRATIONS

PLATES

CONTRIBUTORS

Phyllis Culham Department of History, US Naval Academy, Annapolis

Suzanne Dixon Department of Classics and Ancient History, University of Queensland

Mark Golden Department of Classics, University of Winnipeg

Martin Kilmer Department of Classical Studies, University of Ottawa

David Konstan Department of Classics, Brown University

Ian Morris Departments of Classics and History, Stanford University

Amy Richlin Department of Classics, University of Southern California

Christiane Sourvinou-Inwood Department of Classics, University of Reading

Barry Strauss Department of History, Cornell University

Peter Toohey Department of Classics and Ancient History, University of New England

GENERAL INTRODUCTION

Mark Golden and Peter Toohey

Time is not a solid, like wood, but a fluid, like water or the wind. It doesn't come neatly cut into even-sized lengths, into decades and centuries. Nevertheless, for our purposes we have to pretend it does. The end of any history is a lie in which we all agree to conspire.

(Margaret Atwood, *The Robber Bride*)

This book is about continuity and change and about how we reconstruct past time. Continuity and change are concepts which bedevil thought and research into Greek and Roman culture. To what extent do the major cultural and social forms change through time? To what extent have cultural systems changed or remained the same since? Do historicist approaches, which assume and argue for an 'otherness' of classical culture, and which so often argue for the *periodization* of ancient social, cultural, and affective institutions, represent workable methods for interpreting the culture of Greece and Rome? Or, by ignoring the marked similarities between classical and modern cultures (and equally within the cultures of the Greek and Roman worlds), do they *reconstruct* or even invent an ancient world that is so foreign, so completely different in its characteristics as to be near impenetrable?

A 'hoary question' indeed (as a distinguished colleague wrote in turning down an invitation to contribute to an earlier version of this book). In fact, continuity and change troubled the ancients themselves, from Parmenides and Heraclitus onwards. And the dialectic of continuity and change continues to influence many contemporary approaches to antiquity, informing periods as diverse as the Bronze Age (Deger-Jalkotzy 1988) and the fifth century of our era (I. Wood 1992). Not among scholars alone. 'Recent research seems to indicate that maybe the ancient Britons weren't even very war-like', notes a character in a Margaret Drabble novel (*A Natural Curiosity* 1989: 4). The response is sceptical. 'Really? And the figure of 60,000 Romans put to the sword by Boudicca is just a historical figment too, is it?' 'I don't know', comes the reply. 'I think that's a different period.' An alternative view is offered by another English author, Keith Richards of the Rolling Stones. Explaining his interest in the decline and fall of the Roman empire – he recently read through

1

Gibbon – he observed, 'Well, man, you're doomed to repeat it otherwise. There's continuity and there's foolishness.'

The relationship of the present to the past is as familiar as it is puzzling. We quote from two recent books, both well reviewed, quite contradictory. First, Ruth Padel (1992: 10, 12):

> How difficult, but also how rewarding, it is for us in the late twentieth century to think of the ancient Greeks as astoundingly alien from ourselves ... their daemonology and biology are very different from ours, and play a role in Greek ideas about the self that matches little in our experience.

Next, Bernard Williams (1993: 2, 166):

> I shall stress some unacknowledged similarities between Greek conceptions and our own ... [concerning] the concepts that we use in interpreting our own and other people's feelings and actions ... We are, in our ethical situation, more like human beings in antiquity than any Western people have been in the meantime.

Such startling divergences in opinion are by no means unique to the study of Greece and Rome. The European family was once thought to have undergone a radical transformation as the large household and extended network of kin gave way, with the advent of industrial capitalism, to the nuclear triad's haven in a heartless world. Then Peter Laslett and others found that the nuclear family had prevailed in pre-industrial England and endured with no great structural change in the centuries since. This new orthodoxy – the 'current fashionable historiographical stress on continuity over change' (Pollock 1987: 490) – has in turn been called into question by new work on transformations in family forms and functions in feudal Europe (Seccombe 1992), medieval and early modern England (Ravi 1993, Quinlan and Shackelford 1994) and the United States (Ruggles 1994). Paradigms in the history of emotions have undergone similar shifts (Stearns and Stearns 1988).

It's fun to speculate on the sources for these disagreements and fluctuations in fashion. At the level of individuals, Wally Seccombe (1992: 283, n.1) observes that conservatives naturally feel most comfortable foregrounding continuity; radicals foregrounding change.

Let's consider conservatives. It's not uncommon for those with privilege and with ability to believe in their capacity to communicate between different social classes – lower or higher than theirs. (Could it be that the very maintenance of privilege is based upon this felt capacity to communicate meaningfully with a variety of subordinate groups?) The ability to communicate is grounded upon cultural sameness, on continuity: so, one might argue of Greece or Rome, of twentieth-century Europe, of working or middle class, that the grassroots of human experience (love, death, families, the experience of the passing of time and of ageing itself) remain much the same

2

between different age groups, between different sexes, eras, classes, between different ethnic groups, different nations, and different periods. All that varies is the way these basic experiences are culturally packaged. It is wrapping paper – the *outward* expression of the unchanging psychic modes of human experience – that provides the difference. The communication of the privileged taps instinctively into this psychic continuity and speaks meaningfully across divides.

But such a capacity to communicate is not something readily accepted by all. Those groups less sure of their access to privilege and ability (women, racial minorities, the disabled, the aged, children), those very groups who may have been, or may still be subservient to the privileged élite, are not always quite so sure either of their ability to be understood or of their ability to communicate with dominant groups. Faced with miscomprehension, there has been a tendency for such groups, in their understandable frustration, to deduce that their discourse is self-referential and incomprehensible outside their group. They may even feel that this incomprehensibility places on them a type of cultural aphasia. Such aphasiac exclusion is not always tolerated. When it is not, it is an easy step, utilizing this very incomprehensibility as a political lever, to insist upon the uniqueness of their own voices and to require that their voices, perceived as separate from those of the ruling élite, receive privilege. Uniqueness, otherness, becomes the characterizing quality of the 'disenfranchised'. Otherness, charted through time, leads to the registering of periodicity and change.

The distinction between continuity and change, conservatives and radicals, is only approximate. Golden's (1988) stress on continuity in his conclusion that parents in other times generally cared for their children and were deeply affected by their deaths was not rooted in reactionary essentialism. It was in large part a response to the propaganda of the Vietnam war, in which Western misgivings about the wholesale slaughter of civilians were mollified by appeals to Oriental fatalism, beliefs in the afterlife, the insignificance of the individual elsewhere. It may be more prudent (and less irksome to those who have walked picket lines with Seccombe in the past) to ascribe historians' outlooks in regard to continuity and change to nothing more telling than temperament, and to let it go at that (cf. Strauss 1993a: 92–93).

We are no more inclined to offer explanations of change in emphasis within whole fields of study. It does seem, however, that recent developments in the humanities, sciences, and social sciences combine in making the question of continuity and change more urgent. We single out three here: the work of Michel Foucault, the New Historicism, and non-linear dynamics.

Historicism first: such approaches in Classical Studies have become ever more prevalent since the mid-1980s. The remarkable enthusiasm which greeted Winkler's (1990b) and Halperin's (1990) work offers the most striking evidence. The type of historicism that they practise, one that privileges the periodization of sexuality, thus the change between the ancient and modern worlds – but not within the ancient world itself – differs markedly from the empathetic, intuitive, 'imaginative' historicism of a Dilthey (Gardiner 1961: 29), a Croce (Gardiner 1961: 29), or a Collingwood (1946: 218); or, in Classics, from such empathetic approaches as are reflected in the work, say, of a Wilamowitz-Moellendorff (1922 – cf. Young 1964), a Snell (1953), a Jaeger (1945), or even a Bowra (1964).

How does this 'new' historicism differ from the older variety? The earlier brand stressed as crucial a belief in the uniqueness of historical phenomena. The 'old' historicists maintained that each age should be interpreted in terms of its own ideas and principles and that the actions of people of the past should not be interpreted by reference to the beliefs, motives, and valuations of the historian's own epoch. We could take things a little further. In traditional historicist works devoted to Classical Studies, the spirit of the age, the *Zeitgeist*, resided above all in poetry, in Homer (Snell 1953), or Pindar (cf. Young 1964), and usually in so-called poetic masterworks. There tended to be, in such work, a focus on one or another canonical narrative whose poetry was felt to reflect or express or illustrate a crucial stage in human consciousness. Such narratives grounded the historical critic's interpretation of specific narrative or poetic acts, and, beyond these, of the era itself (so Fränkel 1975).

It has been argued that such traditional historicism expressed itself, at least as far as literary texts are concerned, in three main ways. First, the metaphysical or transcendental, where the literary text is seen as the expression of the moment 'in the unfolding narrative of history' and as 'the self-realization of the absolute'. Second, there is the naturalistic: here the literary text becomes the medium through which the scientific historian imagines himself or herself into another era. Third, there is the nationalistic, in which the literary work is seen as expressing the native spirit of a given culture (Wayne 1991). We might add, as a rider to these basic types of historicist research, that practitioners of traditional historicism all seem to have believed in the efficacy of human subjects as agents of historical change. This is crucial, for it implies, in the literary sphere, that writers write, as it were, their own texts.

What of the new variety of historicism? 'New Historicism', despite its name, is essentially a mode of literary criticism (Veeser 1989; compare Cox and Reynolds 1993 and B. Thomas 1991). Where it intersects with Historical Studies is in its concern that literary texts should be based in an appropriate historical milieu. The milieu favoured by this type of analysis is often what we might associate with sociology or anthropology or the historians of mentalities (cf. Lloyd 1990). New Historicism could never be accused of being apolitical (Himmelfarb (1992: 15) terms it 'a linguistic version of Marxism which interprets "cultural productions" as symbolic forms of "material productions" and "social relations"'; cf. Saul 1992). Spawned of the generation of the 1960s and early 1970s it is, in its politics, patently left-leaning and frequently aiming at social amelioration (Veeser 1989). It comes as no surprise that New Historicism, in most of its contexts, is concerned above all with the analysis of the exercise of power within societal relations. Such a theme, then, is traced in its representations through a variety of genres, or as they may be termed, discourses. A given, for the New Historicist, is that 'discourses' are permeable – a particular way of formulating knowledge, that is, may be evident in, for example, discourses such as law, theology, literature, art, medicine, and so forth (so Foucault 1970 or Laqueur 1990; compare Padel 1992, Dougherty 1993, and Dougherty and Kurke 1993). The New Historicist is as concerned with non-canonical texts (say the Greek novelists) as with the canonical (like Homer – cf. Winkler 1990b or Goldhill 1995). The result of such an analysis of discourse tends to establish a discrete sequence of ways of formulating experience – a periodization. Put simply, this can mean that, for example, the Roman literary attitude to love differs radically from that of the Renaissance, and that in turn from the modern (cf. Veyne 1978). Between such discursive formulations, furthermore, there exists no necessary cause and effect or linear relationship. It follows that the author, as controlling force behind his or her text, is dethroned. Discourse shapes subjectivities.

We could summarize the tendencies of this New Historicism under three points. First, truth (the aim of scholarly research) is not a timeless, abstract quality. Rather it is meaning constructed in and by a particular discourse which is, of course, substantiated in a particular historical period. Second, language, reflective of discourse, is not a timeless, transparent medium. It too is shaped by the historical pressures exerted upon discourses. Third, the individual (the subject) is not in charge of things. She or he does not necessarily enquire and choose freely. The 'subject' is as subject to the pressures of history, of discourse, and the unconscious as are discourse and language themselves. These three points, as we hope is obvious, demonstrate the importance which this new form of historicist analysis places upon change.

We may now turn to flag the writings of Michel Foucault (upon whose work so much New Historical work is based). His work is sufficiently well known within and without Classics not to require detailed comment here (Goldstein 1994; and especially Cohen and Saller 1994). His theories on the cultural relativity, on the *archaeology* of sexuality (Foucault 1978, 1985, 1986) have received their most popular application to Greek and Roman antiquity in the work of David Halperin (1990, cf. 1995; compare Goldhill 1995 and Konstan 1994b). Here we might stress just three points. Foucault, up until *The Archaeology of Knowledge* (1972), examined persistently the interrelations of a variety of discourses (economics, medicine, and linguistics, for example, in *The Order of Things*, 1970) and how these discourses exhibit change. This form of discursive analysis has proved less influential in modern analysis of change. After *The Archaeology of Knowledge*, Foucault's focus moved to such non-discursive practices (practices, that is, which are not necessarily embodied in textual form) as imprisonment and sexuality (Foucault 1977, 1978, 1986).

His concern there was to unmask the operation of power within these systems, but of course from a historical perspective which takes full account of periodization (Gutting 1994). A major concern of the New Historicist, as we have seen, is the operation through time of power.

Our third point concerning Foucault flows from these two. Foucault, chameleon-like in his output, means different things to different people. It may be that Foucault's most lasting, if least satisfactory influence will be as an exponent of the antipsychiatry movement of the 1960s: *Madness and Civilization* (1967), Foucault's first major book (which argued for a change in the concept of madness dating from the European Enlightenment), appeared abridged in English in a collection supervised by the late R.D. Laing. But Foucault's appeal has not been limited to his attacks on psychiatry and the 'helping professions' (Taylor 1989: 508; compare Foucault 1973). Legal theorists may use *Discipline and Punish* (1977) in an attempt to picture how the self (emerging in its modern formulation during the eighteenth century) has been constructed through relations of power and modes of discipline, namely law. New Historicists, as we have just seen, may also focus on those of Foucault's writings that examine the play of power within social and cultural institutions. Activists concerned with Gay or Queer Studies turn to *The History of Sexuality* (1978, 1985, 1986) because it offers a more egalitarian and liberating model of sexuality: one that allows culture to determine sexuality and the type of sexuality to be valued in a particular society, rather than some unchanging aspect of human nature (it is a model based on an abrupt change in the concept of sexuality – sexuality was, through much of antiquity, defined by power; in late antiquity this model was superseded by one based on gender). Classical scholars, taking the lead from Gay Studies, also focus on *The History of Sexuality*. Their concern, it follows, is less with discourse, archaeologies, antipsychiatry, or the play of power within institutions, than with the explanations Foucault offers for the prevalence of homoeroticism in ancient society, its link with active and passive amatory imagery, with the emergence of the dominating role of heterosexual love in late classical culture. It is noteworthy that classicists frequently complain that Foucault's analysis is excessively directed towards male experience, and that it is based on too small a sample of ancient evidence (see Richlin's and Kilmer's essays here (chapters 1 and 2) and cf. Narducci 1985).

We note one other adaptation of Foucault's work (among the many competing). This is neatly stated and exemplified by Ian Hacking (1986 and 1995: 198ff.). Hacking bases his analysis of selfhood on the distinction made in *The Archaeology of Knowledge* (1972) between *savoir* and *connaissance*. *Savoir* (Hacking also terms it 'depth knowledge') may be defined as a body

of elements that would have to be formed by a discursive practice if a scientific discourse was to be constituted, specified not only by its form and rigour, but also by the objects with which it deals, the types of enunciation [roughly, statements] that it uses, the concepts that it manipulates, and the strategies that it employs.

This depth knowledge, suggests Hacking, 'is more like a grammar, an underlying set of rules that determine, in this case, not what is grammatical, but what is up for grabs as true-or-false'. *Connaissance*, or 'surface knowledge', is concerned with items that are counted as true or false. Hacking, therefore, is not concerned with power, nor especially with institutions, but with the way a discipline or belief or practice may reflect a deeper set of rules (a 'grammar') which may be applicable to other disciplines, beliefs, or practices (psychiatric practice and belief, for example, may reflect a 'grammar' that is enunciated in, say, contemporary economics). Hacking is interested in the way that a *savoir*, typical of some of the areas of nineteenth-century thought, may change or be rewritten into the twentieth century. He believes that in the nineteenth century the soul became scientized and that the very concept of soul was transformed into the neutral notion of memory – on to which subject so much therapeutic and often moralistic attention is now directed. Such a concern with the archaeology of emotional states is, of course, predicated upon change.

'Non-linear dynamics', the third recent development to intensify interest in continuity and change, refers to a group of new approaches: to the modelling and understanding of complex natural and social processes – chaos theory, fractal geometry, and non-equilibrium thermodynamics in particular. Some of this work has analogues in postmodern thought, in Foucault and Derrida (Hayles 1989) and in Bourdieu (Dyke forthcoming); much may have important implications for economists, philosophers, cultural critics, and students of social policy (see, e.g., Dyke 1988, Stone 1989, Argyros 1991, Steenburg 1991, Eigenauer 1993, and Smith 1995). Two elements are of special interest to historians. First, non-linear dynamics reverses the onus of Newton's laws of motion. A main feature of Newtonian mechanics is that bodies remain at rest or in motion at a constant rate and in the same direction unless they are subject to some kind of force. In this model, continuity is regarded as the norm, and change requires some explanation. In non-linear dynamics, however:

> it turns out that the world as a whole is far from in equilibrium, as are most regions of the world ... the picture that must emerge to recommend itself to our intuitions is one of the world in a constant flux, with change the norm, and any lasting sameness the result of very special local conditions maintained at cost ... The strong presumption is that [this] is also true of social systems.
>
> (Dyke 1990: 373, 385)

Change and decay in all around we see – and if not, *why* not? Second, non-linear dynamics insists on what is called sensitivity to initial conditions: very small changes in the baseline of a dynamic system can be magnified exponentially over a system's history. Tiny variations in the starting direction or velocity of two pendulums can produce utterly different patterns in their paths; the actions of a single individual can have momentous and unpredictable consequences in an unstable social system. Charles Dyke adduces the late Roman republic as an example of such an unstable society (Dyke 1990: 383). However, this perspective has yet had little impact upon professional students of antiquity. Among exceptions we note here two articles by a contributor to this book, Phyllis Culham: one draws on chaos theory to examine the causes and courses of catastrophe in Greek and Roman battles (Culham 1989); the other analyses the defence-in-depth strategies of the ancient Celts and Romans as self-constructing fractal structures (Culham 1991).

The essays composed for this volume aim to reconstruct the past from a variety of perspectives, but all of them informed by the issues of continuity and change. Sexuality is treated by Kilmer, an art historian, who tests the ancient iconographic representations of pederasty, and by Richlin, a specialist in Latin literature, who looks at body history, gender, and sexuality. Dixon and Golden, both social historians, sceptically examine change and continuity within the institutions of the ancient family. Religion and change is discussed by Christiane Sourvinou-Inwood, who focuses on Eleusis and its mysteries. Barry Strauss concentrates on periodization from a historiographical perspective; Ian Morris examines the periodization of the Greek Dark Ages from the archaeologist's trench; and Phyllis Culham's feminist critique challenges a prevalent classical periodization. And finally, ancient emotional attitudes and their 'archaeologies' are examined by Konstan (from the philosopher's point of view), and by Toohey (from the perspective of cultural criticism). The varied approaches to these varied domains we hope will highlight some of the most important problems facing classicists today: What are the tools which we can bring to bear to interpret the past? What ideologies are helpful in this reconstruction? How *do* we reconstruct the past? To what extent do ancient cultural and social forms persist within antiquity and onwards into modern history? Should we value change or continuity?

It remains for us to thank our benefactors. First partners (Monica and Phyl) and children (our change and continuity, their names are in the dedication). Then institutions. A travel grant from the Arts faculty of the University of New England (Armidale, Australia) brought Golden to Armidale to plan this book. The Classical Association of Canada allowed some of our contributors to present a draft of their chapters at a special session of its 1994 gathering in Calgary. We are grateful for the considerable help provided us by the audiences there. The Department of Classics at the University of Toronto and its head, Emmet Robbins, provided us with space to meet and work in late January, 1995. The Universities of New England and Winnipeg have helped both editors with grants to assist in the completion of this book. Richard Stoneman and the staff at Routledge have been, as always, sympathetic, patient, and discreetly encouraging.

The following individuals and organizations have kindly allowed us to reproduce photographs of material from their collections: The British Museum; Deutsches Archäologisches Institut, Athens; K.J. Dover; Fondazione per il Museo Claudia Faina; the Getty Museum; the Louvre; Museen Preussischer Kulturbesitz; Museo Nazionale di Villa Giulia; Princeton University Press.

Part I

ANTIQUITY AND THE ENLIGHTENMENT: INVENTING THE PRESENT

INTRODUCTION

Whether it is bodies or boredom (Laqueur 1990, Spacks 1995), there is a tendency these days for those interested in the broader field of Cultural Studies to claim that modern perceptions of self (Taylor 1989), modern affectivities (Ariès 1981, Foucault 1978, 1985, 1986), modern societal and institutional structures (Ariès 1962 and 1981, Foucault 1967, 1973, 1977) date from the century beginning with the Enlightenment (compare Saul 1992). The basis for this claim is usually said to be empirical: modern formulations of these matters could not be found before this period. This is an empiricism backed up alarmingly by common sense. The loosening of the ecclesiastical control over society, the weakening of the powers of the European aristocracy, the emergence of a bourgeoisie based on a vigorous mercantile economy, the Industrial Revolution and the empowerment it provided to new social classes, the philosophical and economic championing of reason that flowed from these social changes, all of these forces combine to create a world that more obviously resembles our own than anything that preceded. The mentality of this new world seems to match that of our own.

The five chapters of this first part of our book all confront, directly or indirectly, this pervasive, over-simple, and unhistorical notion. The Enlightenment may indeed have been marked by great discursive and institutional change. But to claim that modern societal institutions and modern formulations of many affective states have their first appearances, even their discovery here is to misrepresent history.

The first chapter concerns body history. When does the modern concept of the body begin? Amy Richlin in her 'Towards a history of body history' (Chapter 1) maintains that many contemporary attitudes to both gender and sexuality are to be found in Roman literature. Following on from Foucault, many scholars (Halperin 1992 and Winkler 1992, for example) have argued that antiquity had a one-sex model (sexual status was defined by power: by who penetrates and who is penetrated) and that the two-sex model is something of very recent provenance (Laqueur 1990). Richlin maintains that there is ample evidence to support a two-sex model in antiquity. That this evidence has been ignored is in part a reflection of the marginality of Classical

Studies within the universities and in part the result of a desire of the disempowered to seek in the past a better, liberating vision.

Martin Kilmer in 'Painters and pederasts: Ancient art, sexuality and social history' (Chapter 2) offers some support for Richlin's revisionism. Kilmer examines the representation of homoerotic relationships on Greek black-figure vases. He concludes that the generalizations made by Dover (1989 [1978]), Foucault (1978, 1985, 1986), Halperin (1990), and Winkler (1990b) are too broad. Kilmer makes two points. First he argues that they privilege the male homoerotic relationships represented in literature by Plato and in art by fifth-century red-figure vase painters. In these the younger, passive partner is pursued by the older, active partner; the relationship is ennobling for the young man, but he ought not to display erotic pleasure in it; he should on maturity take on an 'active' sexual role. But they provide only part of the story. Kilmer maintains that the distinction between young and old, active and passive is not rigidly adhered to in black-figure painting, the form that immediately preceded red-figure. Kilmer's second point is that the popular view which maintains that Athens pursued the one-sex model is too general-ized and is contradicted by some black-figure vases. Kilmer thus (here we should compare Richlin's conclusions) argues for a continuity between modern notions of sexuality and those of black-figure painting, but also argues that change exists between red-figure and black-figure representations of homoerotic acts.

Eros, one expression of sexuality, is also important within Peter Toohey's argument (Chapter 3: 'Trimalchio's constipation: Periodizing madness, eros, and time'). Like Richlin and Kilmer, Toohey is interested in how culture shapes institutions, concepts, and emotional states. He looks at three seem-ingly independent entities – madness, eros, and time – and attempts to link the three into a discursive whole. Toohey argues that the lineaments of the modern views of these cultural constructs are to be found in ancient literature, above all in the texts of the first century of our era. But Toohey's case, like Kilmer's, does allow for change. The 'modern' views (privileging above all a type of affective passivity) are indeed invented, but in this period.

Not sexuality, nor eros, but the calmer emotion of friendship is David Konstan's topic (Chapter 4: 'Philosophy, friendship, and cultural history'). Konstan's elegant argument explains first how modern concepts of friendship (which includes qualities such as self-disclosure, personal intimacy, sincerity, sympathy, informality, openness, voluntariness of association) have been traced primarily to the rise of commodity capitalism in the century following the Enlightenment. Konstan urges that ancient friendship also reflects its cultural context. Friendship for Aristotle is conditioned by the values of the democratic polis of the fifth and fourth centuries. Thus the concept can reflect the modern form of friendship ('a voluntary, informal, intimate, and ex-pressive relationship'), but it can also refer to 'any type of reciprocal love, including that within the family or larger community'. A more particularized and private concept of friendship – one mirroring the modern form – emerged during the third century BCE in response to the emergence of Hellenistic kingship: there too developed 'a new discourse of friendship as a private and personal bond that was . . . independent of and conceptually distinct from the sphere of civic obligations in a more radical way than that which characterized the democratic polis.'

Love, affection, and friendship within the Roman family provide the focus for Suzanne Dixon's paper (Chapter 5: 'Continuity and change in Roman social history: Retrieving "family feeling(s)" from Roman law and literature'). Dixon presents a profoundly sceptical view. Examining the evidence for 'family feelings', she comes to challenge 'the very quest for a historical narrative – that is, a story of change' (cf. now Saller 1994: 4–8, 231–32). Dixon believes that the evidence for such emotions is too vague and too contradictory for us to chart change nor, and this is as important, can one posit continuity. Thus, although Dixon's position provides a sharp challenge to the arguments of Richlin, Kilmer, Toohey, and Konstan, that change and continuity can be mapped both within antiquity and between antiquity and the modern world, it likewise tends to render false, by implication, claims by those who would locate affective and familial change within the Enlightenment or later.

Why has this faith in change so dominated so many disciplines during the last two decades and caused them to valorize the Enlightenment and to downplay the importance of Greek and Roman culture? We think that Richlin has part of the answer. She states that people who study body history, for example, have no one in Classics to talk to. In the major US research universities, Women's Studies, Gay Studies, and body history, were or are not a part of Classics department programmes. When colleagues in other departments came to research topics which might loosely be termed Cultural Studies (for a useful, if hostile discussion of this designation, see Collini 1994), they found that they had no classicists to talk to. What else could they conclude but that, for the study of the history of cultural institutions and affectivities, Classical Studies were of no importance? We also suspect that the focus on the Enlightenment and after offers an easy way out for both individuals (who are thus excused from extensive researches in earlier periods, with their many linguistic and other challenges) and for institutions. These are provided with a convenient rationale for the neglect or excision of programmes no longer deemed relevant for the modern world.

1

TOWARDS A HISTORY OF BODY HISTORY[1]

Amy Richlin

'We ... I', said Leslie that night, 'need to understand how the scream of Dachau is the same, and how it is a different scream from the scream of Hiroshima. And after that I need to learn how to listen to the selfsame sound that rises out of the Hell in which the torturer is getting what he's got coming.'

(Lore Segal, 'The Reverse Bug')

The human body has more often been the subject of comedy than of history. Let me start from a text – one often appealed to as originary – about origin texts. In Plato's *Symposium*, Plato makes the comic playwright Aristophanes into a character in the dialogue and has him define love by telling a mythic origin story about ludicrous huge blobby human beings who lived before the separation of the sexes. Although 'Aristophanes' tells his history of bodies in all seriousness, it is a funny story, entirely appropriate to be put in the mouth of Aristophanes as a character in a story; and indeed Aristophanes in the *Symposium* represents comedy, as the ending of the dialogue clearly shows. There Socrates (philosophy) drinks the last of his fellow guests under the table – first comedy (Aristophanes), then tragedy (Agathon) – in the course of making them admit that the same man could write both comedy and tragedy. The other characters' descriptions of love are much more abstract, less embodied, than Aristophanes' – even the speech of the doctor, Eryximachus, who moves up to take Aristophanes' turn in the lineup when the comedian is overcome by a case of hiccups (the comedian thus embodying the comic body). In the West, bodies have been discussable only in certain kinds of discourse: comedy, horror stories, pornography, medicine.[2] But history has rarely been a language for talking about bodies. Today it seems as if that is changing, and the 'history of the body' and the 'history of sexuality' seem to be turning into recognized fields of history. What is this 'body history'? Why has it begun now, and why does it look as it does? And what does the study of Greek and Roman sexualities have to contribute to body history, and to questions of continuity and change?

Certainly it is possible to take bodies seriously. The epigraph to this essay, from Lore Segal's parable 'The Reverse Bug', suggests how rooted body

16

history is in the specific agonies of the twentieth century; and (hence?) how embroiled it is in moral and epistemological issues. Dachau and Hiroshima unsettle the notion of the impartial historian. Segal's image of a vocabulary of screams, understood by a listener, as both similar and different, I here borrow to represent the history of bodies, studied by scholars, who argue vigorously over whether those bodies are similar or different. Body history itself constitutes a deliberate change; graduate seminars in Classics, for example, used to study the Peloponnesian war or the constitution of Athens and *not* bodies. This change is not arbitrary, but stems from a belief or hope that the study of what was abjected can promote or participate in general social change. In an earlier essay (Richlin 1993b) I talked about what is at stake for people who focus on continuity and similarity versus people who focus on change and difference. But both groups are listening to screams; they are united at some point by their consciousness of human suffering and their urge to end it. They are also listening to screams in another sense: they have chosen to write a history of what other historians have found unintelligible. In this essay, I shall be talking about what I know best, the history of the body as sexual, gendered, and marked; a full history of body history would have to include as well a survey of writing on food, excrement, race, the care of the self, clothing, hair, gesture, and death. Hence the 'Towards' in the title.

BODY HISTORY: WHAT IS IT?

This essay condenses into a small space many arguments I have made previously, and must provide a similarly condensed overview of the field as a whole. The reader should add boiling water (or read more) to get the whole *bouillon*.

Writers of body history might be divided into three main groups, with overlaps: historians, feminists, and classicists.

Most visible as pure body historians, so to speak, have been Americans coming out of the *Annales* school and the Berkeley New Historicists (on whom, see Veeser 1989). The American *Annalistes*, whose published work preceded that of the New Historicists, include Natalie Zemon Davis (e.g. her chapter 'Women on top' in Davis 1975), Mary Russo (for her work on the grotesque body of the old woman in eighteenth-century France, 1986), and Robert Darnton (1984).[3] This work focused less insistently on the body alone than did the work that started coming out of Berkeley in the mid-1980s, epitomized by a 1987 collection edited by Catherine Gallagher and Thomas Laqueur called *The Making of the Modern Body* – which had the telling subtitle, *Sexuality and Society in the Nineteenth Century*, as if that's when the modern body started. This book was based on a 1986 special issue of the New Historicist journal *Representations*. Laqueur's book *Making Sex* came out in 1990, shortly after a three-volume collection published by Zone called *Fragments for a History of the Human Body* (Feher *et al.* 1989). This work had much in common with work being produced at the same time by historians of late antiquity (Brown 1988, Rousselle 1988), and indeed Brown and Laqueur were colleagues (see below), while a piece by Aline Rousselle appears in one of the Zone volumes along with two pieces by Laqueur and one by Gallagher. The excitement caused by this lavishly illustrated and evidently hip work put new life into the field of the history and philosophy of science (a poor stepsister of history when I was in college in the early 1970s), and created an audience for boundary-crossing work like that of Londa Schiebinger, who studies the history of gender differentiation in Western science (1989) and its intersections with the scientific formulation of race (1990).[4] The *Journal of the History of Sexuality*, founded in 1990, by 1992 had developed a speciality as 'an important forum for scholars working in the field of gay studies' ('Announcements and Calls for Papers', *JHS* 2: 506). Under the guidance of historian John C. Fout, who works on masculinity in modern Germany, *JHS* is less committed to social constructionism than are the New Historicists, because open to the idea of a transhistorical 'gay and lesbian history'.

However, all these body historians must be seen in the context of the feminist critique of the ideology surrounding (or constituting) the female body. As Susan Bordo has eloquently demonstrated, not only second-wave but first-wave feminists, going back to Mary Wollstonecraft, developed a critique of 'the material body as a site of political struggle' (Bordo 1993: 15–23). She has in mind not only theorists like Andrea Dworkin and Mary Daly but the critique of beauty culture generated by women's groups in the late 1960s. Other early second-wave thinkers struggled with the association between femaleness and motherhood: Shulamith Firestone in *The Dialectic of Sex* (1970) argued for the separation of reproduction from the female body through technology, an idea worked out in Marge Piercy's noted science-fiction book *Woman on the Edge of Time* (1976); in contrast, another group argued against the evils of technology in the context of the female body (e.g. Corea *et al.* 1987). The politics of reproduction and of the medical profession and medical discourse came in for heavy criticism as women reclaimed their own bodies, most obviously in the Boston Women's Health Book Collective's self-help manual *Our Bodies, Ourselves*, which was reprinted and revised several times from 1969 to 1992. Scholarship followed suit, as in Barbara Ehrenreich and Deirdre English's popular collection of outlandish medical advice to women (1978). Notable recent additions to the corpus include anthropologist Emily Martin's 1987 *The Woman in the Body* (revised edition 1992) and biologist Anne Fausto-Sterling's 1985 *Myths of Gender* (second edition also 1992). Feminist literary critics think about the female body in texts (e.g. Suleiman 1986); feminist film theorists think about the female body in film (e.g. Creed 1993). What differentiates this group from the pure body historians is a constant consciousness of the political implications, for individual women, of the histories they explore.

Meanwhile, in Classics, the current wave of work on the history of sexuality had begun with Jeffrey Henderson's 1975 *The Maculate Muse* (second edition 1991), a study of 'obscene language in Attic comedy', especially the plays of Aristophanes.[5] Henderson was in touch with K.J. Dover, whose *Greek Homosexuality* (1978; revised 1989) is often cited as basic to the field; the books together provide an enormous database on classical Athenian sexual systems and discourse. Henderson, my teacher at Yale, in turn came up with the idea for my dissertation, a Roman version of *The Maculate Muse;* it eventually covered comic and satiric authors from Plautus to Juvenal in the form of a lexicon and motif-index. This work then provided a database for *The Garden of Priapus* (1983; second edition 1992c), which I wrote while reading the work of (and later talking to) Marilyn Skinner and Judith Hallett, whose work on Roman sexuality began coming out in the late 1970s (e.g. Hallett 1977, M. Skinner 1979). Hellenist Eva Keuls' *Reign of the Phallus* appeared in 1985 (second edition 1993). Ironically, in light of the anti-theory bias of Classics as a field, all this potentially radical work came out of solidly, even stolidly, philological traditions of establishing lexical usage and explicating vexed texts. Explaining the database, however, turned out to require forays into various areas of theory, including feminism, anthropology, psychology, and literary theory.[6]

Meanwhile, in France, Michel Foucault was beginning to publish what would be his last work, *The History of Sexuality*, of which so far only volumes 1–3 have been published, with rumours of a possible fourth (on the early church) to be excavated from his notes. Volumes 2 and 3 deal, respectively, with the period of classical Athens and with Graeco-Roman cultures of the first two centuries CE. Some of his earlier studies, especially *Discipline and Punish* (first published in France in 1975), had already provided body historians with key formulations, e.g. those of the regulating gaze and the docile body. Foucault's work proved enormously influential both outside and inside the academy. Among classicists his work had the most influence on that of David Halperin (1990) and John Winkler (1990b). In addition, of course, *The History of Sexuality* has been of great interest to the gay community, along with the work of the historian John Boswell, whose theories run counter to Foucault's (best represented in Boswell 1990). The French structuralists Jean-Pierre Vernant and Marcel Detienne also took up the idea of the body and influenced the work of American classicists, especially Froma Zeitlin; Vernant has a piece in one of the Zone volumes, while Zeitlin co-edited a collection called *Before Sexuality* with Halperin and Winkler (Halperin *et al.* 1990). Winkler, like Jeffrey Henderson, was teaching at Yale when I was there, and was one of the readers of my dissertation.

Elsewhere (Richlin 1991, 1992c, xiii–xxxiii: 1993a, 1993b, forthcoming a) I have spelled out my own position, taking up a stance with some feminists and opposing Foucault. The issue in question is the one that puts me into this volume: whereas Foucault stresses radical discontinuities between ancient and modern sexual systems, I stress continuity. He is interested in differences between ancient and modern definitions of male–male sexuality, I am interested in the persistence of misogyny and homophobia. Questions of method and approach arise. I have argued (forthcoming a) that Foucault's errors and omissions stem from his selection of sources, which produced what I have called 'genre bias', a phenomenon similar to that discussed for the question of Hellenistic childhood by Mark Golden in this volume. Previously (1990: 181) I have suggested that questions of reality can best be settled by an approach that asks the same question of all available kinds of data (including different genres), and extrapolates a three-dimensional answer from the variety of answers obtained (a process I compared to the making-visible of the invisible monster in the movie 'Forbidden Planet'). Obviously at stake here are epistemological and political issues; whereas I espouse (1992c, 1993b) an optimistic epistemology (knowledge can be assessed across cultures) and a pessimistic attitude (but what we get is bad news about the past), Foucault is more doubtful about what can be known and more cheerful about its implications. I should add that, echoing Golden's appeal to Gramsci, I do think that something can be done about it all.

Other major statements about issues of discontinuity in the context of ancient sex/gender systems include those by the historian of science and medicine G.E.R. Lloyd and the cultural critic Page duBois. Lloyd, reacting to the *Annales* school and the question of *mentalités* 'primitive' and otherwise, comes down to the axiom that conflicting systems coexist (1990), a conclusion consonant with that of Suzanne Dixon in this volume (Chapter 5). The position of duBois in *Sowing the Body* (1988) is more complex: unusual among body historians in her choice of psychoanalytic theory as adversary, she posits for archaic and classical Greek culture a developmental model of mindsets characterized by ways of thinking about the female body, a development broken off by Aristotle's radical misogyny. According to duBois, people now might escape the phallocentrism of Freudian theory by historicizing it, and she proposes classical Greek culture as a welcome instance of a time of otherness, before Freud (though not, she says, a golden age, 1988: 58). During this time, ideas of male and female, she argues, were complementary; it is Plato who begins to appropriate the female for the male philosopher, and Aristotle who entirely subsumes the female to the male, a formulation which then continues throughout Western history. The metaphors duBois examines for the female body – field, furrow, stone, oven, tablet – progress conceptually rather than chronologically, though she does partially map them on to a pre-Aristotle chronology; she is thus somewhat in sympathy with Lloyd's idea of coexisting and conflicting systems.

Though I do not myself find the image of woman as furrow to be ploughed much preferable to that of woman as mutilated male – and doubt that the difference is significant – I think duBois breaks new ground (so to speak) by founding her argument on Greek cultural ideas of the female body, which

20

certainly sets her work apart from that of Freud, Foucault, or Lacan, for whom the male always has primacy. Her conclusions might be compared with those of Bella Zweig (1993), who adopts Paula Gunn Allen's model of Native American gender complementarity to suggest a possible way of seeing the Greeks apart from Western phallocentrism.[7] Other theorists save some trouble by simply rejecting Freud and/or phallocentrism; surely the problematical example of classical Greece is not necessary to this move. As I have argued elsewhere (1993b: 279–81), the appeal to antiquity as a lost golden age grows out of a dependence on 'chronological dualism', the view of time as divided into Eden, Fall, and future rapture. I do not myself think it either necessary to justify change by finding a charter in the past or desirable to redeem ancient cultures from modern sins.

WHY BODIES NOW?

The *Annales* school contributed to history-writing a focus on the *longue durée*, on the great, long-lasting structures that underlie the events of day-to-day life; so that individual agents – people – are like the waves that crest and break above the tide.[8] The problem of how body history came to be written in the late twentieth century can be set up as a model *Annales* school study, which would divide up the forces that control history into large, medium, and small, like the Three Bears. Several readers found this model sexist and ageist; let me emphasize that the Bears represent only relative scale, and perhaps should be replaced by the Three T-shirts.

Starting in the middle, at the Mama Bear level, there are the intermediate-level forces, the institutions that made body history thinkable. The *Annales* school itself constitutes one such force; the school's turn from 'Great Men' to a gaze that took in all phenomena, no matter how humble or disgusting (Clark 1985: 186, Braudel 1980: 36), opened the way to a history of the body (and, for that matter, to a history of women). Next I would put the so-called sexual revolution of the 1960s and the second wave of the women's movement. The sexual revolution affected communication as well as practice and made it seem normal to talk about previously taboo subjects. When Jeffrey Henderson began his 1972 Harvard dissertation on obscenity in Aristophanes, for example, it was suggested that he had better write it in Latin; no one was so inhibited about my 1978 Yale dissertation on obscenity in Roman humour (though, as it turned out, people continued to find the subject distasteful for some time). It is hard to realize now how astounding it was in 1975 to see Aristophanes not only translated literally (which involved a lot of 'fuck' and 'cocksucker' and 'cunt') but taken seriously. Trends in feminist theory also emphasized the importance of the personal and concrete (as in consciousness raising) and at the same time laid the foundation for arguments about the social construction of the body, as in Simone de Beauvoir's maxim, 'One is not born, but becomes a woman', a maxim which Monique Wittig developed into a demolition of gender (1981). In the United States, feminist social constructionism has taken a range of forms: a revolutionary call for the separation of reproduction from gender (Firestone 1970); the political analysis of body image, questioning the regime of beauty in women's lives and its place in deciding what is a 'woman' (Bartky 1991, Chapkis 1986); most recently a discussion of gender as performance, tied both to the politics of queer theory (Butler 1990) and to developments in cultural anthropology (Gilmore 1990). Here male as well as female gender is demonstrated to be fluid, a model well applicable to ancient Greek and Roman cultures, as shown most comprehensively in the recent work of Marilyn Skinner on Catullus' Attis (1993) and of Maud Gleason on the rhetoricians of the Second Sophistic (1995).

These institutions together made it possible for certain individuals not only to rise up but to become audible, and for their works in turn to take on the status of institutions, like religious sects. One of the most influential books in body history has been Mikhail Bakhtin's *Rabelais and His World*, translated into English in 1968; his work had previously been little known to the Anglo world. Bakhtin accounted for Rabelais with an optimistic model of a humour of the open body that would 'uncrown gloomy eschatological time' and challenge death. His version of Rabelais seemed to me to be comparable to Roman and other humour, though I questioned his optimism (Richlin 1992c: 70–72). Generally, his work provided scholars with the idea of the 'carnivalesque', which has had wide applications in the cultural history of the early modern (Darnton 1984, Davis 1975, Russo 1986, Stallybrass and White 1986). Similarly, these institutions formed the context for the career of Michel Foucault – who, as Susan Bordo reminds us, arrived on the scene of body politics after feminists had set the terms (1993: 16–17). Writing at a juncture between history, philosophy, and literary history, Foucault forged an understanding of history that emphasized local peculiarities, non-canonical discourses, a holistic approach to cultures that would rightly include the study of the most mundane materials, and the critique of power relations. Sexuality was a logical final destination for Foucault. But that Foucault's final work focused on the history of Greek and Roman sexuality has come to seem almost a mistake to those outside of Classics, since, for the cultural matrix that fostered Foucault himself, Greece and Rome were too canonical and too far in the past. Even writing about *mentalités* cannot escape the conditions of its own *mentalité*.

Likewise, moving to the Baby Bear level, we can see how these larger forces are played out at the most intimate level of the history of the writers of body history themselves, in the networks of people whose everyday dialogues shape one another's ideas. The prefaces and introductions to the books of the new body history writers provide, appropriately enough, some striking examples of confessional writing – which, helpfully, show a lot about the nature of the groups that produce this writing. Where a conventional

22

scholarly work would have mystified its genesis under a chaste blanket of thank-yous, some new historians want the reader to see exactly how it all came to be. For example, Thomas Laqueur, author of *Making Sex*, describes the 'intellectual origins' of his book on the first page of the preface as follows (1990: vii):

> a group of friends started *Representations*; I taught a graduate seminar on the body ... with Catherine Gallagher; I encountered feminist literary and historical scholarship; my almost daily companion in the rational recreation of drinking cappuccino, Peter Brown, was working on his book about the body and society in late antiquity.

A bit farther on, among the friends he thanks is a historian of China named David Keightley, whom he describes as 'leader of the Yuppie Bikers' (Laqueur 1990: ix; the Bikers reappear in the 'Acknowledgements' of Carol Clover's *Men, Women, and Chain Saws* (1992)). Peter Stallybrass and Allon White, authors of the influential *The Politics and Poetics of Transgression*, open their book with an ingenuous confession that it arose out of their arguments over cleaning house: 'Sharing a house together led us, first, to fierce and deeply felt intellectual disagreement about domestic filth ... and thence to a wider discussion of the variety and origins of bourgeois disgust' (Stallybrass and White 1986: ix). Even more intimately, the four co-editors of the collection *Nationalisms and Sexualities* open their preface with these words: '*Nationalisms and Sexualities* was first imagined at Eve Sedgwick's house in Amherst, Massachusetts, during a pyjama party attended by the editors and several members of the editorial board of the newly-launched journal *Genders*' (A. Parker *et al.* 1992: ix). This pyjama party was the birthplace of the 'historic international conference' that was subsequently held at Harvard in 1989.

Now these introductions announce the authors' membership in groups and activities linked to college life since the 1960s, and in a tone that is markedly lighthearted (or precious): the cappuccino, the Yuppie Bikers, the two guys keeping house, the co-ed pyjama party. Yet this link has a serious meaning, and has profoundly influenced what counts as 'history' right now. When Hélène Cixous appealed to her readers to 'write the body' (1980), she was calling for what, in Aristotelian terms, is a big contradiction: a mixing of categories, a conflation of the mind's business with the body's business. Nothing could be so well calculated to appeal to my generation, for whom body and political liberation movements intermingled. And so this idea turned out to be a powerful one.

It produced as well the feminist convention of writing from a defined personal standpoint. The 'Acknowledgements' in Emily Martin's *The Woman in the Body* provide an interesting comparison and contrast to Laqueur's preface (Martin 1987: vii):

This study has rested on the backs of many people besides my own. Foremost are the women who consented to be interviewed, giving their time, spilling their tears, sharing their insights, and opening their minds and hearts. Their collective efforts are the heart of this book and give it its best chance of growing in the hearts of other women. No less important are the women who conducted many of the interviews: . . . [list of names]. For enduring the difficulty of approaching strangers, the agony of trying to find addresses in unfamiliar neighborhoods, the fear of standing in front of a group and asking for help, and for believing in the possibility that ordinary women will have wisdom, I thank them.

Martin here expresses herself in terms of the body (hearts, backs, tears, agony, fear) – the picture is strongly reminiscent of Cixous' description of a woman trying to speak in 'The laugh of the Medusa' (1980: 251), or of the title of Anzaldúa and Moraga's collection of writings by women of colour, *This Bridge Called My Back* (1983). She also claims for her research that it is grounded in talking to ordinary women, and thus is collaborative not only in its method but in a larger sense. And, like Anne Fausto-Sterling (who put out a new edition of her book in response to the hubbub over Simon LeVay's work claiming a physiological basis for male homosexuality, 1992 [1985]: vi), Martin openly believes her work has political implications for the lives of real people.

Laqueur's personal voice in his writing (e.g. 1990: 14–15) may be less connected to a politics, but surely comes from the same desire for social change. It is not a surprise when he gives his motive for writing body history (1990: 24): 'I regard what I have written as somehow liberating, as breaking old shackles of necessity, as opening up worlds of vision, politics, and eros. I only hope that the reader will feel the same.' Certainly in Classics, and presumably in other fields as well, some scholarship produced since 1968 has been produced to mark a generational shift, a change in the idea of what is important, what should be studied, and a move towards a politically engaged scholarship – possibly an oxymoron. This is the scholarship of a particular social group, some of whom believe energy should belong to political activism.

However, all these forces and individuals were still subject to larger forces (the Papa Bear level) that have shaped the writing of the history of sexuality: Marxism, the long tides of misogyny, and the passing of Classics from its traditional position in the academy.

Above all, the writing of body history constitutes a product of the writing of materialist history; Marx's observations that: 'The forming of the five senses is a labour of the entire history of the world down to the present' and that 'The first historical act is thus . . . the production of material life itself' imply that the writing of a history of material life would be a Marxist project.[9] Materialist language imbues body history, from Michel Feher's insistence on the real changes undergone by the body (1989: 11) to Bakhtin's 'material bodily lower stratum'. Though Page duBois says she is not thinking of Engels' 'world-historical defeat of womankind' (1988: 29–30, 36), her study has much more to do with Marxism than with psychoanalysis. The privileging of the body in the mind/body dichotomy reverses a bias in Western thought going back at least to Aristotle, a change that may once again be blamed, like everything else, on the French Revolution. Mark Golden (1990: 169) quotes Mao's remark that it's too early to tell about the long-term effects of the French Revolution; but it certainly made possible not only feminism (Mary Wollstonecraft) but Marxism. Indeed, the two genealogies – of feminism and Marxism – follow parallel and interlinking tracks through the nineteenth century to the present, from Marx to the New Left and from Wollstonecraft to the Second Wave. Alice Echols has shown in vivid detail how second-wave feminists debouched from the New Left, in fact deriving the idea of the personal as political from SDS but going on to develop it beyond what the New Left would tolerate (Echols 1989; cf. also Landry and MacLean 1993). Interestingly, a similar tension characterized nineteenth-century Marxism: for example, though suffragist Victoria Woodhull's newspaper was the first to publish the *Communist Manifesto* in America, Marx called Woodhull 'a banker's woman, free lover, and general humbug', and got her Section expelled from the International (Feuer 1989: xv).

Indeed misogyny (Papa Bear No. 2) continues to structure even the most progressive history, mired once again in the conditions of its production: one of the most conspicuous problems in the new body history is the way it often leaves out women's issues, and how it often seems unconscious of its debt to feminist theory. This takes a variety of forms. Many people have noticed how Foucault's *History of Sexuality*, one of the most influential works in the field, leaves out women and feminist theory (see the acerbic comments of Catharine MacKinnon, 1992: 128; Richlin 1991, and forthcoming a). It is likewise odd to see how Thomas Laqueur's book, which is conscious of work done by Peter Brown and his connections, positioned as feminist, and focused almost exclusively on the female body, shows no knowledge of Page duBois' study of the female body in Greek thought or of work done by feminists in Classics on the history of ancient medicine. The immediate reason for this is systemic, and goes beyond a mere lack of bibliographical searching.[10] There is just nobody like that for Laqueur to drink cappuccino with.

Work on ancient women by feminists in Classics is hard for outsiders to see because feminists in Classics have been marginalized. The study of women in antiquity has grown up in almost complete segregation from the research universities; the result of this, for example, is that in June 1994, working on this essay, I could call the Berkeley Classics department and be told they have no course on women in antiquity on their books. Along with women in the field of Classics, the study of women in antiquity lives elsewhere; students at small colleges have been taught these courses since the 1970s. The demographics of the field determine what it thinks about. In general, the New Left students grew up and became male and female academics, whose fortunes in the academy were determined by pre-existing gender politics there as well as within the New Left. And in particular, during the 1970s and 1980s women's history and feminist theory in Classics were made as marginal as the discipline's gatekeepers (conservative in the first place) could make them be; becoming visible posed a major problem here once again, as feminists in the field were squeezed between right and left (Richlin 1991: 177). Feminists in medieval history have faced similar struggles, as Judith Bennett recently documented (1993) in a special issue of *Speculum* that caused a furore in the field.

Moreover, misogyny itself seems to be unspeakable; once it is named and discussed, these discussions in turn become subject to repression, oblivion, and accusations of whining (as in the term 'victim theory'). Both demographics and silencing may be connected with fundamental gender systems.

Meanwhile, Classics itself (Papa Bear No.3) became isolated from developments elsewhere in the humanities, and is increasingly perceived by other humanities fields as inessential. Rome's grip on élite education in the West seems finally to be dying. The American Philological Association's feminist group, the Women's Classical Caucus, is cut off from the writers of women's history by belonging to Classics. The American Historical Association has its own women's caucus, and the Berkshire Conference on Women's History regularly segregates ancient history into a small group of panels; by far the bulk of the historians who attend this huge conference work on the early modern to modern periods. Like a ruined city, the cultures of the past, so painstakingly excavated by four centuries' worth of classicists, are being overgrown by the lianas of a wilful ignorance.[11]

So, while the ancient world, especially Greek cultures, has been of some interest to the writers of body history, what they say about it is limited by the marginal status both of women and of Classics.

THE SHAPE OF BODY HISTORY

It seems that the theory of history is endlessly implicated in a sort of Zoroastrian struggle between opposite approaches. As Josine Blok has demonstrated (1987), this struggle was played out within Classics in the nineteenth century; and historians and philosophers have played it out all over again in this century, as has been lucidly described by Quentin Skinner (1985). Mark Golden, in a recent essay (1992), compared the debate to the 'big bang' versus 'steady state' universes imagined by physicists: do we see history as forest or trees, *longue durée* or great men, structure or agency? Some people give the sensible answer 'both' (e.g. Ohnuki-Tierney 1990: 24, 'Structure and practice are not antithetical'), and I have argued that the choice of approach often seems to depend more on the writer's temperament than on anything else (Richlin 1993b). But the emphasis on the 'local and contingent' (Q. Skinner 1985: 12) is what seems to be driving the new body history onward. Which in turn puts it at odds with those versions of feminist history that record the oppression of women over the course of millennia. At stake is the definition of 'history': does it mean 'what happened' or 'what changed'?

The whole concept of 'body history' is consciously paradoxical, if 'history' means 'what changed'. Its practitioners, including some feminists, feel that their practice is revolutionary, in so far as the body has been historically perceived as a natural thing, a 'given'; it could have no history if history = change (Bordo 1993: 33, Feher 1989: 11). When Thomas Laqueur says he hopes that his book will be 'liberating' and 'break old shackles', this is what he means: he is going to show that premodern concepts of the body were different in a significant way from modern concepts of the body; and that learning this will make people realize that things do not have to be the way they are. Contingency will set us free.

One problem with this approach is that not everything has changed. If anatomy textbooks alter, what does that mean between the sheets? Catharine MacKinnon expresses doubt that sex has had a history at all, in terms of the status of women (1992: 122–23):

> I would hypothesize that while ideologies about sex and sexuality may ebb and flow, and the ways they attach themselves to gender and to women's status may alter ... the actual practices of sex may look relatively flat. In particular, the sexualization of aggression or the eroticization of power ... such that the one who is the target or object of sexuality is the subordinate, is a female, effeminized if a man, is relatively constant. And that hierarchy is always done through gender in some way ... [V]ariation may not be the most prominent feature of the historical landscape.

I have argued (Richlin 1992c: xvii–xx, 1993b) that misogyny can be conceived of in terms of a *longue durée*; body historians often discard this approach as depressing, for example Lynn Hunt writing on Foucault's *History of Sexuality* (1992b: 82): 'By focusing on bodies, Foucault offered perspectives that help disengage us from a dreary, repetitive, totalizing history of patriarchy and misogyny.' But the idea of a *longue durée* does not imply that nothing can change – just that it has not. And I think it is generally easier for a classicist to take this viewpoint than it is for a modern historian. Like Daniel Boyarin in his book about Rabbinic thought on the body, I like to think of 'our own time' as 'very late antiquity' (Boyarin 1993: ix). The marginalization of Classics means the loss of this long perspective. It is easy for modern historians to believe that the modern is different in kind from earlier times, because earlier times are unfamiliar to them.

Presentism in body history has also produced what look to a classicist like a lot of mistakes (D. Cohen and Saller 1994; Richlin forthcoming a). It seems to me that, at times, what really happened in antiquity is not important; instead, people pick out evidence they like, and leave a whole lot out. Here the preference for the local and contingent is tied up with a strongly felt need to find watersheds.

Examples are not hard to find. Perhaps most important has been Foucault's claim that 'homosexuality', as a concept, did not exist before the nineteenth century. This is a rare example of an academic idea that has had significant impact outside the academy; but I think that it is not true, at least for Rome, and have said as much (Richlin 1993a). Similarly, scholars have followed Foucault's lead in arguing that the idea of sexuality is a modern one; Domna Stanton takes as significant the date of the first appearance of the word 'sexuality' in the *OED*, and talks about 'the emergence of the concept in the early 19th century' (1992a: 2–3, 13; cf. MacKinnon 1992: 119). Titles reflect a preoccupation with claiming the novelty and constructedness of modern institutions: Gallagher and Laqueur's *The Making of the Modern Body* (note that it dates back only to the nineteenth century), Laqueur's *Making Sex*, Halperin *et al.*'s *Before Sexuality* and his own *One Hundred Years of Homosexuality*. Astonishing claims are made for the early modern period, and are warmly greeted: for example, Lynn Hunt entitled her collection on pornography from 1500–1800 *The Invention of Pornography;* Michiko Kakutani, reviewing the book in *The New York Times*, accepts this watershed model without question (1993):

> In the centuries before [the early years of the nineteenth century], pornography was not a separate and distinct genre created to arouse sexual feelings; rather, it was a vehicle used to criticize the political and religious authorities through the shock of sex.

Pornography as obscene is 'a relatively recent Western notion'. But texts designed to 'arouse sexual feelings' were plentiful and understood as such in antiquity, nor could it be said of them that they were designed as political critique – *au contraire*; and which 'centuries' before the nineteenth are meant here, anyway?[12] It all turns into a vague mush.

One particularly mind-boggling juxtaposition: the major argument in Laqueur's *Making Sex*, contrasted with the major argument in Page duBois' *Sowing the Body*. Laqueur argues (1990: 5) that

> in or about the late eighteenth century . . . human sexual nature changed . . . By around 1800, writers of all sorts were determined to base what they insisted were fundamental differences between the male and female sexes, and thus between man and woman, on discoverable biological distinctions.

He goes on to describe this 'two-sex' model as arguing against Aristotle's 'one-sex' model. Page duBois also thinks this biological differentiation is a watershed moment – but she associates it, more justifiably, with Aristotle (1988: 187, cf. 184):

> the erection of the phallus as a privileged symbol . . . the establishment of the male subject as the figure for wholeness to which the female and her body are compared – is not a universal fact of culture. It rather occurs in the philosophical tradition at the moment when women . . . are named as defective, partial men.

She is referring, most obviously, to Aristotle's famous definition of the female as a 'mutilated male', in the midst of a long discussion of ways in which the female body differs from and is worse than the male (*De Generatione Animalium* 765b8). Compare Laqueur (1990: 22): 'In terms of the millennial traditions of Western medicine, genitals came to matter as the marks of sexual opposition only last week.'

This statement and many others like it in Laqueur and Foucault are easily falsifiable, though widely credited in critical theory outside Classics (e.g. A. Parker *et al.* 1992: 4, quoting David Halperin; cf. J.G. Turner 1993: xvi). Carol Clover, for example, in an otherwise convincing account of early Scandinavian sex/gender systems, accepts Laqueur's claims about the prevalence of the 'one-sex' model of sexual difference before 1800 and is then obliged to explain why she sees such a model departing from Norse culture upon its Christianization in the Middle Ages (Clover 1993: 377–78, 385–87). Indeed, Laqueur himself concedes that Aristotle is 'deeply committed to the existence of two radically different . . . sexes' (1990: 28) and that he is 'committed to the genital opposition of two sexes' (1990: 30–31). And it is hard to see why the distinction between 'one-sex' and 'two-sex' matters, since the same culture is evidently capable of holding both models simultaneously, and both models devalue women. The gynaecological works of the ancient medical writers have been well discussed for some time now by Lesley Dean-Jones, Ann Hanson, Helen King, Geoffrey Lloyd, and others, and I cannot improve on their account of sexual differentiation in Greek and Roman cultures.[13] I would just emphasize that the medical writers certainly distinguish women from men on the basis of wombs and menstruation, as do Roman encyclopaedists like Pliny the Elder (Hanson 1990, 1992, King 1983, 1986, Richlin forthcoming b; cf. Dean-Jones 1992, 1994). But I have done most of my own work on comedy and invective (an area acknowledged and dismissed by Laqueur 1990: 34), and would like to illustrate further discussion from those areas.

CONTINUITY AND CHANGE

In what ways were ancient sexual systems different from modern? How did these systems differ from one another in antiquity? It is true that it is easy to make a list of ancient phenomena that diverge from those of the Anglo world today: the rules about male–male and female–female sexuality; the definition of both male and female sexual roles; practices like infibulation and castration; the meaning and treatment of adultery and rape (Richlin 1981, 1993a); the implication of the body in medicine and/or magic (Richlin forthcoming b). It is also easy to see strong similarities: misogyny (Richlin 1984, 1992c); phallocracy (Keuls 1985, Richlin 1992c); the expression of xenophobia through the body (captive Germans in breeches, the circumcised Jew, the Ethiopian); the regulation of sexual activity by law and social pressure (D. Cohen 1991, Edwards 1993, Richlin 1993a). Similarity and difference likewise characterize ancient cultures: the rules for pederasty and marriage were not the same in fifth-century BCE Athens as they were in Sparta, or in Rome at various times, and yet the definition and aesthetic of the boy and woman as sex object remain more or less constant from Attic vase paintings to Byzantine epigrams (Richlin 1992c: 32–56); sex between women shows up, barely, in extant texts in far different guises at different times (more genre bias? – duBois 1984, Hallett 1989, Gordon forthcoming); virulent invective against old women is much more common in Roman texts than in Greek (Richlin 1984, cf. Henderson 1987). Slavery existed throughout antiquity, but the sexual vulnerability of the slave had different meanings in Rome (where household slaves were freed in large numbers) than elsewhere (Joshel 1992: 28–35). Slavery is implicated with prostitution, and with infibulation, castration, and the religious division of women into classes according to the availability of access to their bodies (Richlin forthcoming c).

The differences between sexuality in antiquity and in modern Anglo culture have become familiar through Foucault's work and, to a lesser degree, through work by classicists since Kenneth Dover's *Greek Homosexuality* appeared in 1978. Sexual norms in Greek and Roman cultures, and in other contemporary cultures, depended to a large degree on function – penetrator/penetrated. Adult males were expected to wish to penetrate two kinds of people: boys between the ages of about 12 to 18, and women. Women were expected to fulfil the role of penetrated person; their desire to do so posed a problem. Boys were expected to be conscious of their potential as sex objects and to make a clean transition from (potential) penetrated to penetrator around the age of 20. To this degree, antiquity could be said to have been free from the idea of 'homosexuality', inasmuch as adult males normally desired both boys and women, and boys as they turned into men would move from an all-male world to that mixed world of men, women, and boys.

However, this model does not complete the picture. Greek and Roman texts of all periods emphasize the wrongness of an adult male's continuing to desire to be penetrated after adolescence, and such males are also said to 'want a man', that is, to desire not only an inappropriate action but an inappropriate sex partner. Roman texts emphasize the wrongness of a woman penetrating another woman – and this is their only model for female–female sexuality. I would now suggest that the current impasse in choosing a model to describe ancient sexual systems might be resolved by describing ancient cultures as having had three gender roles: man, woman, and boy. Each of these genders has an appropriate role, either insertive or receptive, thus:

$$\xleftarrow{\hspace{3em}} \qquad \xrightarrow{\hspace{3em}} \qquad \xleftarrow{\hspace{3em}}$$

BOY penetrates ADULT MALE penetrates ADULT FEMALE penetrates *TRIBAS*

$$\xrightarrow{\hspace{2em}}$$

[penetrates *CINAEDUS*]

The 'abnormal' role of the penetrated man was named, and the names were pejorative – for example, *kinaidos* in Greek, *cinaedus* or *mollis* in Latin. In Rome, at least from the time of the Elder Seneca, the 'abnormal' role of penetrating woman was given the pejorative – and Greek – name *tribas*. (Holt Parker argues in addition that the sexually aggressive heterosexual woman reverses gender expectations (forthcoming).) But we note that this system breaks down over Sappho, and presume that a different diagram would have to be drawn for seventh-century BCE Lesbos – if only we had the information to base it on.

These roles were certainly also based, *pace* Laqueur, on differentiation between male and female genitalia (and even between men's and boys', Richlin 1992c: 35–38, 42–43, 55–56, 275–76). To begin with Athens in the fifth century BCE, I would turn to Aristophanes' *Thesmophoriazusae*, a comedy about men spying on the women's festival. At this point in the play, the two main characters, Mnesilochus and Euripides, have just dropped in on the tragic playwright Agathon – the same Agathon who represented tragedy in Plato's *Symposium* – and have overheard him declaiming. Agathon's literary style and personal affect were evidently a noted mix of the feminine and masculine, and Mnesilochus, a regular guy, has this to say to Agathon (*Thes.* 134–43):

> I wish to inquire of you à la Aeschylus
> In his famous trilogy, the *Lykourgeia*:
> Whence hails this woman–man? What his fatherland, what his frock?
> What be the confusion of his life? Why does the lyre
>   babble in a saffron robe? Why a lyre in a hairnet?
> Why a gym-bag [*lêkythos*, lit. 'oil-jar'] and a bra [*strophion*]?
>   These things don't go together.
> What, prithee, does a sword have in common with a hand-mirror?
> Who are you, boy? You call yourself a man?
> And where's your dick [*peos*]? Where's your lumberjacket [*chlaina*,
>   lit. 'cloak']? Where's your hunting boots [*Lakônikai*]?
> Hmm, maybe you call yourself a woman? Then where's your tits
>   [*titthia*]?

I would argue that this text shows a clear association between 'gender' – socially marked appurtenances like frock, robe, hairnet, gym-bag, bra, sword, hand-mirror, lumberjacket, hunting boots – and 'sex' – physical features: 'dick' (*peos*) versus 'tits' (*titthia*).

Similarly, numerous Roman invective texts depend on the association between a person's gender and his or her genitalia. The god Priapus, in the Priapic poems, reserves a special sort of rape for women, boys, and men, allotting a different orifice to each (Richlin 1992c: *passim*): *cunnus* for women, anus for boys, mouth for men. One of Martial's epigrams advises a wife who is jealous of her husband's sex with slave-boys not to bother offering her husband the wrong orifice; she should 'let boys use their own part, you use yours' (12.96.12). This would reinforce the idea of three genders, but also suggest that these roles are normatively enforced.

On the other hand, practices like infibulation and castration expose us to a sexual vocabulary we do not share. Some musicians and actors at Rome wore, and some slaves had imposed on them, the *fibula* (a needle drawn through the foreskin to inhibit erection), or sometimes a sheath covering the penis (Dingwall 1925). It was believed that indulgence in sex hurt the voice; hence vocalists abstained (*Priapea* 77.13–14). Roman satirists claim that infibulation just allows musicians to charge women more money for their sexual services (Martial 14.215, Juvenal 6.73, 6.379) – reflecting a general Roman tendency to class performers with whores (Edwards 1993). Martial elsewhere mocks a man with a huge *fibula* (here a sort of sheath), whom he had thought to be concerned for his voice; the man loses the *fibula* in the baths, and the truth comes out – he is circumcised (*verpus*, 7.82). A woman has her slave wear a *fibula*, also described as a *theca ahenea* ('bronze sheath'), in the baths (Martial 11.75); elsewhere Martial implies that you would need a blacksmith to remove a slave's *fibula* (9.27.10–12). Here a Foucauldian 'care of the self' merges with a decidedly hierarchical policing of sexuality and with Roman alignments of gender with class. The phallocentrism of this practice might strike a feminist reader as familiar, a continuity with her own culture; the materiality of the practice might strike another reader as an important chapter in the history of slavery.

The man who hides his circumcision does so because it breaks Roman norms; here we return to familiar ground. The (male) Jew's body, like that of other Others, marked his difference, as seen in a well-known passage in the *Satyricon* in which the hapless adventurers search desperately for a way to disguise themselves (102.13–14):

> 'Eumolpus, as a student of literature, always has ink about him. So by this remedy let's change our colour from our hair to our fingernails. So, like Ethiopian slaves, we will both be near you, safe and sound, without the risk of torture, and deceive our enemies by our changed colour.'
>
> 'Oh, sure', said Giton, 'and why don't you also circumcise us, so that we look like Jews, and pierce our ears, so that we imitate Arabs, and put chalk on our faces, so that Gaul thinks we're her citizens. . .'

32

He goes on to point out that further work would be necessary to turn them into Ethiopians, and gives a long and unflattering list of Ethiopian physical traits (102.15). Similarly, Giton's pasty-faced Gauls appear in other Roman texts and art, along with their cousins the Germans, as plaid-clad, ponytailed barbarians in chains. These differences are not neutral (Richlin 1995). Thus in Roman satire, it is a matter of insult to say a man is circumcised, and the Jew's penis often forms part of an invective stereotype: a slave's 'Jewish load' (Martial 7.35.3–4); threat of oral rape by a *mentula* that comes from sacked Jerusalem – evidently a big one, not the poet's 'proper little one' (*proba et pusilla*, Mart. 7.55.6–8); the chanted refrain *verpe poeta* in a poem attacking a Jew who is buggering the speaker's boy (Mart. 11.94); a mark of Jewish exclusiveness (Juvenal 14.98–104). Petronius has one of the freed slaves at the *cena Trimalchionis* cite circumcision as one of his prize slave's few faults (68.8), along with snoring.[14] This Roman xenophobia is not only similar to modern othering through the body; in some instances it is identical with the modern practice. If Roman racism included Germans along with Jews and Ethiopians, does that make it significantly different?

Empire, like slavery and prostitution, like gender hierarchy, conditions the sexual experience of all people in a culture. There is no way in which our experience of sex can be the same as the experience of any ancient person. Yet some things persist or repeat. Walking down a city street in Pompeii, you would have been surrounded on all sides by images of the erect penis – stamped on walls and paving stones, decorating shop signs, worn as amulets by children. Today in the West this body part is scrupulously hidden. How significant is this difference?

Is there a history of the body? Yes, by all means; if by this we mean that it is possible to find out about ideas of the body in the past. But to me, what is interesting about the body is not what has changed, but what has not changed, because of the practical implications of the unchanged aspects for women. Even so originary a New Historicist as Stephen Greenblatt has recently rejected what he calls 'the academic left's current dream ... that history will somehow save one from the complacencies of humanism', asking, 'How can the dream of redemptive historical difference survive the end of the Cold War and linger on in the murderous age of ethnic hatreds?' (Greenblatt 1993: 113).[15] He continues (ibid.: 120):

> At the recent United Nations World Conference on Human Rights, it was the most brutally oppressive governments that invoked 'history' and 'difference', claiming that concepts of fairness and justice should be measured against regional particularities and various historical, cultural, and religious differences. These are the 'progressive' arguments of torturers.

Catharine MacKinnon calls for a 'critical history', whose 'task would be to give sexuality a history so that women may have a future' (1992: 127). I would

33

say, and men as well. Like Lore Segal's Leslie, I think we need to listen to screams, to hear both the differences between them and the things they share.

NOTES

1 I am grateful to those who made helpful comments at the Calgary panel, especially Alison Keith. This paper began during a happy month at UC Santa Cruz in the summer of 1993, and owes a lot to conversations with Karen Bassi, Sandra Joshel, and Margaret Malamud; since then, Page duBois and Marilyn Skinner have provided challenging critiques. All of them would disagree with much of what I say, and I wish I could do justice to their requests. Warm thanks to Patricia Parker for getting in touch, and to Peter Rose for long-distance help.
Translations throughout are my own, except where otherwise noted.

2 Indeed, the scholar of tragedy Froma Zeitlin once told me that if I did not stop making jokes in my lectures, no one would take them seriously, because they are about such unserious things; and indeed there is in my own work a tension between comic delivery and gloomy content. Based on my own conclusions in *The Garden of Priapus*, I believe this tension is no accident.
For the *Symposium* as origin text of body history, see e.g. Halperin 1990: 18–21; Bordo 1993: 3–4. For some less jolly Platonic origin texts, see duBois 1988: 171–83. For a comparable overview of feminist theory and body history in the context of Classics, see M. Skinner 1993: 107–11.

3 Darnton notes in his Acknowledgements that *The Great Cat Massacre* grew out of a course he taught in the Princeton History department that began (in 1972) as 'An introduction to the history of *mentalités*' and wound up as a 'Seminar on history and anthropology' team-taught with Clifford Geertz.

4 For a review of the Zone collection that comments on the rhetorical function of its illustrations, see C. Cohen and Robertson 1992.

5 For a learned and witty overview of the question in the nineteenth and twentieth centuries, see Winkler 1990a: 7–13.

6 Work in the field has taken off since 1990; see most notably Barton 1993, D. Cohen 1991, Edwards 1993, Hallett and M. Skinner forthcoming. Eilberg-Schwartz and Doniger 1995 feature cross-cultural work from India to Rome; see especially Molly Myerowitz's essay on hair in ancient Hebrew, Greek, and Roman cultures.

7 For duBois on the 'otherness' of the past as a remedy or useful alternative, see 1988: 1, 14, 17, 22, 24; on complementarity, see especially 147. She envisions her concepts as a conceptual, not a chronological, progression (30–31, 34, 91–92, 107, 109) but sometimes treats them as chronological (65, 86, 110, 127, 129, 130, 149ff., 165). Despite her harshly negative comments on Keuls 1985 (duBois 1988: 185), duBois' model does not explain the copious material Keuls presents to demonstrate Greek phallocentrism.

8 Compare the discussion of Linda Gordon on the structure versus agency debate in women's history in Richlin 1993b: 284–85.

9 The statement about the five senses comes from the *Economic and Philosophic Manuscripts* of 1844, quoted and discussed in Rose 1992: 18–20; the description of material history comes from the *German Ideology*, excerpted in Feuer 1989: 249.

10 On the issue of male scholars' neglect or duplication of female scholars' published work, see Richlin 1991.

11 See Bennett 1993: 327–29 on feminist medievalists' strategies for combating presentism. Bennett's attitude is generally more upbeat than mine.

12 On ancient pornographers, see Holt Parker's definitive essay (1992); for general arguments on the pornographic in antiquity, see Richlin 1992b. On Roman definitions of the obscene, see Richlin 1992c: 1–31. Kakutani's suggestion seems highly implausible to me for other periods as well.

13 These publications have long been available, though none but Lloyd's appears in Laqueur's index (Lesley Dean-Jones seems to appear in the 'Preface' credits as 'Leslie Jones', 1990: ix; a single publication of Hanson's appears at 254, n.30 – though not in the index). Ann Hanson's translation of Hippocrates *Diseases of Women 1* appeared in the first volume of *Signs*, in 1975; and most of the article she published in the Foucauldian collection *Before Sexuality* in 1990 was presented at the 1983 NEH Institute on Women in Classical Antiquity.

14 On circumcision and the Jew's body, see Gilman 1991, esp. 91–95; and work in progress by Daniel Boyarin.

15 For Greenblatt's earlier retreat from political theory, see Greenblatt 1989: 2. The theoretical passion for fragmented differences echoes through titles like *Genders, differences* (note small 'd'), *Feminisms, New French Feminisms, Representations, Nationalisms and Sexualities, Discourses of Sexuality* (which its editor says she would have liked to call *Discourses of Sexualities*, Stanton 1992a: 4, n. 4); see comment by MacKinnon 1992: 119.

2

PAINTERS AND PEDERASTS: ANCIENT ART, SEXUALITY, AND SOCIAL HISTORY[1]

Martin Kilmer

Scholars have long accepted that the view of homoerotic relationships presented by Plato (particularly in the *Symposium*) gives the normal, approved pattern for such relationships between males. The word 'pederasty' comes from the verb *paiderasteuô*, to be a lover of *paides*, with *paides* generally, and quite reasonably, taken to mean 'boys'. The younger partner (called *erômenos*), generally presented as pubescent, is pursued by the older (called *erastês*). It is ennobling for the youth to be in such a relationship, which has a strong element of teaching in it – particularly the inculcation of the manly virtues of courage and the like. On the other hand, any man who continues to prefer being the 'passive' (pursued and especially, penetrated) partner in his homoerotic relationships is viewed as effeminate – though Aristophanes gives fuller information on this than does Plato.

This understanding works, on the whole, fairly well in the literary world presented by Plato, by Xenophon in his philosophical dialogues, and by other writers of the classical period. But a significantly different picture comes from another medium, vase-painting. This material represents a time earlier than the relevant literature, the bulk of it no earlier than about 550 BCE, the latest little more than a century after that. Vase-painting has two very important styles in the archaic Athenian world. Black-figure pottery was the earlier of the two to be produced. Red-figure, whose first decades of production overlap the last generation of important painters of black-figure, began to be made a little after 530 BCE. It gradually supplanted black-figure as the preferred medium for ceramic 'fine wares'. I cannot, at this stage of the investigation, distinguish with certainty which of the changes or distinctions that I shall discuss are due to the difference in medium, which due to the difference in time, which due to some combination of those two factors. But I hope that there will emerge in the course of this discussion precisely the sort of 'moderate variation and development' or 'mid-range change' which Mark Golden has suggested (1992: 13) is most likely to reward the fortunate researcher into the social history of the Greek and Roman worlds. I think it very likely – at the very minimum, it is an economical proposition – that the differences in presentation of homoerotic relationships reflect some differences in the experience of homoerotic relationships in the two time periods represented by these two disparate sources of evidence.

The modern scholarly view of pederasty – the love of the older man for a youth or an even younger boy – as an almost universal standard for homoerotic relationships in the Greek world was supported by misunderstanding of a fundamental 1947 article by Sir John Beazley, 'Some Attic vases in Cyprus', which appeared to extend this pattern from the late fifth/early fourth-century context of the main literary evidence back into the archaic period. Beazley was unquestionably the twentieth century's greatest authority on Attic pottery, and had seen and handled a very large proportion of surviving vessels and fragments known in his time. But Beazley certainly did not include in that article all the vases he knew which included homoerotic scenes; nor did he intend it to give a definitive summation of his understanding of the topic. The vases illustrating homoerotic scenes which Beazley includes in that article are those that have close iconographic parallels with the homoerotic scenes found on vases and fragments in the Cyprus Museum. Thus, the scope of the article is much more limited than has sometimes been assumed. Sir Kenneth Dover's *Greek Homosexuality* (1989) [1978], a very important book, a pioneering work in many respects, reinforced the view that the conventions of archaic pottery corresponded to the customs explicit in the later literary record. Dover's illustrations – many of them selected from vases cited in Beazley's article – give incomplete, and so to some extent inaccurate or misleading, information.

H. Alan Shapiro's article 'Courtship scenes in Attic vase-painting' (1981), though it added more illustrations, worked apparently on the basis of the same assumption that Beazley's seminal article covered the full run of homoerotic scenes that he knew. This further compounded the error. Shapiro drew political conclusions from this material, reckoning that homoerotic scenes on vases declined in popularity in the period following the expulsion of the Peisistratids (*c.* 510) because pederasty was associated with the aristocracy. This contention has serious difficulties. It is not true that homoerotic scenes involving ordinary mortals disappear from vase-painting shortly after the Peisistratids were expelled: a number of them occur in red-figure in the period between *c.* 500 and *c.* 470 – there are examples by (e.g.) Onesimos (*GE* 463*, though this could be a little before 500), Makron (*GE* R651*), the Brygos Painter (*GE* R520*), the Briseis Painter (*GE* R539* = Plate 1), Douris (*GE* R573* = Plate 2). Rather, explicit sexual scenes (both heteroerotic and homoerotic) seem to fall out of fashion in red-figure pottery *pari passu* in the decade after *c.* 470 (the date is much 'softer' even than this appears to make it). The reason (or reasons) for this fall from grace surely applied with rough equality whatever the sexes of the participants depicted. Political motivation – particularly, pro-democratic and/or anti-aristocratic sentiment – seems to me unlikely to have been the sole cause, or even the principal cause.

Plate 1: Red-figure vase, *c.* 500–470 BCE by the Briseis Painter,
Paris G278, Florence ZB27. *ARV²* 407.16 (Briseis Painter);
Add² 232 (=R539).

In fact, explicit homoerotic scenes in red-figure have come down to us in
very much smaller numbers than their explicit heteroerotic counterparts.
Contrary to what Shapiro's discussion might lead us to expect, I know of no
red-figure explicit homoerotic scene which must be earlier than 510 BCE, and
only three which may be earlier than 500 (a fragmentary cup related to the
early work of Douris, *GE* R1123*; Peithinos' Berlin cup, *GE* R196*; perhaps
Onesimos, *GE* R463*). Because the overall numbers are very small, and the
accident of preservation may play an even larger role than it usually does with
archaeological material, statistical analysis would not be helpful. (For discussion of these issues, see *GE* 205–208.) Besides all this, the apparent dis-
appearance of explicit erotica from one medium (red-figure pottery) tells us
nothing about what happened in other media. We know virtually nothing,
for example, about painting on wood panels, except that we know it existed,
and almost nothing about mural painting in private houses during this period.
Keith DeVries of the University of Pennsylvania has been working on a
book, provisionally entitled *Homosexuality and Athenian Democracy*, of
which he has been kind enough to send me an early draft. The picture that

Plate 2: Red-figure vase, *c.* 500–470 BCE, by Douris. Munich
2631. *ARV²* 443.224 (Douris) *Add²* 240; *GH* R573 (=R573)

arises from his examination of archaic Attic pottery, particularly archaic black-figure, is much more complex than we had been led to expect. A briefer discussion by the Dutch scholar Charles A.M. Hupperts (1988) already raised several key points about male–male sex in black-figure, anticipating some of DeVries' conclusions.

Before examining 'heretical' material, let us discuss some scenes which fit into the generally accepted scheme for male same-sex erotics. First, from the mild end of the spectrum, a red-figure cup in the Villa Giulia, by the Ambrosios Painter (*GE* R283* = Plate 3, inv. 50458). The scene is a symposium: we can see two wine cups (a *skyphos* and a *kylix*) in use, and some sort of friendly interaction between the bearded male to our left and the couple to our right. The couple is our point of focus here: a bearded man puts both arms around a beardless (but none the less clearly adolescent) boy. The man has one hand on the youth's breast; his right arm is around the

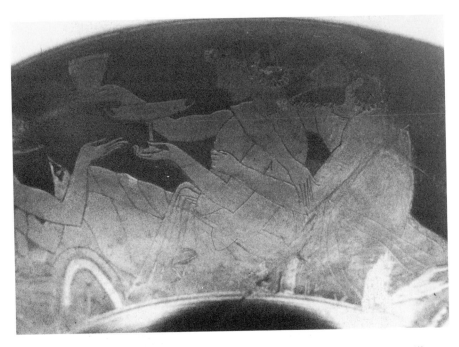

Plate 3: Red-figure cup, *c.* 510–500 BCE, by the Ambrosios Painter. Rome, Villa Giulia 50458. *ARV*² 173.5. *Para* 338; *Add*² 184 (Ambrosios Painter); (=R283).

youth's neck, the hand resting on his own upper arm. The man's erotic interest is evident, even though we can see no unavoidable proof of sexual arousal. The youth's engagement in the episode is less clear. He shows no direct sign of response to the man on any level other than the most basic. He does not reject the man's advances. He is co-operating at least to the extent of taking care of both drinking cups, which allows the man to have both hands free for embrace and caressing.

The late fifth/early fourth-century homoerotic ethos as expressed in the literary record insisted that the *erômenos* exhibit no sexual response to his *erastês'* advances; and we can use this scene as an early example of that ethos – but perhaps a note of caution is in order. Few of us would hesitate to assign a strong connection to her sexuality in the young girl's enthusiastic response – perhaps even initiation of the engagement – in the Kiss Painter's name cup (*GE* R303*, Berlin 2269=Plate 5). Halperin's description of a related vignette by the Carpenter Painter is telling (*GE* R308.1* = Plate 4, Malibu 85.AE.25; Halperin 1990: frontispiece caption):

> This scene might be entitled 'More than he bargained for.' A vase-painter teases the erotic conventions of male society in classical Athens by depicting an amorous boy responding more enthusiastically than

Plate 4: Red-figure vase, *c.* 515–500 BCE, by the Carpenter
Painter. Malibu 85.AE.25. Bothmer 1986 (attr. Carpenter Painter)
Dierichs (1988) 117d; Halperin (1990) Frontispiece (=R308.1)

expected to the overtures of an evidently startled adult suitor. Note,
however, that the boy is not portrayed as *sexually* aroused by physical
contact with the man whom he wishes to encourage: he is shown
without an erection.

In fact, the youth shows no erection at least in part because his draped cloak
won't allow any to show, though this is of the vase-painter's choice. The man
shows none either. We deny sexual involvement at our peril – and if Dover
and Halperin had not told me that this youth is not responding sexually, I'm
quite certain I should not have come to that conclusion on the evidence of
the scene itself. A companion scene by the Briseis Painter (*GE* R539* = Plate
1), this one apparently set in the *gymnasion*, seems to me also to suggest
enthusiastic sexual involvement on the part of the youth. It is risky to place
too much weight on comparisons between heteroerotic and homoerotic
scenes. It is probably at least as dangerous to try to treat one without
thorough knowledge of the other.

A more advanced stage of the operation, with intercrural copulation shown
under way, or about to begin, is fairly common in red-figure of the early fifth

Plate 5: Red-figure vase, *c.* 500 BCE, by the Kiss Painter.
Berlin 2269. *ARV²* 177.1 (Kiss Painter); *Para* 339; *Add²* 185;
Dierichs (1988) 117a; *GH* R303; Keuls (1985) pl. 174 (=R303).

century: I cite two examples, one by the Triptolemos Painter, in Mykonos
(*GE* R502*, Mykonos, no number = Plate 6); the other by Douris, in Munich
(R573*, Munich 2631 = Plate 2). In both the penetrating partner is adult, the
more passive partner youthful. This scene has many parallels in black-figure
– as on an unattributed tripod pyxis in Mississippi (St Louis, Washington
University, University Museum 1977.3.72) or on an amphora by the Painter
of Berlin 1686 (London 1865.11–18.39 [formerly W39], *ABV* 297.16, *Para*
128, *Add²* 78). Also akin are courting scenes with the 'up-and-down' hand
positions of the *erastês*, – that is, he touches his (usually younger) lover's chin
and genitals – for example one by the Phrynos Painter (Würzburg 241, *ABV*
169.5, 688, *Para* 70, *Add²* 48) which has an added martial element indicated
by the slender lance. Scenes of courtship, including gift exchange, are even
more common: the Amasis Painter's Paris cup-*skyphos* (Paris A479 [formerly
MNB 1746], *ABV* 156.80, *Para* 65, 90, *Add²* 46) shows that some specific gifts
are appropriate for either male or female love-objects.

Illustrations on pottery by the black-figure artist known as the Affecter
show a quite different scenario, with men of similar ages or youths of similar
ages carrying out the same sorts of courtship and sexual culmination as we

Plate 6: Red-figure vase, early fifth century BCE, by the
Triptolemos Painter. Mykonos. *ARV²* 362.21 (Triptolemos
painter); *Add²* 222; Koch-Harnack (1983) fig. 15;
GH R502; (=R502).

already know in the more familiar youth-meets-boy, man-meets-youth age
formats. This on its own is sufficient to call the traditional view into doubt.
Two examples: on an amphora in New York (MMA 18.145.15, Rogers Fund.
ABV 247.90. 691, 715, *Para* 111, *Add* 64, Hupperts 1988: fig. 4), in front of a
benign Dionysos and a male onlooker, a beardless but fully grown youth
approaches an older, bearded man. The youth's hands take the 'up-and-down'
positions normal for the hands of the *erastês*, clarifying still further the
atypical age relationship the Affecter is showing here. In a second amphora,
in London (BM 1836.2–24.46 [B153]. *ABV* 243.45, *Add²* 62, Hupperts 1988:
fig. 5 = Plate 9), a youth showing what must be his first beard – it is substantially
thinner and shorter than that of his companion – touches the chin of an older,
full-bearded man. The younger man holds a circular wreath in his left hand –
a rather common courting gift. Below the handle to our right of these figures,

Plate 7: Black-figure Tyrrhenian amphora, *c.* 550–530 BCE, by the Guglielmi Painter. Guglielmi Painter (Bothmer), Tyrrhenian, Orvieto, Faina 2664 (1955 VG 38). *ABV* 102.100, 684; *Para* 38; *Add²* 27; Wojcik (1989) figs 1.1–1.4.

a more typical scene shows a bearded man (substantially smaller than the figures in the first group: he must fit into the restricted space under the handle) offering a live hare to a youth or boy. Only the hare shows signs of displeasure. Given the clearer eroticism of the first couple, we are probably correct in accepting this, too, as a courting scene.

Still more significant is a scene on a Tyrrhenian amphora in Orvieto and from Orvieto. (Orvieto, Faina 2664 [1955; VG 38], *ABV* 102.100, *Add²* 27, Wojcik 1989: 46–49, figs 1.1–1.4 = Plate 7) Tyrrhenian amphoras have been found most commonly in Etruria ('87 per cent of the 250 that survive' – Spivey 1991: 141), and have been thought at times not to be of Attic manufacture, and perhaps not of Greek manufacture at all. However, they are now generally taken to be of Attic (read 'Athenian'?) production. Their clay looks Attic; the decoration – both figure painting and subsidiary ornament – fits comfortably within the Attic tradition even though their animals often seem to owe more to Corinthian style than to the style of other Attic painters working around the same time. The letters used in their inscriptions also clearly fit the Attic tradition, even when the inscriptions' meaning is obscure and even when they are manifestly and intentionally meaningless. (On the script, see Immerwahr 1990: 39 and Carpenter 1983, 1984. On their place in

44

the Attic tradition, see Spivey 1991: 141–42 and especially Carpenter 1983, 1984).

The painter is the Guglielmi Painter, a painter of modest gifts.[2] The B side shows a fairly typical Dionysiac revel, with Dionysos seated on a folding stool near a laden grapevine and a large container suitable for wine. One nymph (or maenad?) and two satyrs dance attendance on him, one satyr with large but flaccid penis, the other grasping his enormous erection in both hands. The inscription which runs below his phallus, unfortunately unreadable, has its letters placed much as droplets are placed in scenes which show satyrs ejaculating. Should we see the letters as substitutes for droplets of seminal fluid? This works best if there is a rather strong wind from the right; but unfortunately there is no confirming evidence.

The A side (Plate 7) is the one which most concerns us here. Three men (two of them ithyphallic) move in from our left. At far right, flanking a krater, we see a naked woman and a naked man who seems to stroke his erect phallus. Both look towards the main vignette. Here we have a bearded man on his knees, bent forward so that his beard seems to touch the ground. Coming up behind him is a beardless youth – in profile, with the whole of his facial profile shown unobscured: the absence of beard is conscious and important to the artist's intentions for the scene – who begins anal penetration of the older man. Two things which we have seen scholars treat as major taboos in the visual arts for Attic craftsmen are here violated. First, there is clear anal penetration, not the intercrural copulation which normally stands in as the visual substitute for that. Second, the person doing the penetrating is obviously younger than the penetrated person, reversing the relationship which we have been conditioned to anticipate.

Plate 8: Tripod pyxis, *c.* 525–515 BCE, by the Amasis Painter, from the Aphaia sanctuary on Aegina.

Before moving to my conclusions, two puzzles. A small tripod pyxis in Berlin, unattributed, shows heroic scenes on two of its legs; the third is devoted to sports – including homoerotic sex. We 'know' immediately how to interpret the erotic scene. There is a variant of the up-and-down position. The male to right, crouching slightly, is still taller than his standing companion, and should be seen thus as older – and his crouched position makes him ready to engage in intercrural copulation. There is just one problem: the faces of both characters are completely effaced. We 'know' their relative ages because we are applying *our* understanding of *their* artistic/sexual conventions. It is surely unsafe to assume that no youth was ever taller than any man. We will not learn from this picture by applying our standardized template. We may in fact be misinterpreting – and we may never know.

The second puzzle is another tripod pyxis, this one found in the Aphaia sanctuary on Aegina, and painted by the Amasis Painter (Aegina, Museum, no number. M. Ohly-Dumm 1985 = Plate 8). The vessel has very complex decoration – it seems to me highly probable that it was made specifically to

Plate 9: Black-figure amphora, *c.* 550–520 BCE, by the Affecter. London, British Museum 1836.2–24.46. *ABV* 243.45; *Add²* 62 (= B153).

46

be dedicated – with one leg showing a homoerotic scene of three couples and two male spectators. The scene is set in the *palaistra* – there is at least one oil-jar – and includes a dog, which we know from elsewhere as a common love-gift in homoerotic relationships (*GE*, Index, under 'courting-gifts'). Publications of this piece have assumed that we can determine on the evidence preserved which male in each couple is *erastês* and which is *erômenos*. We have now seen, however, that there is more than one pattern possible for homoerotic relationships in Attica in the sixth century. Rather than the 'pattern' for homoerotic relationships in the black-figure tradition, we should instead refer to the 'patterns'. We make this kind of age distinction at our peril where the evidence preserved is in itself inconclusive. Without the heads of the courting couples on these two pyxides, we cannot be certain of the age relationships of the courting couples.

CONCLUSIONS

The first two of these conclusions have particular significance for the overall theme of this book, since they demonstrate that there was a change in the conventions of visual representation of a significant social phenomenon. They additionally suggest that there is a substantial difference between the conventions of homoerotics as shown in painted pottery of the late archaic period and the mode espoused by some writers of the classical period.

1 The conventions for black-figure male–male homoerotic scenes are very different from the conventions explained by Plato and others in the late fifth/early fourth centuries. There are some significant (though less strongly marked) differences between the conventions of red-figure and the conventions of the literary material. There is no question that, according to the evidence currently available, there appears to be a substantial shift between what is approved for representation of sexual fantasy in black-figure pottery and what is approved for visual fantasy in early red-figure. There are further differences between each of these and the conventions as presented in the literary evidence of the late fifth/early fourth centuries.

2 Between what is permitted in visual erotic fantasy (which commonly gets part of its appeal from breach of taboo), what is permitted in literature (Aristophanes is one thing, Plato something substantially different), and what happens in real life, there are – or there may be – gaps of unknown dimensions. While the law-courts of the fourth century provide some evidence with which to bridge the gaps at that date, the clear presence of change of conventions in the visual arts warns that it is dangerous to extrapolate the conventions of the fourth century on to the society of Athens a century and more before.

3 The conventions for representation of male–male homoerotic relationships in Attic painted pottery are different in black-figure from what they are in

early red-figure, with black-figure showing a much wider range of patterns of age and of sexual role(s). Black-figure pottery continues in production substantially later than the beginning of red-figure pottery; but the black-figure examples examined here are all earlier than any of the red-figure.

4 Parallels from heteroerotic scenes suggest that we need to re-evaluate the convention that Dover and others have seen at work in red-figure erotica: that the younger and presumed penetrated partner is never to show signs of physical arousal. Attic pottery had limited ways to show physical signs of sexual arousal in women – erect nipples show up from time to time, but there is no convention apparent for showing vaginal lubrication (see *GE* 151–52) – and yet there are many heteroerotic scenes in which we need have no hesitation at all in saying that the female participants are aroused or at the least enthusiastically co-operating, even initiating sexual interaction. The same is surely true of scenes using the same and similar iconographies in male–male homoerotica.

5 Even the single case of black-figure homoerotic anal penetration presented here challenges the belief that anal penetration of one male by another was such a shameful thing for the penetrated partner that it could never be visually represented. For the Gugliemi Painter (and for his client, who need not have been Greek) this taboo was certainly not operating in the anticipated way.

6 The same Tyrrhenian amphora by the Gugliemi Painter also provides the single case of anal penetration of an adult male by a youth. While this scene does not on its own provide a new orthodoxy, it does raise the possibility that two current orthodoxies about 'sexuality' in the Athenian world need to be re-examined: first, that homoerotic sex is always to involve the elder acting on the younger partner; second, that for the archaic Athenians, 'sexuality' was not divided into 'males', 'females', and 'homosexuals', but into those who penetrate and those who are penetrated, the latter considered as social inferiors of the former. If the younger can penetrate the older, even this once, the value system posited for late fifth/early fourth centuries cannot have held for the time when our Tyrrhenian vase was painted.

NOTES

1 David Halperin's *One Hundred Years of Homosexuality* (1990) and the late John Winkler's *Constraints of Desire* (1990b), along with Foucault's *History of Sexuality* (1978, 1985, 1986), have had considerable impact on recent investigations of homoeroticism among the ancient Greeks. My debts to them are at least as significant as are my disagreements with them.

This essay, though commissioned separately from the project, falls within the confines of the long-term project on the Social History of Athens undertaken by me in collaboration with Dr Robert Develin. I am, as always, grateful to him for his comments and suggestions, some of which I have incorporated. Any errors that have persisted are, of course, entirely my own. Does this remind anybody else of 'Mission Impossible'?

In the identification of vases, the 'R-numbers' (e.g. R283 = Plate 3, R303 = Plate 5) are the catalogue numbers of these vases either in Dover's *Greek Homosexuality*, in my *Greek Erotica*, or in both. These numbers, which follow the order established by Beazley in his *ARV*, by virtue of that fact give the approximate chronological order of the pieces. The asterisk (*) accompanying such numbers indicates that a vase is illustrated in my *Greek Erotica*. I use the following abbreviations: *ABV* = Beazley (1956); *Para* = Beazley (1971); *Add²* = Carpenter (1989); *GE* = Kilmer (1993).

2 The attribution is by Dietrich von Bothmer.

3

TRIMALCHIO'S CONSTIPATION: PERIODIZING MADNESS, EROS, AND TIME[1]

Peter Toohey

INTRODUCTION

Madness, eros, time: these have become canonical subjects for modern Cultural Studies. The three have been powerfully linked in a variety of ways. The Enlightenment, it is often argued, provides one of the most interesting of links: beginning in this revolutionary period the modern concepts of madness (Foucault 1973), eros (Foucault 1978), and time (Elias 1992, Borst 1993, Foucault 1977: 149ff.) first emerged. Of madness it has been argued that, because of the development of a more sophisticated form of mercantile economy, there emerged for the first time concepts of mental illness with these matched by institutions to incarcerate the mentally ill and medical systems to legitimize such 'clinics':

> in the bourgeois world ... the cardinal sin ... had been defined ... [as the] inability to participate in the production, circulation, or accumulation of wealth (whether or not through any fault of their [the mads'] own). The exclusion to which they were subjected goes hand in hand with that inability to work, and it indicates the appearance in the modern world of a caesura that had not previously existed.
>
> (Foucault 1987: 68; but cf. Porter 1987: 6–9)

In similar fashion, it has been argued, time was rewritten by a bourgeoisie determined to extract the maximum financial gain not just from the physical commodities of trade, but also from their workers. Time became money. Everything was organized by the clock (Foucault 1977: 174). Producers, like products, required quantification. The regulation of time into easily recognizable periods apportionable to one's workers became one means of regulating production and controlling its producers (Foucault 1977: 160). Time thus, requiring monitoring and instrumentalization, assumed the linear, evolutive, serial, cumulative, progressive, and compartmentalized shape that it has today.

Eros and sexuality can be said to succumb to the same social forces

(Foucault 1978, Laqueur 1990). These changes coincide with what might best be described as a new way of speaking of the body. This, as we have just seen, may enunciate itself as a lesser discourse on madness or on time. So it may be with eros and sexuality, where changes emerge too in response to a common imperative. We could explain this as follows. The formulation of the body, up until the Enlightenment, was based upon the effects 'of a system of production in which labour power, and therefore the human body, has neither the utility nor the commercial value that are conferred on them in an economy of an industrial type' (Foucault 1977: 54). Such a system resulted in a contempt for the body which was reinforced by the demographical and biographical situation of the day: people died younger and more often through the 'ravages of disease and hunger, the periodic massacres of the epidemics, the formidable child mortality rate' (Foucault 1977: 54–55). Inchoate capitalism, nascent industrialism, and the beginnings of the medical control of disease usher in a new regime of bodily treatment and hygiene. For the new industrial state to prosper, it is often argued, the body must be controlled and husbanded. Medical hygiene, sexual hygiene, a sexuality that is directed into the industrially productive practice of reproduction (hetero-sexuality), an eros that is controlled and channelled accordingly, a use and application of time that encourages such profitable 'health', all of these factors encourage a new vision, a vision which manifests itself in the segregation and removal of those qualities or folk deemed unsuitable to the new commercial world. So eros and sexuality, it has been argued, are channelled along with madness and time into more efficacious modes.

Madness, eros, time, and their articulation within the ancient world (and thus their periodization) will be the focus of this chapter. I shall concentrate on particularized manifestations of these conditions: melancholia (a particu-larized manifestation of madness) and boredom, lovesickness (a particularized mode of expression for eros and sexuality), and time's passing (as we see it in Petronius' *Satyricon* and Ovid's *Fasti*). I hope to demonstrate not just that they exhibit a periodization, but that these particularized states also manifest discursive patterns and relations (using discourse and discursive in the technical sense – as the sum total of the conventions according to which genres, textual forms, and fields of knowledge are organized and classifiable in any given period) that are shared and that are applicable to madness, eros, and time within the ancient world.

The Enlightenment, I also hope to demonstrate, has been overprivileged. Amy Richlin and Martin Kilmer argue in this volume that the shift in the perception of sexuality purportedly ushered in by the Enlightenment was already present in the ancient world. David Konstan makes a similar case for 'friendship'. Suzanne Dixon argues thus for childhood and affection within marriage. I too will argue that, while historicist analysis is vital (that *culture* rather than *nature* determines a particular subjectivity or discourse) and that my three thematic concerns most certainly betray periodization, crucial

51

aspects of the modern, post-Enlightenment conceptions of madness, eros/sexuality, and time are to be observed within the texts of the ancient world.

TRIMALCHIO'S CONSTIPATION

'Pardon me', he said, 'but for many days now my stomach has not answered the call.' So announced Trimalchio to his guests (Petronius, *Satyricon* 47). Trimalchio has been absent for some time from his remarkable banquet. He seems to feel that his guests deserve an explanation. Constipation was the excuse. Trimalchio's cure was pomegranate, resin and vinegar. But constipation makes Trimalchio think of dying.[2] 'The doctors', he explains to his friends, 'forbid you to hold back ... Believe me if the gas goes to your head it produces feebleness throughout the whole body too. I've known many to die that way, because they were unwilling to be honest with themselves' (compare Suetonius, *Claudius* 32).

The passing of time and death provide persistent organizational motifs within the banquet scene of Petronius' *Satyricon* (Arrowsmith 1966, Slater 1990: 54–55). I suggest that Trimalchio's anxiety over constipation exemplifies these themes.[3] I suggest further that how Trimalchio describes his condition echoes the language and conceptual formulation which are used of some forms of madness and eros in contemporary literature.

First let us look at the how the themes of time's passing, and this intertwined with death, are evident within the *Satyricon*. When we enter Trimalchio's house with Encolpius (*Satyricon* 26) we discover that Trimalchio has a 'clock [*horologium*] in his dining-room and a well-dressed trumpeter to tell him how much of his life he's lost'. The trumpeter lets forth timely blasts which notify the millionaire how much remains of his thirty years, two months, and two days (we learn of Trimalchio's residual lifespan in 77 – compare Manilius' computation of lifespans at *Astronomica* 3.560–617). Trimalchio's 'morbid, although whimsical, preoccupation with death', as Martin Smith (1975: 53) puts it, is made even more plain in the closing scenes of the banquet. There (77) he gives this command: 'Stichus, bring out the material in which I want to be laid out. Bring some unguent too, and a draught from that wine jar in which I want my bones to be washed.' The *cena* ends with a reprise of that with which it began. The clock and the trumpeter match Trimalchio's funerary evocation of that for which the trumpet blares (so Arrowsmith 1966: 306–07).

But Petronius is not satisfied to conclude his *cena* with Trimalchio merely looking at the unguent and the wine for his bones. He has him experiment with the nard and urge his guests to try it too. Trimalchio even opens the wine in which his bones will be washed and seems set to share it. Worse still, after showing the guests his shroud, he lies along the couch as if he had already passed away. 'Imagine I'm dead', he announces, 'and say something nice.' As if to chase away his own fear of death, Trimalchio begins to enact his very funeral. He has his cornet players blow a funeral march.

An obsession with time's passing and with death can be observed in other places within the *cena*. Early on in the banquet (34) Trimalchio's slave brings in a miniature silver skeleton with flexible joints. Trimalchio plays with this, casts it on the table, then recites a ditty:

> Alas for us wretches; little man is nothing!
> We'll all be like that after death has taken us away.
> So let's enjoy ourselves, while we can.

Later, in section 48, Trimalchio brags that he has seen the Sibyl at Cumae and that she said 'I want to die'. Nearer to the close of the banquet (as he grows more and more drunk – 71) Trimalchio reads his will, something that reduces his whole household to tears (72). And when his wife, Fortunata, picks a fight with him (74) for being too lavish in his affections towards a boyfriend, he responds with a blow from a thrown cup and these angry words:

> Right, I'll make you go after me with your bare nails. And, so that you'll know right now what you've done for yourself: Habinnas! I don't want you to put her statue on my tomb, in case I have this squabbling when I'm dead. One more thing: so that she'll know I can give it out too, I won't have her kiss me when I'm dead.

Trimalchio, when not worried about death, continues to fuss over time and its symbols. In the colonnade to his home (29) Encolpius spots a shrine in which there is a golden casket containing Trimalchio's first beard – another reminder of the passing of time (as it is also a sign of sexual maturity). Later, in 73, we read: 'Today, friends', said Trimalchio, 'my servant had his first shave: so help me, he's a careful man and close with his money. So let's drink up and eat till dawn.' And there is of course the famous zodiac dish, itself a bizarre, celestial timepiece (35 and 39; compare Manilius, *Astronomica* 5.32–709). Of it Trimalchio states (39), 'so the heavens turn like a millstone and always brings something bad – people being born and dying.'

Little surprise in all of this that at least one of Trimalchio's guests (referred to in 38) has been an undertaker. And Habinnas and Scintilla arrive late at the banquet (section 65) because they have been at a ninth-day funeral feast for a slave called Scissa. Little surprise too that one of the favourite topics for conversation at the banquet is death. Seleucus (in 42), after recounting aspects of the funeral and of the life and death of his friend Chrysanthus, concludes: 'We're walking sacks of wind. We're less than flies – they've at least got some worth. We're nothing more than bubbles.' When Ganymedes puts in his piece (44), he intones on contemporary decline: 'It gets worse every day. This town is growing backwards like a calf's tail.' Echion, the sadistic rag-merchant, speaks cheerfully (45), but it is all about death struggles at gladiatorial shows or killing off a young boy's pet birds.

Experiencing time for Trimalchio and his guests is a passive business. Petronius' discourse represents humans as time's playthings. They register time's passing passively and play no active role in its unfolding. For them its climax is death. Trimalchio's comic but understandable attempts to manage and to master time amount to little more than an admission of fear and failure.

It is in this light that we ought to understand Trimalchio's constipation. Trimalchio's intestinal regularity seems to provide a woeful means for tracking the proper advance of time. Just as does the regularity of the clock and the trumpet, so too does bowel routine provide for Trimalchio's life a series of foreseeable punctuations and predictable events. Their regularity, their predicability, and the fact that they can be controlled, in some degree mitigate the depressing, unpredictable, and uncontrollable reality of death. I doubt that Trimalchio (or Petronius) was conscious of this, at least when all was normal. But irregularity of bowel movements, which Trimalchio has been suffering, renders void the pretence of controlling death. Irregularity may even hasten one's death. Little wonder that Trimalchio and his friend Habinnas are so conscious of what they eat. Trimalchio expounds in section 56 that 'a doctor has to know what people have in their insides and what causes fever – although I do hate them terribly the way they put me on a diet of duck'. (M. Smith 1975: 150–51, tells us that duck is very good for digestive troubles.) Habinnas in section 66 even commends wholemeal bread.

Trimalchio's constipation, therefore, reflects a larger discourse on the experience of time's passing.[4] We may well be right to describe this constipation as a *somatization* (a sign or symbol) of Trimalchio's fears. The passing of time for Trimalchio, I am suggesting, could produce an actual *debilitating* and *physical* manifestation.

ANOTHER TIME

Time's passing was not always expressed in this strange and maudlin fashion. Trimalchio's time is a far cry from the conception of time broadcast by Augustan writers such as Virgil, Horace, and Ovid. We could illustrate this traditional Roman attitude to time by referring to Ovid's great Augustan poem on time and the calendar, the *Fasti*.[5] The *Fasti* details the major events of the first six months of the Roman calendar. Time's passing is at the heart of this poem. For Ovid, at least as he broadcasts it in the *Fasti*, time is social and cyclical (for this type of 'social' time, see Elias 1992 and Borst 1993: 1ff.; for time as a social construct, see Bettini 1991). It is not progressive (linear as it is for Trimalchio), nor is it degenerate (despite Janus' half-hearted reference to a decline from a golden age at *Fasti* 1.247ff.). Ovid's calendar embodies a process of re-enactment and constant re-creation: Roman origins and key Roman mythological and historical or quasi-historical events are annually re-created through the various festivals of the calendar. Such events are persistently related to contemporary events. Thus is created a link between mythological time and time now. What Ovid tells us of the activities of the Luperci (2.267–424), for example, could be applied throughout his version of the calendar and its festivals: 'they bring back the memory of ancient custom and give witness to the resources of the ancients' (2.301–02).

In Ovid's traditional temporal world, mythological and early historical time is revivified above all by Augustus' royal family. The Megalesia (4.179–372) is striking in this regard. Transplanted from Greece to Rome, it early on gained particular connection with the imperial family (4.293–348). It is still practised (4.349–72) and is still relevant now. Thus, for example, the 'Trojan' legend concerning Dido's sister, Anna (3.523–710), leads imperceptibly to Roman foundation legends and, significantly, is juxtaposed with a brief lament on the murder of Aeneas' descendant, Julius Caesar (3.697–710). Anna and Caesar, both victims, become, eventually, divine beneficiaries.

A systematic appraisal of time's passing within Ovid's calendar would be impossible within the constraints of the space I have available here (I cannot touch, for example, on the way Augustus politicized time and how he came to use it as an instrument of power – see Wallace-Hadrill 1987 and Zanker 1988). But allow me to offer, through the Carmentalia, one last example of how this circularity is operant (and thus offer a hermeneutic template which may be applied throughout much of the rest of the poem). The Carmentalia was a festival begun on 11 January for Carmentis, the mother of that first inhabitant of the site of Rome, Evander (1.461–586). It begins with a straightforward description of Evander's birth and exile (for crimes not of his own making) from Arcadia in Greece (1.469–508). Then, after arrival at Tarentum, it shows us Carmentis enthusiastically greeting the new homeland (Rome itself – Carmentis and Evander have sailed up the Tiber) and predicting its future greatness (1.509–42). What does Carmentis tell of Rome's future? After greeting Rome and exclaiming in a generalized fashion on its future (1.509–18), she prophesies the arrival of the Trojans (1.519), subsequent war (1.520), Lavinia, Aeneas' bride-to-be (1.520), the death of Pallas, Evander's son (1.521–22), the belated triumph of Troy over Greece (1.523–26), and Aeneas (1.527–28). At this point Carmentis jumps one thousand years (*in annos nostros*) and forces, arbitrarily, a comparison between that family which includes Julius Caesar, Augustus, Tiberius, Germanicus, and the founders of Rome (1.529–30; note the reference to Vesta in 1.528). Augustus' clan thus comes to be seen as another instance of the sorts of things which were manifest in Rome even from its beginnings. Ovid drives home the point. He goes on to link in Augustus, Tiberius (1.530–34), and Augustus' to-be-deified wife, Livia (1.535–36).

But this is enough of Ovid and of the concept of time's passing evident in his *Fasti*. One crucial point, however, remains to be made. In Ovid's concept of time's passing, the individual is not envisaged as a passive player. Rather, human beings occupy a position of considerable significance. Through their participation in calendrical rites, they may play their piece not just within the great cycle of time, but within the very formative and restorative acts of their Roman culture.

MADNESS

Have we not witnessed in the cases of Petronius and Ovid hints of a periodization of the representation of time's passing? In Ovid (who lived 43 BCE–17 CE) we noted the refraction of a way of looking at things which estimates time's passing in a manner that implies that one participates', collaborates, and plays a partner with time and its restoration of the Roman state. Significantly, one does not name time. Being no oppressor, it needs no nominal privilege. In Petronius (d. 65 CE) Trimalchio's representation of time's passing is utterly passive: time controls; it humiliates; humans attempt to escape its net; and time is named. Time, furthermore, is a linear, serial, and cumulative process (Slater 1990: 55). Do we not see a sharp break – hence a periodization – in this reflection of modes of conceptualizing the effects of time's passing? Do we not witness a shift from a viewpoint which respects individual participation in a cyclical temporal movement, to a viewpoint which descries subjects as passive victims of an essentially disinterested (but potentially malevolent and degenerative), linear, and serial temporal movement?

Madness plays its role within this spectrum. I cannot hope to touch upon madness in all its ancient manifestations (surveys: Rosen 1968, Simon 1978, Milns 1986). Instead I would like to focus on just one of its forms, namely melancholia (surveys: Starobinski 1962, Klibansky *et al.* 1964, Flashar 1966, Jackson 1986, Rütten 1992, Ferguson 1995: 1ff.). I have looked at the information on this matter elsewhere (Toohey 1990). Perhaps it will suffice here to point to the evidence of the pseudo-Aristotelian *Problema* 30.1. This text maintains that melancholia is the product of a superfluity of black bile. Black bile was a mixture of cold and hot. Melancholics, accordingly, fall into two broad groups, those in whom the black bile becomes very hot and those in whom the black bile becomes very cold. Where the black bile is hot, one would expect what we term the manic phase of this condition; where the black bile is cold, one would expect the depressed phase. Subsequent theorists, whether humoralists or not, associate the illness with one, the other, or both of the two poles, mania or depression. So Celsus (*De Medicina* 2.7.19–20), Soranus of Ephesus, and Caelius Aurelianus all associate the disease with depression (see Drabkin 1950: 19, 561). Aretaeus of Cappadocia (Jackson 1986: 40) and Galen (Jackson 1986: 41–45, Siegel 1976), on the other hand, allow the bipolarity of the *Problema*.

The literary depictions of the condition of melancholia, I have argued (Toohey 1990), indicate that these two forms just mentioned seem to cluster or to predominate in two different periods. The more common literary depiction of melancholia is of the manic variety (Cicero states typically at *Tusculan Disputations* 3.5, 'what we call *furor*, the Greeks call *melancholia*'). The pseudo-Aristotelian *Problema* 30.1 provides us with a number of examples of this type of character who, when faced with frustration, reacts in a most violent manner. Heracles (especially as we see him in Euripides and in Seneca) is typical, as is Lysander (compare Plutarch, *Lysander* 2 and 28), Ajax (violent towards his companions), and Bellerophon (compare *Iliad* 6.200–02). The *Problema* also adds supposedly manic characters such as Socrates, Plato, and Empedocles.

Beginning in the Alexandrian period, melancholia takes on a second face. Here we see isolated cases of a depressive form of melancholia. As the centuries pass, the ranks of the depressives swell but little. One of the earliest depressive melancholics may be Jason in Apollonius' *Argonautica* (Beye 1982: 81). Jason broods and becomes *amêchaneôn* (*Argonautica* 1.460–61); he grieves when faced with possible doom (2.622–23) and becomes excessively fearful (2.276–8); he despairs (4.1316–18, 1347); he sometimes becomes excessively silent in his anguish (1.1286–89); and is prone to tearfulness (1.534–35, 4.1703–04). The depressive form of melancholia does not assume any prominence in literary experience until the era when Celsus, Soranus of Ephesus, Caelius Aurelianus, Aretaeus of Cappadocia, and Galen begin to produce their analysis. So we find M. Annaeus Serenus, the addressee of Seneca's *De Tranquillitate Vitae*, suffering from a condition (melancholia, surely) which is characterized (2.6–15) by a variety of colourful terms: nouns or noun phrases such as *adsidua mutatio propositi, cunctatio vitae, displicentia sui, sibi displicere, fastidium [vitae], fluctus animi, inertia, levitas, maeror, marior, oscitatio, residentis animi volutatio et otii sui tristis atque aegra paenitentia, taedium, tristitia*; adjectives such as *instabilis* and *mobilis*; or the adjectival clause *inter destituta vota torpentis animi situs*. Persius' third satire offers us another glimpse of a melancholic individual who, it is implied at 3.63, requires the standard cure for melancholia, hellebore, for he displays symptoms of a pervasive purposelessness (3.60–62) as he lolls about yawning (3.58–59), and because, through a personal inertia, he lives his life in the same inadequate circumstances in which it began (3.24–33). Other non-medical examples may perhaps be drawn from the Greek novelists, in particular from Persius' contemporary Chariton who, in his romance *Chaereas and Callirhoe*, offers a group of male leads who are all of them a most melancholy and depressing collection. Faced with adversity of almost any kind, but particularly with the prospect of losing Callirhoe, these men are cast into a depressed state of black hopelessness. They fret, tend to weep, and begin to lose weight in a dangerous manner.

Again we witness what seems to be a periodization of emotional repines. On this occasion what is privileged is a passive emotional state. It is as if there were an invention or discovery of depressive melancholia. The periodization may be localized: to speak approximately, acute frustration tends to provoke a manic melancholic reaction throughout the literary experience of antiquity. But, beginning with the third century BCE, but more pronouncedly within the literary experience of Rome in the early empire, acute frustration may produce a reaction best described in terms which match those which we use of melancholia. It 'becomes' a passive condition, an utterly depressive and fretting condition. What is notable, however, is that this invention displays no clear stratigraphic line of demarcation. It begins to become prominent in Alexandrian literature for the first time. It disappears. Then, displaying a pendulum-like motion, it comes back in the first century of our era. Of its own this melancholic periodization is, I believe, a rather interesting thing – if, that is to say, my rough and schematic diagnosis is correct. Depression, something to which nearly all of us are prone, was, as it were, 'invented' in a more systematic way twice, first in Alexandria and then again some time in the first century of our era. Now I say 'invented' with all due caution. What I mean by this term is merely that it seems suddenly and unexpectedly to have been judged a topic worthy of serious textual contemplation.

Earlier in this essay I spoke of the need to demonstrate how a single set of discursive rules defines the relations between madness, eros/sexuality, and time. I would like now to allude briefly to an emotional state related to, but not quite comparable to madness, namely boredom. (But note that ethologists, amongst others, have posited a relationship between these conditions; frustration, boredom, and depression have been marked as an experiential logical continuum – Wemelsfelder 1985, 1989.)[6] Boredom's formulation (its symptomatology) and its periodization exhibit patterns comparable to those of melancholia.

The incidence of boredom – as it is depicted in literary texts – seems to rise as we move later into antiquity. Greek of the classical period seems to lack both a clear-cut term for the condition (*alys* assumes the unambiguous sense of 'boredom' late in antiquity) and clear-cut descriptions of circumstances implying boredom (see Toohey 1988: 153–55). Roman literature of the classical period presents us with the same case. The *horror loci* of Lucretius' or Horace's dissatisfied Roman who rushes aimlessly between city and country (*De Rerum Natura* 3.1060–67 and Horace, *Satires* 2.7.28–29, *Epistles* 1.11.27, 1.14, 1.18.12; *Epistles* 1.11 produces the famous term for boredom, *strenua inertia* – see Negri 1988) certainly resemble boredom, though we are not specifically told that is what they are suffering, for Lucretius' and Horace's concern are more with philosophical issues than with psychological ones. It is under the early Roman empire that boredom becomes a condition sufficiently invasive as to be able to infect a whole life. We may witness this in Seneca's *Epistles* (24, say, where boredom is a Sartrean *nausia*; one ought to compare again the *De Tranquillitate Animi*) and in Plutarch's life of Pyrrhus. That king was driven to his death by boredom (Plutarch, *Pyrrhus* 13): Pyrrhus, after taking early retirement, returned to the general's life, just to alleviate the boredom of civilian existence (his boredom was a *nausia*, Toohey 1987).

We could summarize as follows. Greek literature to the Hellenistic period seems to lack reference to anything more than the simplest form of boredom. Serious or unequivocal consideration of boredom begins in the first century BCE in Rome, but here it is limited to the less complex form of *horror loci*. It is in the first and second centuries CE that a 'spiritual' form of boredom is first referred to. Boredom in Seneca, for example, can be depicted as an emotion which affects a person's life not only sporadically but can spread to influence one's every waking action.

In Seneca, Persius, and Plutarch, I believe, there is registered the 'invention' of the modern concepts of the emotion. The incidence of boredom in ancient literature, as I read things, seems not unexpectedly to match the literary 'invention' of melancholia. Do we witness the operation of a generalized affective formulation, one whose very hallmark is passivity, one that inscribes the world as something which one merely registers, something which acts upon one, something over which one has no ready control?

TRIMALCHIO'S MELANCHOLY CONDITION

What is so profoundly interesting in the instances of boredom and melancholia is that, like most psychological conditions in the ancient world, these emotional states manifest themselves in somatic terms. Melancholia and boredom were seen in most periods of the history of the ancient world as physically debilitating conditions. These were conditions which could mani-fest a somatization that might be dangerous to others (thus the violent melancholia instanced by *Problema* 30.1 of manic characters such as Hercules,[7] Lysander, Bellerophon, and Ajax), but that might also be dangerous to oneself (thus the depressive inertia of Apollonius' Jason [see Toohey 1990: 156ff.], Seneca's M. Annaeus Serenus in *De Tranquillitate Vitae* 1.4–14, 2.1–15 or the melancholy and suicidal tendencies of the heroes of Chariton's *Chaereas and Callirhoe* [1.4, 1.5, 3.1, etc.].

Trimalchio's constipation at this point becomes again a pressing matter. That Trimalchio's somatization of the experience of time's passing carries con-siderable danger for himself we have already seen. The danger is described in a language that is strangely familiar. It is a language or symptomatology which echoes in part that provided by medical writers for melancholia itself. Constipation, we learn from Petronius' near contemporary Celsus (*De Medicina* 3.18.17), is to be associated with melancholia (*tristitia*) or an excess of black bile (*bilis atra*, the very substance which causes melancholia) (compare Jackson 1986: 38). This is what Celsus says (translation W.G. Spencer I 1948):

> There is another sort of insanity ... depression which seems caused by the black bile. Bloodletting is here of service; but if anything prohibit this, then comes firstly abstinence, secondly, a clearance by a white hellebore and a vomit.

A few lines later, Celsus points out that if health is to be maintained, then 'the motions are to be kept very soft'. Constipation, thus, is to be avoided.

Now Trimalchio, though alluding to constipation and to purges, does not use hellebore (*veratrum*) as an emetic, the standard treatment for insanity

(Celsus 2.12; see also W.G. Spencer II 1953: lviii–lix) and melancholia (Starobinski 1962: 16–21, Toohey 1990: 159–60). He uses pomegranate, resin and vinegar. Constipation of itself, of course, is no proof of melancholy (Celsus describes its symptoms and cures at 1.3.23–27), although it was associated with melancholy (by such as Aretaeus – see Starobinski 1962: 23). We could leave it there were it not for Trimalchio's suggestion that the stool might overheat and send up an exhalation which might damage the higher portions of the body. Although such damage is an expected concomitant of excessive constipation (according to Celsus 1.3.23–27), Trimalchio, by describing the dangerous vapour produced by the constipation as *anathymiasis*, must inevitably point to a humoral context. Galen, for example, uses the word of 'an exhalation from the humours being drawn to the head' (M. Smith 1975: 128). (Indeed, for Galen, it was the combustion within the body of black bile and the resultant dangerous vapour which cause insanity – Starobinski 1962: 25–26.) What other humour would Trimalchio have us associate with his condition than the atrabilious one, the black humour often associated with constipation?

Trimalchio, as I have stated, has not specifically described melancholia when he refers to his constipation. Yet his outline – constipation, dangerous overheating of the stool thus damaging higher portions of the body – seems to reflect, however indirectly and however unintentionally, the language and concepts used of melancholy. What are we to conclude? Evidence of a conceptual contagion, in part, the permeability of discourses, in part, but above all evidence of a larger discourse of which boredom, melancholia, and the experience of time's passing represent individual enunciations.

Trimalchio's condition does not just help us in the search for discursive rules. It also provides a fascinating match for the periodization which I have attributed to madness as it is manifested in melancholia and boredom. Trimalchio's fears manifest themselves precisely within the period during which Seneca's Serenus and, possibly, Chariton's doleful heroes make their melancholic, depressive, and passive laments. Trimalchio's constipation, therefore, provides another instance of the affective caesura to which I have already alluded.

EROS

Madness, eros, and time: these are the subjects for my chapter. Eros and sexuality, of course, intersect. Their mapping has been repeated again and again during the last ten years. I can only describe one small corner of this vast realm. Lovesickness, my interest here, must reflect not just the discourse of love, but in turn that of eros and sexuality.

We associate lovesickness with depression. Yet depressive lovesickness is not at all common in the literature of the classical world. Typical of the dominant amatory cliché is Apollonius' depiction of the growing love of Medea for Jason. The symptomatology of Apollonius' portrait is explicit and consistent (*Argonautica* 3.284–98). The initial attack of love produces a violent, physical reaction (Eros' shaft is 'like fire'; Medea's heart is full of 'agony'; the shaft, furthermore, causes forgetfulness, mental turmoil, and pallor alternating with rose-coloured flushing). Subsequent frustrations recapitulate, though in a more pronounced manner, this manic, violent, and emotional reaction (3.444–71, 3.755–65, 4.16–23).[8] One might contrast depressive lovesickness. One of the earliest unambiguous examples comes from Theocritus, *Idyll* 2 – this is the portrait of Simaetha depressed (2.82–86) and even balding (2.88–90) from frustrated love. The majority of such ancient examples, however, are to be drawn from the first century of our era and later.

One of the very first is the story of Antiochus and Stratonice, a tale which may be found in Valerius Maximus (*Facta* 5.7.1) and Plutarch (*Demetrius* 37.2–3). It concerns young Antiochus, the son of King Seleucus, who fell in love with his equally young stepmother, Stratonice. Antiochus, either unwilling or unable to reveal his passion, fell ill, took to his bed, and began to waste away. The physician Erasistratus, called to attend Antiochus, noticed how, when Stratonice entered the room, his pulse and breathing quickened, and how he flushed. Erasistratus realized that the cause of Antiochus' troubles was frustrated love. King Seleucus so loved his son that, on hearing Erasistratus' diagnosis, he passed on his wife, Stratonice, to Antiochus. That selfless action afforded the cure. A number of other comparable tales could be cited. There is Ovid's Echo and Narcissus (*Metamorphoses* 3.339–510), Marcus Aurelius' wife, Faustina, and her conception of Commodus (*Historia Augusta, Marcus Antoninus* 19.12), and above all the love-struck players in the Greek novels: Callirhoe and Chaereas in Chariton's *Chaereas and Callirhoe* (1.1), Habrocomes (1.5) and Anthia (1.5, 1.6) in Xenophon of Ephesus' *Ephesian Tale*, or Charicleia in Heliodorus' *Aethiopica* (3.5, 3.7–9, 3.19, 4.7). The onset of eros for all of these characters is physically dangerous, causing debilitation and threatening death.

It is striking that the appearance of this sort of lovesickness in literature (I have no strong opinion concerning lived experience) coincides approximately with the earliest medical discussions of the condition. What the doctors say of ancient lovesickness (the little that there is is confined to Aretaeus, Galen, Oribasius, Caelius Aurelianus, and Paul of Aegina) interprets the condition as a depressive illness (brief surveys in Jackson 1986, Beecher and Ciavolella 1990, Wack 1990, and Toohey 1992). Aretaeus of Cappadocia (*c.* 150 CE), for whom melancholy was a depressive rather than a manic illness, may be typical. He describes one man who 'appeared to the common people to be melancholic'. In fact his trouble was merely a case of 'serious dejection due to unrequited love'. His doctors, like the common people, must have assumed the illness was melancholy, for their treatments were unsuccessful. The truth of Aretaeus' diagnosis was demonstrated by the man's cure. This took place when he declared his love to his beloved (Jackson 1986: 353). Galen (*c.* 130–200 CE) offers us a comparable story. A woman had fallen in love with a dancer, Pylades. She had become 'emaciated, pale, sleepless, and even feverish'. Galen at first took her condition to be melancholy. Her pulse rate, however, which rose when the dancer's name was mentioned, gave indication of the true nature of her illness (Jackson 1986: 353, Wack 1990: 7–9, Beecher and Ciavolella 1990: 51). Oribasius (fl. 326–403 CE), Paul of Aegina (fl. 640 CE) and Caelius Aurelianus (sixth century CE, but translating the Trajanic medical writer Soranus of Ephesus) offer comparable analyses. We could summarize as follows: lovesickness, according to the major surviving medical view, was a condition typified by sadness, insomnia, despondency, dejection, physical debility, and blinking. Aretaeus and Galen do not seem to have thought of the condition as a specific illness (unlike melancholia), but rather as a psychological disturbance which could best be cured by therapeutic intercourse. Oribasius and Paul of Aegina conceived of lovesickness as an actual illness, but one not based on an excess of black bile.

These medical discussions of lovesickness seem to confirm the proposed periodization of the affective disease. While Theocritus may demonstrate that depressive lovesickness was a condition from which people always suffered, or at least that there was a minor literary outbreak in the third century CE, the remaining 'literary' instances and the medical discussions of the condition suggest that, as a discursive, even sociological phenomenon to be taken seriously, depressive lovesickness was 'invented' in the early imperial era. Until that point, the reaction to eros' invasiveness was violence.

While ancient medical theory seems in practice to recognize only one form of lovesickness, the depressive form, I hope to have indicated that, in the literary sources, there were two distinct forms: the medically recognized depressive form and also the more widespread manic form. The symptomatology of lovesickness, then, seems to match the views of ancient medical theory on melancholia. As we have already noted, melancholia was categorized as depressive or, more commonly, as violent and manic. Thus the two types of melancholia mentioned in, say, the *Problema* and depicted later in various medical contexts seem to match the two types of lovesickness I have been attempting to outline (despite the fact that the medical writers did not pick up the match). Just as melancholia could be manic or depressive, so could lovesickness be manic or depressive. The congruence is remarkable and perhaps tells us something of the popular formulation of melancholia and lovesickness. We might add that these two forms of melancholia and of lovesickness seem to match those identified in the instance of boredom. Depressive lovesickness, what is more, echoes the language used of Trimalchio's constipation.

This curious congruity is of particular importance, therefore, when we attempt to isolate the rules governing the greater dialogue to which these conditions belong. It is also of help in allowing us to establish a periodization for this condition. The shift in the perception of the effects of this *morbus* parallels precisely those which we have observed in the case of melancholia, boredom, and the passing of time.[9] This periodization seems to mark the inception of a recognition of the symptoms of lovesickness which runs to this day. Consider this recent description of lovesickness. It matches closely those which we witnessed in young Antiochus (García Márquez 1988: 61–62):

> After Florentino Ariza saw her for the first time, his mother knew before he told her because he lost his voice and his appetite and spent the entire night tossing and turning in his bed. But when he began to wait for the answer to his first letter, his anguish was complicated by diarrhoea and green vomit, he became disorientated and suffered from sudden fainting spells, and his mother was terrified because his condition did not resemble the turmoil of love so much as the devastation of cholera. Florentino Ariza's godfather, an old homoeopathic practitioner who had been Tránsito Ariza's confidant ever since her days as a secret mistress, was also alarmed at first by the patient's condition, because he had a weak pulse, the hoarse breathing, and the pale perspiration of a dying man. But his examination revealed that he had no fever, no pain anywhere, and that his only concrete feeling was an urgent desire to die.

CONCLUSION

I hope that my comparison of the specific examples from the three seemingly discrete realms of madness, eros, and time has allowed us to establish between them certain correspondences and certain dissimilarities. The correspondences could be said to reflect 'textual dialogue' between these affective domains (the perception of time is manifest as an affective state), which might best be termed a discourse. The shared dissimilarities within the formulations of these conditions allow us to establish a periodization for this discourse, both within the ancient world and between the ancient and the modern worlds.

I doubt that I need detail the characteristic polarities of this discourse: key qualities, however, are a contrast between activity and passivity, between assertion and yielding, between participation and withdrawal, between complicity and estrangement, between the cyclical and the linear, between the mark (the visible) and the sign (the hidden), between body and mind. The list could be continued.

The periodization established by the dissimilarities within this 'textual dialogue' is of considerable significance. It supports the conclusions drawn here, but within different ideological parameters, by Richlin, Kilmer, Dixon, and Konstan. Sex, gendering, even erotics as we know them, are not inventions of the late eighteenth century. Nor, to press the point, are affectivities like depression (which, in Jackson's 1986 survey, seems to assume the modern form in approximately the same period) or boredom (which, though lacking a proper history, is associated more with the nineteenth century and the emergence of capitalist economies – Spacks 1995). Claims for these states which privilege their novelty require modification (we have seen Foucault 1987: 68 assert of madness that, during the Enlightenment, there appeared 'a caesura that had not previously existed'). If these emotions do assume a prominence and do assume a form recognizable to us, it is during the two periods to which I have alluded: the Alexandrian era, and the first century of our era.

I would like to finish with one curious piece of evidence for this periodical continuity. Think back first to Trimalchio's trumpeting timepiece and the lifespan, allotted to him by an astrologer, which the trumpet and the doomsday clock announced. Recently, in the *Sydney Morning Herald* (1 September 1994: 21), I found the following report. I will let it speak for itself:

> A clock which forecasts how long someone has left to live is being sold in the United States. Based on an average life span – 74 years for men and 79 for women – it is programmed with the owner's age and gender and calculates his or her remaining hours and minutes.

NOTES

1 My thanks for help in the composition of this chapter to Mark Golden, David Konstan, Amy Richlin, Elaine Fantham, and the audience at the 1994 conference of the Classical Association of Canada in Calgary, at which a first version was read.
2 Arrowsmith (1966: 307) notes of Trimalchio's circumstances: 'wealth brings thoughts of defecation (for wealth is symbolically a satiety that cannot evacuate itself)'.
3 Compare Arrowsmith (1966: 309): 'food consumed to the point of satiety is an instance, a symbol, of *luxuria*; the end of satiety is constipation; and flatulent vapours "go straight to your brain and derange your whole system", and especially the reason which should, at least in Epicurean ethics, control the appetites. "I know some who've died . . . from holding it in." That is, *luxuria* is death, extinction of the rational will.'
4 Petronius' novel may be *sui generis*, but his concept of time is not. Seneca periodically alludes to the serial nature of time's movement. The best place to see this is in his moral essay *De Brevitate Vitae*. It may be worth noting that this essay finishes with a mock funeral, that of Sextus Turannius. Bettini 1991 has some observations on Seneca and time. For Stoic time there is Goldsmith 1979, cf. Munn 1992.
5 Although temporal decline is a persistent *topos* (see, for example, Virgil, *Georgics* 1.121ff. and 1.463ff., Horace, *Epodes* 7 and 16, and compare Lovejoy and Boas 1965 and Dodds 1985), much *public* literature affirmed a cyclical (agrarian or seasonal) concept of time. Thus, in the *Aeneid*, Augustus completes a cycle in that he embodies the mythical Roman founder Aeneas (6.752–853, 8.608–731). So he does in Ovid's *Metamorphoses*, which we learn through Pythagoras' teachings on metempsychosis (15.60–478). In Horace's *Carmen Saeculare*, Augustan Rome

renovates time, as it were, by its continuation of an ancient festival. For this theme in architecture, see Zanker 1988.

6 Wemelsfelder (1985, 1989) believes animals experience boredom, for what it is worth. Spacks (1995), citing Thomas (1993), denies this, just as she denies the experience to the ancients.

7 The most prominent of the violent melancholics in *Problema* 30 is Hercules. So Euripides' version of Heracles in the *Hercules Furens*. On his melancholia, see Wilamowitz 1959: 92–95 and Collinge 1962: 48. Virgil was aware of the tradition of *Hercules melancholicus*. See *Aeneid* 8.219–20. Seneca seems to use atrabilious terms of Hercules at *Hercules Furens* 939ff.

8 Virgil's Dido reacts in similar fashion: 4.1–2, 67, the wound; 4.5, 9ff., anxiety and insomnia; 4.300–03, anger. Compare Valerius Flaccus' Medea, *Argonautica* 7.144–52.

9 There seems to be a pendulum-like movement between the manic and depressive phases. The depressive phase is hinted at in the literature of Alexandria, then seems to disappear, only to be replaced apparently by the manic in republican and Augustan Rome, only to be met again in the depressive form under the early Roman empire. Pigeaud 1987 seems to link the depressive form with the Alexandrian period and a mind–body split in medical thought of this period.

4

PHILOSOPHY, FRIENDSHIP, AND CULTURAL HISTORY

David Konstan

For we should not forget that we are speaking first of all from within the tradition of a certain concept of friendship, within a given culture, let us say ours, in any case the one on the basis of which a certain 'we' here tries its luck. Now, this tradition is not homogeneous, nor is the determination of friendship within it. Our principal concern will be to recognize there the major marks of a tension, perhaps ruptures, and in any case scansions, at the interior of this history of friendship, of the canonical figure of friendship.

(Derrida 1993: 366–67)

Ces difficultés rendent totalement illusoire la prétension de rapprocher anciens et modernes du seul point de vue de la *philosophia perennis*, et imposent le rejet de toute méthode qui ne soit pas purement historique.
(Fraisse 1974: 20)

In speaking of 'friend' or 'friendship', one uses a term that existed a thousand years ago, unlike the tricky terms 'feudalism' or 'courtly love', which moderns invented to describe medieval patterns of life. The very sharing of terms between our age and an earlier one, however, makes it difficult to distinguish between our own experience of friendship and the medieval one. Two dangers appear: either we posit a facile similarity of all human experience, with no historical dimension, or else we conclude that the identity of vocabulary actually hides the fact that we know little or nothing about individual friendships in another age so different from our own.

(McGuire 1988: xvi)

In a study of eighteenth-century theories of friendship in the writings of the liberal Scots thinkers Adam Ferguson, David Hume, Francis Hutcheson, and Adam Smith, the sociologist Allan Silver observes: 'Sociological studies of modern personal relations are not historically grounded, and the comparisons some make or imply with the past often strain an awkward join between contemporary and historical research.' Silver notes that modern scholars

66

frequently write as though relations such as friendship remain more or less stable over time, and he comments: 'This large inference is indeed fragile for, among other problems, it assumes that personal relations in times past are sufficiently similar to those prevailing in modernculture to warrant inferences comparing their magnitudes, distributions, and structures.' For the Scottish liberals, however, ancient friendship was different in kind from modern: 'precommercial societies do not offer the possibility of disinterested relations, ungoverned by the clash and calculation of interests; only the development of the market does so, in those domains falling outside the market itself and therefore newly distinguishable from the interplay of interest'. This is why in pre-modern societies such as ancient Greece 'the purpose of friendship ... was to help friends by defeating enemies'; this sordid and calculating mode of interaction was unavoidable, Silver writes in his summary of Ferguson's argument, because 'in such settings vital resources are obtained largely through what modern culture and theory see as personal relations ... In contrast, the Scots conceive of personal relations in commercial society as benefiting those involved at no cost to others; friendship becomes simultaneously a private virtue and a public good' (Silver 1990: 1484–85, 1487, 1496).

I have cited Silver's article at length because he elegantly shows how the analysis of social relations, and in particular of friendship, over different historical epochs depends on a theoretical perspective. Against the contemporary tendency in the social sciences to assume that modern categories are broadly applicable to the experience of other societies, Silver adduces not Foucault but the tradition of eighteenth-century rationalism. These thinkers celebrated the modern ideal of sympathy as a function of the differentiation of social space into a newly emerged economic sphere governed by market relations and a personal domain, constituted in counterpoint with the commercial realm, in which disinterested individual bonds were now free to flourish. Their analysis is, in a sense, doubly historicized: they recognize that their interpretation of modern forms of friendship is a reflex of the new social conditions which they are seeking to describe. Correspondingly, it may be supposed that the theorization of classical modes of friendship by thinkers such as Plato and Aristotle differs in form and substance from modern treatments, both because the subject of their investigation is distinct and because the modes of analysis at their disposal are, or at least may be, different from modern methods to the extent that they too are a product of particular historical conditions.

Indeed, it is precisely on the subject of friendship that Plato and Aristotle appear to be furthest removed from modern definitions and approaches. The notion of *philia*, which Aristotle investigates in Books 8 and 9 of the *Nicomachean Ethics* (as well as in other ethical treatises), manifestly refers to a much wider range of relations than the English term 'friendship', since it pertains as well to kin, fellow citizens, and in general to people associated in any common enterprise whatever. As Paul Millett notes, Aristotle includes in his discussion of *philia* 'parents, brothers, benefactors, fellow-tribesmen and fellow-citizens', as well as 'husbands and wives, fellow-voyagers, comrades-in-arms, guest-friends, and cousins' (Millett 1991: 113). If *philia* is the closest that the classical Greek language comes to a conception of friendship, then we might reasonably conclude that the assumed continuity between ancient and modern treatments is in principle problematic, since they apparently deal with two quite different concepts.

That a language lacks a term to represent a particular relationship does not necessarily prove, of course, that the relationship does not exist. It seems natural to suppose that the Greeks recognized and prized the bond between friends at least as much as we do. The famous pairs of friends celebrated by the ancients, such as Achilles and Patroclus, Orestes and Pylades, or Theseus and Pirithous, would seem to be *prima facie* evidence for the existence and value of friendship in the classical world. But was the nature of the relationship between these men in fact that same as that which we identify as friendship today? Allan Silver (1989: 274) defines the constitutive characteristics of the modern ideal of friendship:

> Especially in the urban core of Western society, particularly in its more educated sectors, friendships are judged of high quality to the extent that they invert the ways of the larger society. In this ideal, friendships are voluntary, unspecialized, informal and private. They are grounded in open-ended commitments without explicit provision for their termination ... Friendships so conceived turn on intimacy, the confident revelation of the self to a trusted other, the sharing of expressive and consummatory activities ... The behaviour of friends to each other is appropriately interpreted through knowledge of the other's inner nature.

It is not obvious that this account captures the essential qualities of the bond between Achilles and Patroclus and the other famous pairs, not to mention more ordinary comradeship in the classical Greek world. For example, the association between Achilles and Patroclus is not strictly speaking informal or private: Patroclus is the squire or *therapôn* of Achilles, as Sthenelus is to Diomedes or Glaucus to Sarpedon, and he is at Achilles' service. Prior to the departure for Troy, Patroclus' father had instructed him, Nestor says, to offer good counsel to Achilles, for Achilles, though he is the younger man, is his superior in lineage (*geneê*) as well as in strength (*Iliad* 11.785–88). Achilles' father had adopted Patroclus into his household as *therapôn* to Achilles after Patroclus had slain a fellow youth in his home country (23.89–90). It is impossible to doubt the intensity of the love that Achilles feels for Patroclus (e.g. 18.80–82: 'my dear companion has perished, Patroclos, whom I loved beyond all other companions, as well as my own life'; 19.321–22: 'there is nothing worse than this I could suffer, not even if I were to hear of the death of my father' (trans. Lattimore 1951)). But their mutual affection is embedded in a structure of duties and responsibilities that seems contrary to the spontaneous and unobliged ideal of modern friendship. Thus Percival (1940: xvi) flatly affirms: 'Affection, in fact, may exist between friends in the Heroic Age, and sometimes does; but it is no essential part of friendship. The essence of friendship is its duties.'

Self-disclosure, which plays a very large role in modern discussions of friendship from Montaigne to Emerson and contemporary pop-psychology handbooks (see Jourard 1971, Chelune 1979, Bell 1981: 22, Duck 1983: 27, 67), is not an important feature of the friendships praised by the Greeks. Neither in the narrative examples nor in the classical philosophical discussions of friendship does there appear to be an emphasis on understanding a friend's 'inner nature' (on the inner self in modern thought, see Taylor 1989, Gill 1994). We might suppose – provisionally – that this absence of what we think of as personal intimacy corresponds to the more socially embedded or formal quality of friendship in classical antiquity. The classical ideal of friendship is not necessarily imagined to 'invert the ways of the larger society'.

The apparent distance between the classical instances of friendship and modern conceptions would seem to find its reflection in Aristotle's treatment of friendship as one aspect or form (Aristotle's word is *eidos*) of the more general bond connoted by the term *philia*, extending from kinship to civic or ethnic identity. These latter relations are not elective; rather, they are ascribed statuses. If Aristotle embedded his discussion of friendship, that is, of the bond between unrelated persons based on altruistic affection, in a larger treatise concerning the several types or species of *philia* generally, the reason is perhaps that he conceived of friendship as part of a matrix of social relations defined by roles. Accordingly, Aristotle did not organize his discussion of friendship around the opposition between informal and formal, or private and public spheres that informs modern theory and contemporary social practice.

In fact, a widespread – possibly the prevailing – view among modern classicists defines *philia* entirely in terms of abstract obligations rather than personal feeling. Thus Malcolm Heath, for example, writes:

> *philia* is not, at root, a subjective bond of affection and emotional warmth, but the entirely objective bond of reciprocal obligation; one's *philos* is the man one is obliged to help, and on whom one can (or ought to be able to) rely for help when oneself is in need. The family, therefore, is a group, reinforced by special ethical and religious sanctions, the members of which are, to a greater or lesser extent, mutually dependent.
>
> (Heath 1987: 73–74)

We may note the easy transition from mutual assistance among *philoi* to the specific obligations entailed by family ties. If *philia* is an 'entirely objective bond of reciprocal obligation', and those related as *philoi* include everyone from 'parents, brothers, benefactors, fellow-tribesmen and fellow-citizens' to 'husbands and wives, fellow-voyagers, comrades-in-arms, guest-friends, and cousins', then one may reasonably doubt that the subject of Aristotle's analysis in the eighth and ninth books of the *Nicomachean Ethics* (abbrev. *NE*) is related to the modern notion of friendship in any significant way whatever.

Now, I do not believe that the distance between the classical Greek view of friendship, in particular as it is expressed by Aristotle, and the modern notion is in fact as great as that. A close examination of relevant passages demonstrates that the primary meaning of *philia* in fifth- and fourth-century Greek texts is love or affection; among family members, for example, *philia* denotes goodwill as opposed to the fact of kinship, which is expressed by various terms such as *syngeneia*. What is more, while *philia* does indeed refer to a wide range of affective ties including those between family members and fellow citizens as well as between friends in the modern sense of the term, the noun *philos* is more restricted in its application, and indicates a relationship very much like friendship as the term is used today, in principle excluding kin, compatriots, and other formal social relations. Aristotle discusses friendship in this restricted sense in the first seven chapters of book eight of the *Nicomachean Ethics*, and then turns to other types of *philia*, in the analysis of which he generally eschews the term *philos*. We have Aristotle's explicit formulation of the distinction between loving in general – here he employs forms of the verb *philein* – and the more specialized term *philos* or 'friend' in a passage from the seventh book, devoted to the topic of *philia*, of the *Eudemian Ethics* (abbrev. *EE*):

> As has been said, there are three kinds of *philia*, according to virtue, utility, and pleasure, and these in turn are divided into two, the one set according to equality, the other according to surplus. Both sets are *philiai*, but friends [*philoi*] are those according to equality; for it would be absurd for a father to be a friend [*philos*] to his child, but of course he loves [*philei*] him and is loved [*phileitai*] by him.
>
> (*EE* 7.4.1–2.1239a1–7)

Toward the beginning of book eight of the *Nicomachean Ethics*, Aristotle identifies three properties of the relationship between *philoi* or friends in the limited sense. Friendship involves (1) reciprocal goodwill or affection; (2) mutual awareness of the disposition of the other; and (3) disinterestedness or altruism, that is, a desire for the other's good for that person's sake rather than one's own (8.2.1155b33–1156a4). Aristotle does not mention here such values as self-revelation, nor does he stipulate that friendship must be voluntary; nevertheless, his definition and his subsequent discussion seem to have enough in common with modern conceptions of friendship for critics to take Aristotle as a point of departure in their own analysis, thereby honouring Aristotle as a participant in a common enquiry into the nature of the bond between friends. For example, Elizabeth Telfer, in a justly famous essay entitled 'Friendship' published originally in 1970, writes:

> Now it is clear that Aristotle is mistaken in supposing that a man's virtue is not a contingent and changeable fact – as indeed he later admits. But his other assumption – that we care for friends 'in themselves' rather than for any contingent facts about them – has a certain plausibility. How far is it valid?
>
> (Telfer 1991: 255)

I omit the subsequent interrogation, subtle as it is, because my point is to illustrate the way in which Telfer assumes that she and Aristotle are investigating recognizably similar concepts when they speak of friends and virtue.

But even if it is the case that the Greeks had in the noun *philos* a term that singles out relations that resemble those we think of as obtaining among friends, as opposed to other bonds such as family or civic ties, there may remain a deep incommensurability between Aristotle's conception of *philia* in this restricted sense and the modern notion of friendship. On the one hand, the three constitutive elements of *philia* between *philoi* in Aristotle's account might be thought to apply not only to friendship conceived of as a voluntary, informal, intimate, and expressive relationship but to any type of reciprocal love, including that within the family or larger community. On the other hand, the very fact that Aristotle slides so readily from friendship in the narrow sense to affective bonds generally, all identifiable as forms of *philia*, might be taken as a sign that for him the bond between *philoi* is more continuous with these other affiliations than we would be inclined to allow, and hence that it is different in kind from modern friendship. Though Aristotle's usage, like classical Greek usage generally, may have discriminated *philoi* from other categories of relationship such as kin and fellow-tribesmen, it is not without significance that they are all, in his mind, closely connected. It is just this tendency to assimilate *philoi* to other kinds of attachments that has obscured the distinctiveness in Aristotle of the *philos* relationship itself (see e.g. Schollmeier 1994).

I have argued elsewhere that Aristotle's treatment of *philia* reflects the values of the democratic polis in the fifth and fourth centuries BCE (Konstan forthcoming). The ideology of the democracy encouraged a massive identification of the citizen with the community at large, and minimized the expression of differences between the public and private spheres in the domain of personal relations among males. Friendships were accordingly conceived of as distinct from but continuous with other forms of civic solidarity, from family ties to identification with fellow citizens. Rather than emphasize the differences and indeed the potential opposition or conflict between voluntary ties and social bonds, the culture of the democratic city-state interpreted friendship as a kind of virtue, and thus in principle consistent with other manifestations of virtue in the social sphere, such as responsibility to one's family and service to the community. Richard Bodéüs (1993: 43) affirms that for Aristotle 'there can be no contradiction in principle between what is required for the good of the city and what is presupposed for the happiness of human beings', since 'according to Aristotle, the city (*polis*) and the particular person (*hekastos*) are not opposed, but are distinguished only as whole (*holon*) and part (*meros*)'. Correspondingly, ethics is not an autonomous discipline in Aristotle (there is no mention of an *epistêmê êthikê*); rather, the discussion of ethics is part of the science of politics (Bodéüs 1993: 39–40). A person who was a good friend was the model of a good citizen.

Aristotle's treatment of friendship thus answers to the role of personal relations in the context of the classical city-state culture. In identifying an ideology specific to the democratic polis, however, I am not positing a primary division between premodern and modern societies, according to the model developed by the eighteenth-century Scots theorists. The embeddedness of personal relations between *philoi* in the nexus of social bonds within the city-state is not necessarily to be explained by the absence of a developed market economy, over and against which the personal sphere is constituted as the space of private sympathy, free of interested motives. In the first place, Aristotle's ideal of friendship is a disinterested one precisely because it is implicated in a larger notion of civic virtue. This is so whatever the actual practice of ordinary Athenians, which was arguably no more selfish than that of modern individuals, despite the emphasis in all genres, including philosophical treatises, on mutual assistance or advantage as a major reason for cultivating friendship (Dirlmeier 1931: 50–53, Percival 1940: xx). Second, and equally important, the coalescence of the private and the public spheres, at least so far as friendship is concerned, is not necessarily characteristic of Greek society as such. Rather, it is a feature of the civic culture of the democratic city-state, which was hegemonic at least in parts of the Greek world for a restricted period of perhaps two or three centuries: the sixth to the fourth centuries BCE. It cannot be assumed that this ideal obtained in the archaic period or in the Hellenistic and Roman periods in the Greek east. Indeed, there is evidence to suggest that the conception of friendship, and its relationship to other civic values, loyalties, and bonds, underwent important shifts over the course of ancient Greek history, just as it has done in the modern era. An adequate periodization of the concept of friendship in classical antiquity, and correspondingly of the philosophical discussions devoted to it, will have to be more fine-tuned than the gross contrast between the world of modern commerce and pre-capitalist societies posited by Ferguson, Adam Smith, and the other Enlightenment thinkers and their followers.

We have already seen that the loving bond between Achilles and Patroclus, as it is represented in the *Iliad*, seems to be inscribed in a hierarchical relationship of lord and squire or attendant. Patroclus anxiously caters to

Achilles' commands: 'You know yourself, aged sir beloved of Zeus', he tells Nestor, 'how *he* is; a dangerous man; he might even be angry with one who is guiltless' (11.652–53; trans. Lattimore 1951). The sense of duty and fear blended in Patroclus' deference seems remote not only from modern notions of the uncoerced spontaneity characteristic of friendship but also from Aristotle's ideal of perfect reciprocity and selflessness. As we saw in the passage cited from the *Eudemian Ethics*, a major element in Aristotle's conception of the bond between *philoi* is equality: in the *Nicomachean Ethics*, Aristotle quotes with approval the popular jingle, *philotês isotês* or 'amity is parity' (8.5.1157b36). The emphasis on equality is consonant with the democratic ethos that subtends the relationship of friendship in Aristotle's treatment. In Homer, on the contrary, the bond between lord and henchman is adapted to the aristocratic or 'strong-man' culture projected by the archaic epic (Donlan 1980: 9–10).

While Achilles is certainly capable of feeling and expressing his intense love for Patroclus, as we have seen, there does not appear to be a special term or category for friends in epic comparable to the use of the noun *philos* in Aristotle and classical Greek generally, which identifies a subset of the affective relations covered by the word *philia*. In Homer, the term *philos* refers to the people of one's own community or side: it may designate Odysseus' fellow Ithacans or, in the *Iliad*, the entire army of the Achaeans when they are addressed by their leader, Agamemnon (2.110). The opposite of *philos* in this sense is *xenos*, which primarily means 'stranger', that is, a person whom one does not know, rather than a foreigner in the sense of an inhabitant of another city or country, which is what the word comes to mean in the classical period. Among those who are in Achilles' privileged circle Patroclus is especially favoured, but the term *philos* does not pick him out uniquely from the group of Achilles' companions or *hetairoi*.

Here again, it may be misleading to infer the absence of an institution from the want of a specific nomenclature, and given Achilles' passionate attachment to Patroclus, it may seem perverse to deny them the appellation of friends. In the classical period, to be sure, the inequality between the partners inclined readers or auditors of the poem to believe that the relationship between the two was one of erotic love rather than friendship, since *erôs* was conceived of as a relation between dominant and subordinate partners, one of whom was the active lover or *erastês* while the other was the beloved or *erômenos* (Plato, *Symposium* 179D–180A). Such a conception of Achilles' and Patroclus' bond is clearly foreign to the *Iliad*. But this is not to say that we must settle upon the classical conception of friendship as the relevant description. For it may be that among the various intersecting ties such as lord and henchman, king and followers, kinsmen, comrades in arms, members of the same *ethnos* or community, and other kinds of relationship that collectively constitute Homeric society, there is no special space reserved for an elective association based chiefly on personal affection. Achilles and Patroclus certainly love each other (Hooker 1989: 34–35), but this fact is not the basis of a culturally recognized and privileged relation distinct from the several formal or ascribed roles in which personal attachments, as described by Homer, are situated or embedded.

The embeddedness of friendship in social relations determined by status is not unique to the culture of the Greek epics. Silver (1989: 278) remarks: '"Bond friendship" and "blood brotherhood", like other forms of institutionalized friendship studied by ethnographers, sharply differ from freely elective and non-institutionalized friendships characteristic of modern culture – their ritual and socially sanctioned character, and their frequent connection with imperative necessity seem to stamp them as involuntary' (cf. Evans-Pritchard 1933, Pitt-Rivers 1954; on Homeric friendship, see Silver 1989: 280, 282–84). Ritual bonds themselves, however, are complexly determined; Gibbs (1962: 67), for example, insists that 'ritual brotherhood is a type of friendship and is, therefore, an individual as well as a societal phenomenon'. Indeed, the metaphor of blood may serve to shore up voluntary bonds among men just when such relations seem threatened (L. White 1994). The Homeric poems, in any case, offer no evidence of ritual ties among friends (*contra* Herman 1987).

Both the intensity of the bond between Achilles and Patroclus and the apparent absence of a distinct social classification that designates a circle of friends may perhaps be understood as features of a relatively complex communal society. Eric Wolf (1966: 11), who divides friendships into the two classes of 'emotional friendship' and 'instrumental friendship', suggests that emotional friendship is likely to be found 'primarily in social situations where the individual is strongly embedded in solidary groupings like communities and lineages, and where the set of social structure inhibits social and geographical mobility. In such situations, ego's access to resources – natural and social – is largely provided by the solidary units; and friendship can at best provide emotional release and catharsis from the strains and pressures of role-playing.'

In the period following the defeat of Athens by Philip of Macedon and the imposition upon the city (after the death of Alexander the Great) of a regime supported by foreign armies, the values of the democratic polis underwent a profound change. For example, the freedom of speech or *parrhêsia* recognized by the members of the classical city-state as the characteristic right of free citizens was reinterpreted as frankness or candour, a virtue manifested especially by subordinates who had the decency to prefer honesty to flattery and falsehood (Scarpat 1964, Hunter 1985: 488). Such frankness was seen as the particular mark of the true friend, who subsumed his personal interests to those of his partner, patron, or monarch in the Hellenistic state: indeed, the monarch's inner council in Egypt, Syria, and Macedon was known officially as the *philoi* or Friends. To the classical discourse concerning mutual assistance and the danger of the fairweather friend was added an entirely new *topos*, namely the contrast between the sincere friend and the flatterer or toady who insinuated himself into the company of the rich or powerful in the interest of personal advancement. Hence such treatises as Plutarch's essay entitled 'How to distinguish a flatterer from a friend'.

The problem of the flatterer introduced into the philosophical and ethical discussions of friendship two other dimensions that played only a minor role in Aristotle's analysis. First, there is the new issue of sincerity, which bears a certain resemblance to the ideals of self-disclosure and intimacy that are so central to modern conceptions of friendship. Just how close the resemblance really is would require a more extended treatment than I can provide here (see Gill 1994). Second, the fact that people in positions of power, such as rulers and patrons, were making claims on the loyalty of their followers under the description of friendship raised the issue of a potential conflict between personal and political attachments in a way that had been largely suppressed or displaced in Aristotle's investigation and, I would argue, in the democratic discourse generally. In particular, with the development of the Hellenistic monarchies and, later, with the crises that wracked the Roman republic and the emergence of the principate, the problem of private associations as a locus of possible resistance or opposition to the political order became a central concern of treatises on friendship, nowhere more clearly so than in Cicero's *De amicitia* (Konstan 1994a).

Thus, in the post-classical discussions of friendship we find simultaneously a new emphasis on unequal or hierarchical relations that tend to coalesce with semi-formal or institutionalized structures of patronage in a way that may appear quite removed from modern conceptions of voluntary and personal attachments (Saller 1989: 57; but see P. White 1993: 14), and an equally new preoccupation with ideas of candour and the private world of friendship as opposed to the public or political sphere that seem to anticipate the ideal of personal intimacy characteristic of modern friendship.

The shift in the philosophical treatments of *philia* and *philos*-relations from the classical works of Plato and especially Aristotle to the Hellenistic and Roman treatises like those of Plutarch and Cicero corresponds, according to the analysis presented above, to a change in the political character of the ancient community. Aristotle was responding to a communitarian social order in which the tension between private and public interests tended to be repressed in the collective discourse. Especially in the domain of personal loyalties such as friendship, which was assimilated to the virtue of sociability generally, the suggestion of potential conflicts between personal attachments and the demands of the state was raised only in the special case of tyranny. Tyranny was precisely the deviant political form in which there arose a distance between the demands of the state and personal conscience: Sophocles' *Antigone* is a study in this problem, and Creon's suspicion of private attachments as the source of political rebelliousness (182–91) marks him as the type of the tyrant.

With the development of Hellenistic kingship and the aristocratic Roman state, the distance between private and public, personal and political, became more sharply articulated. This in turn inaugurated a new discourse of friendship as a private and personal bond that was both linked to the institutional order in so far as it crossed with patronage (although the spheres of patronage and friendship were never simply assimilated) and at the same time was independent of and conceptually distinct from the sphere of civic obligations in a more radical way than that which characterized the democratic polis. One form taken by the new modality of personal relations was the bonding that occurred within the philosophical schools. Discussions of *philia* and *philoi* among Epicureans such as Philodemus, for example, who lived in Italy during the first century BCE and was in contact with figures such as Horace and the aristocratic Piso family (Armstrong 1994), appear to have concentrated on the personal aspects of discipleship and the therapeutic effectiveness of individual attention and instruction.

The political transformations from the world of the Homeric epics to the democratic city-state and beyond that to the Hellenistic kingdoms and the Roman empire are not directly comparable to the economic changes inaugurated by the rise of commodity capitalism, as this was understood by the Scots thinkers and, in their wake, by Karl Marx, Max Weber, and their intellectual heirs, as well as by the founders and framers of the American republic (Rahe 1992:55–79). The Scots liberals were themselves reacting to an earlier tradition within British culture in which the domain of friendship was not so narrowly circumscribed as they would have it be by contrast with the impersonal relations of the market place. Silver (1990: 1487) cites a study by Randolf Trumbach (1978: 64) for the view that the word 'friend' in eighteenth-century England 'could mean a distant or close relation, a patron or a client, an individual to whom one was tied by mutual sponsorship, or someone attached by warm affection' (see also Perkin 1972: 46–51, G. Wood 1992: 58; but the evidence I have reviewed suggests to me that the distinction between friendship and other bonds was nevertheless clear throughout this period: cf. Brain 1976: 86, 93). This state of affairs, in which friendship was integrated or aligned with formal bonds rather than polarized with respect to them, would seem to mirror the broad range attaching to the term *philia* as it is analysed by Aristotle, even though, as I have argued, the concrete noun *philos* marks off in Aristotle and his contemporaries the more specific relationship of elective friends as opposed to kin and other institutionalized relations.

Broad social concepts such as friendship, and the philosophical accounts that they invite, do not evolve according to a universal pattern or teleological ideal. They respond to deep political, economic, or social changes in ways that are constellated by the particular contours of a given culture. The development and periodization of Greek and Roman notions of personal bonds in part parallel the modern transformations of the idea of friendship, and in part have a trajectory specific to ancient ideals. The modern vision of sympathy and intimacy is neither more advanced nor more natural than classical conceptions; nor does it represent the necessary form that personal relations must assume under the regime of commodity capitalism. The periodization of notions such as friendship, and of the philosophical analyses to which they are subject, must be the product of a close examination of the discursive practices of a culture and their intersection with particular social formations.

By the second century CE, when the Greek scholar Aspasius was composing his commentary on Aristotle's *Nicomachean Ethics*, the distinction that Aristotle had drawn between the love constitutive of the relationship between friends and that obtaining in other relations such as parent and child had already become obscured – a problem that has, I believe, continued to cause confusion in the interpretation of Aristotle down to the present day. Soon after emphasizing the importance of reciprocity in the relation between *philoi*, Aristotle mentions certain relationships under the heading of *philia* that do not exhibit mutually conscious affection. Aristotle characterizes as the most natural form of *philia* that between a mother and her child. He then describes an instance of its extraordinary power:

> For some [mothers] give out their own children to be raised, and they love [*philousi*] and know them, but they do not seek to be loved in return [*antiphileisthai*], if both [loving and being loved] are not possible; but it seems to them to suffice if they see them [i.e., their children] doing well, and they love them even if they, as a result of their ignorance, provide in return none of the things that are due a mother.
>
> (*NE* 8.8.1159a28–33)

This bond is manifestly asymmetrical. Aspasius, who does not appear to recognize that Aristotle has shifted the discussion to a different form or species of *philia* that is not subject to the constraints of his earlier definition, suggests that Aristotle is speaking here of *philêsis* or affection rather than *philia* in the narrow sense, which Aspasius takes to be defined by the earlier discussion involving the reciprocal relationship between *philoi*. Aspasius notes that parents' love of their children contains a 'trace' (*ichnos*) of *philia*, since, although it is not necessarily reciprocal, it at least has the characteristic of altruism (text in Heylbut 1889: 180.2–6). It is a shame that Aspasius feels obliged to derogate the maternal bond, which for Aristotle is the most natural (*physei*) form of *philia* (the second-century BCE Epicurean Demetrius Lacon, it may be noted, denied that love for offspring is natural in humans; text in Puglia 1988: 182–83).

Between the philosopher and his commentator there intervened six centuries of social and cultural change. Perhaps it is not to be wondered at that Aspasius failed to address the possibility that what Aristotle conceived of as the personal bond between *philoi* or, loosely, friends did not correspond precisely to the conventions determining the connection between this and related categories of *philia* in his own time. If I am right, the problem has persisted in philosophical discussions of Aristotle down to our own day and age. An awareness of the challenge of periodization, combined with the disposition characteristic of the new cultural history to read texts in the context of larger cultural values, may encourage an alertness to shifts in the primary terms of the cultural discourse that come in for philosophical analysis. In the process, philosophy itself may abandon some of its pretensions to timeless objectivity and accept its own subjection to history.

5

CONTINUITY AND CHANGE IN ROMAN SOCIAL HISTORY: RETRIEVING 'FAMILY FEELING(S)' FROM ROMAN LAW AND LITERATURE

Suzanne Dixon

This volume is testimony to the extent to which historians and literary specialists are now prepared to discuss the emotions and personal relationships of the ancients.[1] I shall consider how we might go about the attempt to identify Romans' feelings and to plot historically any significant changes in those feelings. This chapter is essentially a theoretical, historiographic discussion, but I shall explore the issues in relation to some specific questions: first, how Roman parents might have regarded their young children – 'family feelings'; second, how Romans might have viewed the responsibilities of husbands towards their wives' dowries and of others (especially parents) towards the inheritance 'rights' of family members – an area better termed 'family feeling' in the more general sense of propriety.[2] My argument will be essentially conservative, particularly in the realm of 'love', for it seems to me that the feelings of others – however expressed – are very difficult to read in any genre or culture (including one's own) and that apparent historical change might be a product of imperfect comparisons or silences. I am a little more hopeful of plotting some change in institutions such as dowry and inheritance, but even there the 'change' might be more a new legal response to specific difficulties (the 'bad husband' who breaches and therefore clarifies the ideal or norm) rather than a general change in community or personal expectation. I am therefore also sceptical of claims for any consistently 'liberalizing' tendencies in Roman law in relation, for example, to *patria potestas* or the legal independence of Roman citizen women.[3] Most negatively of all, I challenge the very quest for a historical narrative – that is, a story of change.

Historians of marriage, family and childhood in the ancient world have tended to pursue much the same questions as their colleagues working in other periods of history and geographic areas. Some of these questions

79

include the nature of the household (whether it was nuclear or multi-generational); whether there was a concept of childhood as a separate stage of human development; whether children were valued as individuals or simply for their function in the family; and whether there was any concept of conjugal love. The influential *Annales* school – most significantly, through Bloch, Febvre, and LeRoy Ladurie, put the human life-cycle and lower-class private life on the historical agenda even before the women's movement and other radical political approaches of the 1970s promoted women's history and 'history from below' (see the introduction to Hunt 1989 and Dixon 1994). These trends gradually brought respectability to social history, a category which included history of the family.

Household demography and economics soon led to studies of social and even emotional relationships among family members. Individual historians such as Stone and Ariès set the stage for those who wished to trace the development of the 'modern European family', for which they offered explanations somewhat different from the classic Marxist–Engelian model, although capitalism, industrialization and Protestantism continued to be viewed as crucial factors in a presumed change of household structure and family style in the modern period.[4] Whether the author in question is led by a particular line of reasoning to interpret the development of modern family relations as a sad decline from an idyllic earlier state (e.g. Engels 1972 [1884], Ariès 1962) or as the triumphant emergence from a horror-filled past (e.g. Stone 1977, deMause 1974), each provides a historical narrative with a happy or unhappy ending which, in classic Whig fashion, ends up with and explains the present.

An equally significant aspect of these studies is the presumption that certain relations and emotions date from the early modern period. Companionate or bourgeois ideals of marriage[5] and easier relations between parent (especially father) and child are represented as modern developments. Indeed, Ariès argued that the very concept of childhood as a separate stage of human development was a modern invention. Manson, French and I have, rather, argued that there *was* an identifiable concept of childhood and appreciation of childish qualities in the Roman world, at least by the late republican period (see especially Manson 1983, Dixon 1988: 104–14, 1992: 98–108, French 1991). I would not press this much further – certainly not to suggest that Roman conceptions of childhood mark a stage in a steady evolution of adult–child relations or that their conceptions of childhood had much in common with modern ones.

Until recently, all of those who wrote on the subject agreed that there was a new, identifiable, modern family which emerged in Europe in the late eighteenth or early nineteenth century. One of its agreed characteristics was a new emphasis on the role of the mother. Shorter (1977) and Badinter (1981) have gone so far as to see intimate and responsible motherhood as a modern invention.[6] In my 1988 book, *The Roman Mother*, I analysed dominant

Roman ideals of motherhood and concluded that, in contrast with the stress in modern (i.e. wealthy urban Western Anglo) dominant ideals on nurturing, 'soft' maternal qualities, the Roman cultural emphasis was on the role of mothers in moral transmission, particularly their influence on adolescent and young adult sons. If anything, Romans favoured maternal severity, a marked difference from modern post-Freudian emphasis on the intimate and affectionate bond between mother and infant and on retrospective mother-blaming. I did not suggest that Roman mothers of any social group avoided affectionate physical contact with young children, merely that that was not the defining element of the mother–child relationship. I repeatedly insisted that I could do little more than discuss dominant cultural ideals. This still seems to me the best we can hope for in discussing parent–child relations in the past.

As I have already noted, the conclusion that there was a Roman concept of childhood as a distinct stage of life clearly contradicts Ariès' argument that childhood is a wholly modern invention, but it need not follow that every subsequent age retained and elaborated the concept. Like knowledge of (or interest in) creating sewers or Greek fire, an appreciation of childhood can change or disappear from a culture and, even when it is found, it can coexist with indifference to the maltreatment of some or all children. I have been inclined to link Roman interest in children's childish characteristics with a stress on conjugal ideals of companionship and loyalty in the late republic and early empire (a period which is the focus of most of my work) to demonstrate in particular that marriages arranged by the wider family for material and political reasons might still be formed in expectation of the development of conjugal love after the event (Dixon 1985a, 1991).

In the *Roman Family* (1992), I presented a flexible – but, I hope, not idealized – portrait of family life which included generation conflict, economic exploitation of family members, norms of obligation and the kind of support Romans might have expected of their families. In general, I am uneasy about attempts to read uniform universal feelings into relationships (husband–wife, parent–child), or to read human social development as consistently going from harshness to happiness (i.e. social evolution) or from a glorious past to a decadent present (moral decline). I have instead favoured a cautious cultural relativism based on connections between social and economic factors and the culturally privileged norms (e.g. *pietas* towards parents).

This approach might seem to accord with Richard Saller's suggestion that we link the history of the family more clearly to other aspects of Roman history:

> The Roman family has a history, not in the dramatic sense that a date and cause can be found for the invention of the affectionate conjugal family, but in the more subtle sense that the Romans used legal

institutions and customs in characteristic patterns to pursue certain familial goals within the social, economic, political, and demographic contexts of their time. The goals, circumstances, and institutions changed, albeit slowly, and their configuration differed from those of other societies. Since the family was the primary social group transmitting legal status and wealth, its history is linked to many facets of political, institutional, and military history, and hence should interest mainstream historians more than it has.

(Saller 1988b: 263)

The problems of investigating such questions lie not only in general theoretical difficulties but in specific problems concerning the types of evidence we might use to assess changes in Roman family relations over time. These could include the linguistic and iconographic representations of the life stages, legal evidence for changing inheritance practices and *patria potestas*, and some literary and epigraphic conventions for referring to parent–child relations. One immediate problem is apparent in considering parent–child relations: while children's diaries and letters are available to early modern historians (see Pollock 1983), ancient evidence for young children all emanates from adults. Even first-hand information about adolescence is typically from an older person looking back and making an older-generation identification, as in the case of Agricola's story that his mother, Iulia Procilla, had rescued him from an excessive youthful zeal for philosophy (Tacitus, *Agricola* 4). Such an example needs also to be assessed in the light of its conventional quality. Similar stories are told in biographies of other men,[7] so I suspect the value of such anecdotes lies primarily in their indication of ideal or appropriate relations between young adult sons and their mothers. They fall into the same category as the motif of father–son conflict which features in moral tales and comedy. It, too, reinforces conservative stress on the authority and wisdom of the older generation, an ideological buttress of the legal institution of *patria potestas*. The moral tales, in which noble fathers execute their own sons, have the additional dimension of exhibiting the priority of civic responsibility over private preference and affection.[8] These stories appear to be timeless. Like proverbs, they are passed on to successive generations and could almost be said to reflect an aspect of cultural continuity. Or do they simply reflect, like our own transmission of fairy stories, nursery rhymes and Aesop's fables, an unthinking conservatism in passing on stories out of their original context with no serious interest in their inappropriateness to the children who hear them, who have never seen a muffin man and regard a wolf as a fluffy puppy to visit in the zoo?

Perhaps it is too much to expect our ancient texts (whether written, iconographic, or material) to provide us with circumstantial information, when they primarily encode ideologies. In this sense, Agricola's fond recollections of his mother's intervention in his philosophical enthusiasms probably represents at least one factual incident, but also – and perhaps more significantly – signals the fact that he held the appropriate attitudes towards his mother and towards maternal and older generation control of youth. It performs a role analogous to the erection of a funeral monument or to Tacitus' pious publication of the *Agricola*, itself a *laudatio funebris* of his father-in-law and a political pamphlet which contains and therefore transmits the anecdote as part of the family history.

Such distinctions between the aims and content of different types of evidence (good old source criticism, in other words) are of prime importance in reconstructing family relations from the past. Even in everyday life, we routinely discriminate between different sources of information, for purposes of varying gravity: creative conversational analyses of the sex life of the English royal family; the somewhat better-informed dissections of the emotional (and sex) lives of our friends; the decisions about which car manufacturer's claims to believe; the merits of a student appeal against an examination result; our confidence in alleged connections between undesirable medical conditions and eating, exercise, or smoking habits. History, like many other disciplines, has adopted epistemological standards based on the vaguely defined 'scientific' models which have affected not only academic reasoning but even our administrative and legal practice. Our laws of historical evidence bear some resemblance to those of criminal trials in their distinctions between observation, inference, speculation, and second-hand reportage. I should not therefore seem unduly pessimistic if I insist on the need to distinguish between our ability to reconstruct mourning customs and mourning prescriptions – which is difficult enough – and our absolute inability to retrieve the feelings of the bereaved (cf. Morris 1992b, especially chapter 1). Such inferences are difficult enough in one's own culture, where the people and the codes are much better understood. It is certainly easier to establish that parents were assumed or expected to love their children than it is to establish that they did. It is easier to establish the incidence of conflict and cruelty than to conclude from such behaviour that people in families hated each other. It is certainly easier to determine conventions of mourning and the fact that some people flouted them (as in the case of 'excessive' mourning for young children) than it is to distinguish the emotions felt by the mourners.

From the premise that we cannot recover the actual feelings of mourning spouses or parents from the past, it follows that we cannot trace changes in such feelings. We can, perhaps, note changes in conventions and ideals – or their expression – but even that exercise is vitiated by the lack of comparable evidence over a lengthy period of time (see Dixon 1991). The epitaphs which have survived are often difficult to date and seldom representative of the total populations. Any attempt to plot change from archaic Rome or even the mid-republic must confront the concentration of literary testimony in the two centuries spanning the late republic and early empire. Attitudes that are expressed in writing in the 60s BCE might simply not have been recorded in this form before – that is no reason to suppose they are new. Even apparently objective criteria invoked in the eternal debate of whether childhood is a modern invention are questionable: depictions of children as miniaturized adults might not indicate that the artist – let alone the whole contemporary adult society – necessarily perceived children only as potential adults. The separation of Christian babies in a special cemetery can be interpreted as emphasis or exclusion (Golden 1992: 16–17). I do not question that community and subculture feelings and attitudes do alter over time, but manifestations of such change can be interpreted in so many different ways that the discussion becomes more interesting for what it reveals of the position of the disputing parties. This is evident in the continuing moral debate about whether child abuse is a modern phenomenon or a shameful legacy which we have only now begun to challenge.[9]

Paul Veyne's well-known (1978) attempt to tie an alleged change in family relations to political changes in imperial Rome has met with general criticism, as exaggerating the distinctions between republican and imperial élite competition for public honours and inventing a 'new' model of family affection which has ample attestations in late republican sources (e.g. Garnsey and Saller 1987: 133). Paradoxes also tempt historians into arguments about changing attitudes over time. The reciprocal ideal of *pietas* and the respect due elders are emphasized at all periods in Roman culture and *patria potestas* as a legal institution changes relatively little over centuries. Yet detailed examination of actual relations between fathers and children – inevitably belonging to that late republican-early imperial period when literature provides such anecdotes – reveals a much more flexible approach (cf. Saller 1988a, Dixon 1992: 47–48, 146–49). It is tempting to leap to the conclusion that the traditional tales represent a dourer period of single-minded austerity and that the clashes within the Cicero family show a decline or improvement in family relations (according to the stance of the historian writing).[10] The ancients certainly believed in linear change. They persistently saw their own epoch – whenever that was – as falling short of an earlier standard in religion, marital fidelity, youthful comportment, maternal breast-feeding, wealth, civic dedication, and oratory.[11] Ariès has provided a modern equivalent in his insistence that an earlier, idyllic state of childhood has progressively become controlled by adults since the early modern period, and Marxism also paints a picture of decline from an earlier, happier era of gender relations. The moral perspective is reversed in deMause's social evolutionary reading, when he argues that 'the history of childhood is a nightmare from which we have only recently begun to awaken' (deMause, 1974: 1), but in each case we are presented with a reductive, satisfying portrait of consistent progress or decline.

At the centre of all such attempts is the recurrent, almost obsessive need of historians to locate and explain change, to force history into a narrative of some kind. It is almost our defining professional characteristic. At times, the most fundamental indicators of change (periodization) have been challenged seriously, and we are left with the awful prospect that there might be no clear, definable difference between Roman republic and Roman empire, that there might not exactly have been a Renaissance, an Enlightenment or even a clear-cut process of industrialization. Yet we resist the *Annaliste* recourse to *continuité* and the Foucauldian vision of history as discontinuities, persisting in the attempt to describe human behaviour as a series of changes (from indifference to love; from autocracy to democracy; from the Dark Ages to the Renaissance) and to refine such changes. This stubborn quest almost inevitably involves a distorting reduction by characterizing each age in an oversimplified way. Mark Golden has – rightly, I think – criticized attempts to identify specific developments in parent–child relations and to assign them to particular periods.[12] He raises more general questions about the need to look for change over time and the basis of such claims.[13]

It is arguable that the most important difference between historians and social scientists lies not in their necessarily divergent techniques (since first-hand observation or interrogation of the ancients is out of the question) but in this driving historical preoccupation with change and causation. There is otherwise a strong community of interest. Social historians and social scientists both tend to generalize from a set of closely studied examples, although there are often differences about how wide the generalizations can be – e.g. whether findings about household structure or inheritance rights can be extended from the group studied to a whole region, class, nation, or even century. We engage in similar debates about the extent to which we should accept the categories and rationales of the groups we study or feel free to apply our own constructions to them.[14] When the disciplines meet, the social scientists also expect our distinctive contribution to be the introduction of change into their more synchronous construction of social relations.

I have already pointed out that the temptation to read father–child relations at Rome as a liberalizing narrative might stem from a wish to explain the gap between traditional stories of paternal savagery and the more circumstantial accounts of family relationships in the very different genres of letters and law-court speeches. In the area of 'family feeling', there are similar temptations to explain away apparent paradoxes by then-and-now progressions. Much of my own work has sought to explain how Roman women, apparently bound legally by lifelong *tutela*, were able in practice to exercise such freedom over their fortunes (see especially Dixon 1984). The paradox of inheritance rules which continued to propagate rigidly agnatic succession within a much more flexible system (in which children inherited from both parents, even when their mothers were technically members of a distinct family) has also led me to argue that there were changes in notions of family duty and the proper uses of wealth from the time of the fifth-century BCE Twelve Tables (see, e.g., Dixon 1985b, 1988: 44–47, 51–60). Yet the Cambridge anthropologist Jack

Goody, capable of arguing from an awesome comparative perspective, has put forward the possibility that in such comparisons of archaic practices deduced from the Twelve Tables and later practices, attested by literary sources from the mid-republic, we Romanists fail to allow for the special and very limited character of the early legal code:

> It is possible to interpret a gap between 'law' and 'practice' as the result of a change over time, as many authorities have done. But such a gap often exists as a matter of course, especially when 'codes' are initially written down.

(Goody 1990: 410)

He points out that such codes are rarely comprehensive and their very existence and subsequent use in legal proceedings might expose important omissions which can lead to perceived inequities and need to be rectified by legislation or the creation of special suits, if they cannot simply be circumvented by alternative means.

> As a result 'legal reform' may take a long time to catch up with an earlier state of affairs; the history of such movements may look like a continuous process of rationalisation, of modernisation of 'primitive law', whereas their very existence stems from the initial failure of written law (perhaps because of particular interests, perhaps for more neutral reasons like an inadequate understanding, or inadequate tools for understanding, the complexities of the present situation) to encompass or reflect the process of actual decision-making.

(Goody 1990: 410)

If this fits the Roman picture – and it has a certain plausibility – it suggests that basic patterns of inheritance and family affiliation might not have changed as much as we imagine. Historians have always acknowledged that the Twelve Tables were not comprehensive. Dowry, for example, was not mentioned, as far as we know, in its provisions, but legal historians generally assume that it existed in Roman society of the fifth century BCE (Peppe 1984, Watson 1975: 31–39). In 230 BCE, Carvilius Ruga divorced his wife but refused to repay her dowry, although she had been blameless.[15] It emerges from the semi-mythic context that Ruga's behaviour offended contemporary notions of propriety, for it marks the establishment of the *actio rei uxoriae*, a legal action for the recovery of dowry by a divorced wife (and her father) or the father of a deceased wife in the absence of a specific pre-nuptial agreement. If this was intended to remedy a perceived inequity or loophole, Goody's suggested approach is apposite. The creation of a new legal procedure might not represent a new development in attitudes to marriage, divorce, and women's claims so much as an *ad hoc* response to a social breach of understood conventions. This reasoning may not necessarily fit every case of apparent reform or change in marital and familial obligation, but it could often be appropriate. Indeed, it is likely that some apparent discrepancies, construed by scholars (including myself) as indicating historical shifts, are in fact the usual inconsistencies to be found in any culture (modern stress on romantic lifelong love versus divorce is only one fairly obvious one). Perhaps we all tolerate such inconsistencies unwittingly in our own societies but feel the need to explain them elsewhere, because of a desire to fit human behaviour into patterns which are both familiar and aesthetically pleasing. Perhaps as historians we have been so convinced that our task is to explain change that we are incapable of accepting that certain institutions might change so little – or be impossible to chart.[16]

One change which has never been satisfactorily explained is the shift in Roman marriage preference from the corporate form, in which a woman entered her husband's *manus* and therefore his legal family, to the form of marriage whereby she retained legal membership of the family of her birth. Yet many consequences flowed from this change, particularly the legal distance it set up between a married woman and her children for purposes of inheritance on intestate death. Roman family feeling, however, saw this relationship as central, and Roman mothers employed testaments to overcome the legal anomaly. Eventually, statutes even addressed it in part for cases of intestacy.[17] Again, this seems to represent a moral view – that children ought to inherit from their mothers – which apparently remained constant for several centuries. Yet the structure of inheritance on intestacy was based on the system of agnatic succession more suited to the merged property regime of families formed by *manus*-marriage, and gives no help in determining why the marriage preference did change. As Saller pointed out in the above quote, 'the family was the primary social group transmitting legal status and wealth'. It also transmitted ideologies, and some would argue that legal and other institutions employed to achieve such goals are themselves expressions of ideology.[18] The traditional Roman rules of inheritance on intestacy can be read as reflecting dominant ideologies of sibling equality, the ascendancy of the masculine line of succession, and the essential stability of physical holdings and of marriage. The demonstrable concern in later periods to ensure inheritance through the maternal line as well as the agnatic confuses the question of whether this ideology continued to have any force, unless we can accept a degree of paradox or inconsistency.

Such acceptance goes against the academic grain. I have been as ready as any to over-systematize material into a progressive historical narrative, arguing in many works that there was a change in ideology which led men and women to collude in modifying inheritance in practice while retaining the traditional inheritance structure out of Roman respect for the past (another ideology). I have suggested in others that many rules operated by common consent governing 'proper' lines of inheritance or 'decent' behaviour in returning dowries after divorce, and that legal intervention was invoked only when these systems broke down, offering this as a likely explanation of developments such as the institution of the *actio rei uxoriae* in 230 BCE or Augustus' statutory limitation on a husband's right to mortgage or alienate the real component of a dowry, or of second-century CE laws acknowledging intestate succession between mother and child, who belonged legally to different agnatic groups (thus diverging from traditional, strictly agnatic lines of succession on intestacy). In conventional fashion, I have attempted to identify apparent ideological shifts like these with economic and political developments, such as Roman territorial expansion and changing uses of land and wealth. This is risky enough. It is equally possible that there were changes in patterns of affection and emotional expectations within families in Roman Italy – such transformations are as likely to affect personal feelings as residential units or testamentary conventions. It then becomes a matter of courage and faith as much as intellectual preference whether one takes the plunge to determine such questions as whether Roman parents were un-happy when their children died, and whether Roman husbands and wives loved each other.

In sum, a case can be made for certain changes in some important areas of Roman social history: children do appear more in art from the late republic; wives are less likely to be *in manu mariti* from about that time; literature contains affectionate references to wives and young children; divorce becomes more frequent and bilaterally initiated; women seem quite untrammelled by the institution of *tutela perpetua* which ought in theory to have limited their financial capabilities; daughters in the top property group inherit from their parents in spite of the second-century BCE Lex Voconia; mothers make wills and leave their estates to their children, not to their heirs on intestacy in the agnatic line (such as their brothers and sisters). Are we wrong in accepting that they represent a change from earlier practice? In each case, it would be possible but relatively perverse to claim that we might be exaggerating the departure from earlier practice. Perhaps children figured in art which disappeared for some or no reason. It is just possible that a woman's *tutor* had never been a serious limitation on her transactions, but it is difficult to make any sense of the institution if that is the case. On the other hand, we know that Roman men were within a few generations quite puzzled about the motives for passing the Lex Voconia provision preventing women of the top census group from being instituted heirs in wills, and that the spirit of the provision was already being circumvented soon after its ratification.[19] This suggests either a change in ideas about daughters' rights or that traditional, continuous ideas were consciously violated by a clause of the particular statute for reasons specific to the early 160s BCE and subsequently lost not only to us but to succeeding generations of Romans.

Nevertheless, it may be wiser to remain sceptical about change in general. We can determine enough about feelings to counter negative generalizations (the Romans had no concept of married love; Romans had no concept of childhood; Romans never cared when their young children died), but not to make counter-generalizations about happy marriages or parental devotion and bereavement. Other than that, it may be more productive to focus on identifying specific norms, ideologies, and obligations and not to expect them to form a coherent system overall or in any given historical period. Plotting change even in concepts of authority within the family is very difficult. Charting histories of emotion seems to be to beyond our capacity. And in the end, I wonder whether we should be trying, for the better approach might be to accept incongruity and discontinuity as features of every artificially constructed period.

NOTES

1 Keith Hopkins' remark (at the conclusion of the second International Roman Family Seminar in Canberra in 1981) that there was little point in discussing families unless you also discussed feelings within families seemed bold at the time, but many have since pursued the subject. See Dixon 1992: 15–16.

2 Throughout this chapter, I refer to my own published writings in an endeavour to draw together the kinds of themes and arguments relevant to this discussion of continuity and change. Far from holding up my work as a model, I cite past studies in most cases as examples of possibly wrong-headed determination to discern and explain change in Roman social and legal institutions.

3 As argued most powerfully by Schulz (1951). There are, to be sure, many steps in Schulz's argument with which I agree, but I do not see Roman law as pursuing a consistently 'humanistic' trend from the republic to the early principate.

4 This is a very brief overview relevant to the questions discussed in this chapter, not a state-of-the art account, for which see my 1994 review essay. That also contains a brief history of trends and works on the Roman family, and references to earlier reviews.

5 The term depends on whether one draws on Stone or Marx and Engels to discuss the institution.

6 Both authors support their argument with a catalogue of seventeenth- and eighteenth-century horrors which they contrast with the caring behaviour expected of nineteenth- and twentieth-century French mothers.

7 E.g. of the emperors Nero (*Suet.* 52.1) and Marcus (Iul. Cap., *SHA*: *Marcus Ant.* 2.6).

8 Liv. 8.7; Val. Max. 5.8 QUI SEVERI ADVERSUS LIBEROS. See Eyben 1993: 47–49.

9 DeMause 1974: 4–5 castigates social historians who have played down the abandonment and cruelty of the past, but Demos (1986: 72) sees all such references as distorted, and argues that pre-industrial communities checked child abuse effectively by means of social mechanisms.

10 Cf. Golden's comments (1992: 7–8) on the assumptions of early modern historians and other scholars on the agreed shift in Western parent–child relations since the eighteenth century.

11 Dixon 1992: 21–24. Such comments about the decline of desirable customs are so moralizing and subjective that their circumstantial value is suspect, however much we may wish to use them. Consider Pepys' self-satisfied comments on his own old-fashioned hospitality in contrast with the behaviour of a colleague:

> we to Creed's, and there find him and her [his wife] together alone, in their new house ... Here they treat us like strangers, quite according to the

fashion – nothing to drink or eat, which is a thing that will spoil our ever having any acquaintance with them; for we do continue the old freedom and kindness of England to all our friends.

(Pepys, *Diary*, 14 April 1669 in Wheatley 1962: 277)

12 Golden 1992: 9–11. He concludes that 'investigators find a significant shift in adult attitudes towards children in every era they examine'.

13 See the examples he adduces (1992: 10, n.14) of similar scepticism about attempts to trace the origins of modern individualism and the modern family in different periods. Cf. his comments pp. 11–12.

14 I am thinking of debates about whether there was a concept of 'a market' or 'an economy' in the ancient world.

15 Aul. Gell. *N.A.* 4.3.1–2. See Watson 1965, Gardner 1986: 48–49.

16 Cf. the comments of Bashar (1984) on the role of change in the traditional historian's self-set task, and the *Annaliste* commitment to *l'histoire immobile*.

17 See esp. Gardner 1986: 196–200 and Dixon 1988: 51–60.

18 E.g. Yanagisako and Brettell, in Kertzer and Saller 1991.

19 See Dixon 1985b on the Lex Voconia and daughter inheritance. Devices might have been used even in the second century BCE to thwart some of the provisions of the Lex Voconia, such as the will of Aemilia (widow of Scipio Africanus maior) which allowed for lavish final payments of so-called dowries in 162 BCE, many years after their marriages (Polybius 31.26–28). See Pomeroy 1976: 223, Dixon 1985c: 156.

Part II

RECONSTRUCTING THE PAST: THE PRACTICE OF PERIODIZATION

INTRODUCTION

Part I examined the problems of continuity, change, and the periodization of institutions and affective states, particularly between the ancient and modern worlds. It was argued that more heed should be paid to classical origins and that the current esteem in which the Enlightenment is held as an institutional and affective watershed is unfairly exaggerated. In Part II of *Inventing Ancient Culture* our authors narrow their focus. The five chapters here examine continuity, change, and periodization *within* the ancient world. These essays aim to test the usefulness of periodization as a tool for the reconstruction of the past. The sorts of questions which they will address are: What sort of events deserve periodization? How does one go about the process of establishing periods? How reliable are schemes of periodization? What sorts of constraints do periodizations exert upon their users?

Ian Morris (Chapter 6: 'Periodization and the heroes: Inventing a Dark Age') looks at how periodization (which he sees as crucial to an understanding of the past) is shaped and controlled by contemporary intellectual beliefs. His topic is the years from about 1200 to 700 BCE, more particularly 'the principles which have led this period to be characterized either as a "Dark Age" or a "Heroic Age"'. Morris maintains that the reconstruction of this period has been conditioned primarily by 'disciplinary structures and professional goals'. The act of periodization, as he sees it operant in research on the Dark Age, 'is intimately bound up with the organization of the profession of classical studies'. Morris contends that the only way to break the dependence of periodization upon one's intellectual milieu is through 'historical analysis of the process of writing history'.

A remedial strategy for Morris's trenchant scepticism is provided by Christiane Sourvinou-Inwood in her 'Reconstructing change: Ideology and the Eleusinian mysteries' (Chapter 7). Sourvinou-Inwood argues that there was a radical change in the conception and practice of the Eleusinian mystery cult of Demeter and Persephone and its place in Athenian religion in the late seventh or early sixth century BCE. This 'transformed an agricultural cult with poliadic content to one that included a significant eschatological/ soteriological component'. She believes that this shift, echoed in contemporary 'attitudes to death and funerary ideology', is the result of political tensions that emerged during the archaic period (here we might compare Konstan's stress on the shift in the concept of *philia* in the third century BCE). Where lies the remedial strategy? In this case it can be provided by pursuing 'different lines of investigation that pertain to different sets of evidence', by treating independently three 'separate grids': archaeological evidence, textual evidence, and epigraphical evidence. Should they provide a convergence of detail, then (argues Sourvinou-Inwood) there are grounds for drawing conclusions. By hunting out polarities and analogies within these separate domains, she believes that it is possible to avoid the 'preconceived moulds' of contemporary or previous scholarly discourse – precisely those constraints which Morris was at pains to elucidate.

Barry Strauss examines periodization, change, and continuity within the historiographical tradition. His 'The problem of periodization: The case of the Peloponnesian war' (Chapter 8) takes a specific *ancient* example of periodization, that of the Peloponnesian war (431–404 BCE) as it is mapped for us by Thucydides. Strauss reminds us that other ancient periodizations for the Peloponnesian war existed. Some ancient witnesses believed that there were three or even four great wars in this era, not one. After pointing out how Thucydides' unitary view of the Spartan and Athenian conflict has become the dominant one, Strauss shows how periodization (that 'invented' for us by Thucydides' masterwork) changes our perception of ancient history. If we do not follow Thucydides' periodization, then the distinct nature of the Archidamian and the Iono–Decelean wars becomes plainer. The first was an inter-Greek affair, the second was 'terrible and unexpected' because a foreign power, Persia, intervened. If, furthermore, we see the Corinthian war as the finale of the conflict between Sparta and Athens, then history takes on a less tragic hue than that implied by Thucydides' version. The Athenian reverse in 387/86 was far less conclusive than in 404.

The Greek attitude to children has often been said to change during the third century BCE. Mark Golden (Chapter 9: 'Change or continuity? Children and childhood in Hellenistic historiography') tests this hypothesis through an examination of Greek historiography, specifically of the Hellenistic historian Polybius. It is true that Polybius provides some evidence of a change in mentality towards children. But Golden maintains that, although Polybius does demonstrate a sympathy for children, Herodotus, hardly a Hellenistic historian, exhibits a greater interest. Golden concludes that change in the attitude to children within this period may not be as marked as we like to believe. Genre may influence how one represents life: Polybius was more influenced by Thucydides than he was by Herodotus, and Thucydides was less interested in children. The easy assumption that there was affective change in the Hellenistic period (asserted by Konstan and Toohey) and that this is reflected in a shift in attitude towards children, should therefore be treated with some scepticism. Golden's agnosticism may be compared to that of Dixon.

Our final chapter looks at women in the early Roman empire. Phyllis Culham ('Did Roman women have an empire?') asks whether Roman women shared any of the advantages of the Roman power which developed under the early empire. Do the standard periodizations of Roman political history (broadly into republic and empire) 'produce results which help us understand both women and politically defined eras better'? Or do such concepts (particularly such grandiose notions as empire) distract us from a proper understanding of the position of women in Roman society? Culham believes that the standard political periodization is of use. The advent of the empire and of the emperor Augustus marks out a new period for women's history in Rome too. Augustus' attempt to enforce public morality, particularly sexual morality among the aristocratic élite, had the paradoxical effect of shoring up women's status: it caused for them a flow-through of the public status enjoyed by their husbands. This, Culham believes, increased both their status and their personal freedom. In that sense they did indeed have an empire.

6

PERIODIZATION AND THE HEROES: INVENTING A DARK AGE[1]

Ian Morris

INTRODUCTION

Periodization distorts. That much everyone would agree on: when we draw lines through time, artificially dividing the continuous flow of lived experience, we may obscure as much as we reveal. So why do we do it? The obvious, but facile, answer is that it makes the practice of history easier. It gives us a shorthand: everyone knows what we mean when we talk about archaic and classical, or early, middle, and late, or phases I, II, and III. But there is more to it than that. Periodization is also characterization – it is a basic part of the process of historical understanding, which *requires* us to draw lines, to say that some common thread unites a block of human experience, and that this block is qualitatively different from other blocks of time that can be identified before and after it. Stanley Fish has rightly argued that 'you cannot not forget; you cannot not exclude; you cannot refuse boundaries and distinctions' (Fish 1989: 311). Periodization constrains thought about the past, but also enables it.

But it is equally obvious that we do not all want to draw the *same* lines through the past, or all want to say that the lines mean the same thing. The international treaty which marks a decisive turning point for the diplomatic historian may be a mere epiphenomenon for the Marxist; or worse, it may draw attention away from what is really important, as Joan Kelly argued in her well-known (1984) paper 'Did women have a Renaissance?' In this chapter, I examine the historiographical processes by which the evidence surviving from ancient Greece between about 1200 and 700 BCE has, since about 1890, regularly been grouped together to form a single period, and discuss the principles which have led this period to be characterized as either a 'Dark Age' or a 'Heroic Age'. I argue that in this particular case, while historians have regularly changed their interpretations in the light of significant increases in empirical knowledge, these changes have always taken place within higher-level frameworks determined by the interplay of disciplinary structures and professional goals. These factors have had decisive effects on what we have imagined this half-millennium to have been like. The struggle

96

between the Dark Age and Heroic Age does not provide a general model for processes of periodization, which can be applied to any instance; but it does show the kind of role that non-empirical factors can play in how we approach our data. In short, it shows that whatever span of time we find most interesting, and whatever the reason we have for that, we need to problematize the activity of periodization, so central to historical practice, but so little discussed.

THE ARGUMENT: PERIODIZING PERIODIZATION

In what follows, I identify three major breaks in thought which have led to the current conception of a homogeneous period of Greek history filling the years from *c.* 1200 to *c.* 700 BCE. The first rupture falls in the 1870s. Before 1870 there was no real concept of a Dark Age; instead, Greece before the lyric poets of the seventh century was generally imagined as an Early or Heroic Age, represented by Homer. In the nineteenth century this period was caught up in the Anglo-German polemics of the Homeric Question, but by the 1860s most members of the first generation of professional academics were starting to agree that we could in fact know very little about it.

This burgeoning consensus was shattered after 1870 by two unexpected sets of new data: first Schliemann's discovery of the Greek Bronze Age, and then Petrie's 1890 synchronism of the fall of the palaces with the Egyptian Nineteenth Dynasty, around 1200 BCE. This left a five-century gap between Schliemann's finds and the lyric poets. Classical scholars quickly reversed the 1860s consensus and revived the older idea of a historical Heroic Age, now to be set before 1200 BCE. Bronze Age archaeology was seen as important and interesting, because Homer filled in the background to the finds, and the finds illustrated Homer, who stood at the beginning of the Western tradition. But Homer told us little about the succeeding period, and its archaeology cast little light on the bard. This was thus a Dark Age, or the Greek Middle Ages, which meant that it was uninteresting. Archaeological research was driven by its subordinate relationship to classical philology. The scientific ideals of classical archaeology fortunately meant that most fieldworkers did excavate and record Dark Age materials if they came across them, but virtually no one wanted to devote a significant part of his career to this period (for women archaeologists it was a slightly different story). The Heroic Age was interesting, important, and worthy of serious scholars' attention; the Dark Age was not.

The notion of profound discontinuities around 1200 and 700 BCE has survived more or less intact from the 1890s to the 1990s, but the interpretation of these breaks has not. The distinction between a pre-1200 Heroic Age and post-1200 Dark Age began to break down after 1945, beginning a third phase in the history of these periods. The diffusion of Parry's theories of an oral poet, the decipherment of Linear B, and the accumulation of post-Mycenaean archaeological finds combined to undermine the older assumption that Homer was a faithful guide to Bronze Age life. Some historians suggested that we would learn more about Homer by studying a later period, between the tenth and eighth centuries; and Moses Finley began to argue that this period held part of the key to understanding the long-term economic and social development of ancient society.

At the same time, but for very different reasons, a group of British archaeologists was also rethinking the period. Driven more by a positivist urge to fill the gap in the archaeological literature than by an interest in linking material to literary culture, the scholars of this school retained the old concept of a Dark Age, but now felt that it *was* worth study. The pre-war distinction between a Bronze/Heroic Age and an Iron/Dark Age was transformed into a post-war distinction between a philological Heroic Age and an archae-ological Dark Age. Both groups of scholars agreed that the post-Mycenaean period was vitally important, but wrote their accounts of it in totally different ways. But there was no confrontation between the two models. Instead, a series of great syntheses of the archaeological data in the 1970s quietly swept the field, although in the process the archaeologists' art-historical agenda became increasingly fragmented.

By 1980, the archaeologists' Dark Age model commanded near-universal support, but in the last fifteen years it has been called into question. It is too early yet to see what kind of post-synthesis periodization will emerge, but various trends can be identified. To some extent, the positivist programme of the 1950s–1970s may have simply exhausted itself; by 1980 the gap was filled, and there was little room to say anything new within this framework, except for incorporating the latest finds into the old syntheses. But there were also other factors at work. The influence of post-processual prehistoric archae-ology made a reconciliation between archaeological and literary approaches easier, encouraging new questions, at a time when those who studied ancient Greece came under increasing pressure to justify themselves in an academic environment where nineteenth-century Eurocentric ideologies could no longer support the weight of a huge classical establishment. Some have responded by blurring the boundaries which constituted the Dark Age, seeing greater continuities between the Bronze Age and classical Greece than previously, and following Martin Bernal's lead (1987, 1991) in emphasizing the role of the Near East in the formation of Greek culture. From this perspective, the very notion of a Dark Age is questionable.

Disciplinary historians tend to fall into two broad camps, which we can call internalists and externalists. The former concentrate on what goes on inside the discipline, the latter on the interaction between practitioners and various kinds of outside forces. This distinction is often cross-cut by another: between cognitivists, who privilege the substance of research and the rational factors in its development, and noncognitivists, who emphasize political, ideological, psychological, and other forces. In this chapter I emphasize forces that were internal, but also noncognitive. New evidence, such as Schliemann's digs in the 1870s, the discovery of Homeric orality in the 1930s, or finds at the Lefkandi Toumba heroon in the 1980s, has generally been incorporated into, and interpreted within, pre-existing disciplinary structures (the distinction between historical and archaeological studies, and the subordination of both to classical philology) and professional agendas (the relevance of research to a relatively inflexible canon of Greek authors), rather than being used to overturn these programmes. These structures and agendas, I suggest, are ultimately the most important forces in the current periodization of the Dark Age. They have been resistant to the challenges of new data, and have mitigated the influence of ideas from other parts of the academy. The act of periodization is intimately bound up with the organization of the profession of Classical Studies; any serious rethinking of periodization leads inevitably to questioning why we continue to pay so much attention to ancient Greece and Rome, and vice versa.

PHASE I. BEFORE THE DARK AGE

The earliest narrative account of Greece before 700 BCE comes from Thucydides (1.1–12). He relied on similar categories of evidence to those which we use twenty-five centuries later: legends, Homer, archaeology, and ethnographic analogy. He saw a steady growth in wealth and preparedness up to the time of the Trojan war, followed by a period of disturbance and population movements. Progress was then renewed, continuing to his own day. He dated the Dorian invasion eighty years after the fall of Troy, adding that 'Greece enjoyed scarcely any peace for a long time' (1.12.4), but moved straight on from this to describe the Ionian settlements and the eighth-century colonies in Sicily, saying simply that 'All these were founded after the Trojan war.' As Snodgrass (1971: 7) points out, in contrast to the dominant modern model:

> Thucydides' story is one of a consistent, if extremely slow, progress; there is no 'crest' in the heroic age followed by a 'trough' in the dark age, partly because one of his aims is to modify the poets' assessment of the achievement of the heroic age.

Thucydides wanted to show that despite the difficulty of finding out about early times, the Peloponnesian war of 431–404 BCE was 'the greatest disturbance in the history of the Hellenes' (1.1.2). Contrary to the implication of Homer and the other poets of the Epic Cycle, he was at pains to insist that the Trojan war was not particularly significant from a logistical point of view. Connor (1984: 21) observes that this made his *archaeologia* 'a polemical essay on the nature of early Greek history ... a revisionist argument about the remote past'. Yet the first serious modern attempts to read Homer as history consistently imagined an early period of Greek history by forcing the details of the epics into a Thucydidean narrative. Abandoning earlier allegorical readings (Clarke 1979: 60–105), some eighteenth-century Homerists started to understand the poems in a Romantic vein:

> Blackwell and Gravine, Wood and Merian labored to knock Homer off his Ionic pedestal, to strip him of his austere classic robes, and to deck him out with the rough staff and furry cloak appropriate to a storyteller at a tribal campfire.
>
> (Grafton *et al.* 1985: 10)

Romantics found a primitive Homer more interesting than a polished Virgil, and were often attached to an idea of Homer's poetry as a spontaneous effusion of original genius. Grittiness and reality were all-important. As Simonsuuri (1979: 119) argues:

> The eighteenth century's original contribution to the Homeric debate can be seen emerging when writers begin to look at Homer as a poet from a primitive culture or as one whose work gave poetic expression to Greek popular thought. These writers made the theoretical assumption that what they were considering in Homer were manifestations of reality.

This reality was especially important for British Homerists, who tended to imagine a single, fairly homogeneous period stretching from the peopling of Greece in the remotest antiquity until the first Olympiad in 776 BCE. The treatment of early Greece in the two best-known British historians of this century illustrates this well. Temple Stanyan in his *Grecian History* (1739) divided the chapters covering Greece down to 510 BCE geographically rather than chronologically, with each treating one city-state within a single Heroic Age. He generally followed Bishop Ussher's dating system, identifying a period of roughly one thousand years before the Trojan war, which, following Eratosthenes, he placed in 1184 BCE (preface: 12, main text: 55). For Stanyan, the war 'properly put an end to the *infancy* of Greece' (ibid.: 39), but apart from noting – like Thucydides – that 'Whatever *Troy* suffered, the *Grecians* had no great reason to boast of their conquest' (ibid.: 55), he identified no significant changes between pre- and post-war Greece. Again like Thucydides, the detail of his story declines after the return of the sons of Heracles; after devoting forty-three pages to Argos from its foundation to the fall of the kings, which he put around 1000 BCE, for the next 250 years he simply commented, 'In this state the *Argives* flourished for many ages' (ibid.: 61–62).

The obvious reason for the change in Stanyan's account after 1000 is the lack of stories about the post-war period in his sources. Stanyan insisted, 'The first from whom we receive any tolerable light into the *Grecian* affairs, is *Heredotus*' (1739: preface, p. 5 [misspelling in original]), but relied almost entirely on Homer and later collectors of myth in his first five chapters. And while he professed equal scorn for those who denied the reality of Homer's characters and those who 'greedily catch at the least remains of antiquity', he was determined to save Homer from the critics. He held that Homer had good information about the Trojan war period. He did not discuss the poet's date relative to the war, but did argue that 'neither was Homer the first and only author, (as some will have it) who gave an account of this expedition. There are several recorded before him, from whom undoubtedly he copied' (ibid.: 40–41).

In 1784, William Mitford began publishing his ten-volume *History of Greece*. Mitford was more critical of authorities than Stanyan, and disagreed with both Ussher's and Isaac Newton's high chronologies for the foundation of Sicyon, the oldest polis. Stanyan had noted the problems with believing in a thousand-year period of kings at Sicyon, but still followed Ussher (Stanyan 1739: 15). Mitford, however, asserted that 'scarcely a wandering hunter had ever set foot in Peloponnesus so early as the period assigned by chronologers even to the founding of Argos' (1784: 25–26). Mitford put an explicitly present-minded political slant on early Greek history, but differed little from Stanyan in his outline of pre-archaic times. He identified a single phase from the coming of man to the archaic period. Like Stanyan, he called the capture of Troy 'a dear-bought, a mournful triumph' (ibid.: 80), but described no consequences beyond dynastic problems. In the marginal notes, he cited Thucydides 1.1–12 as his only source.

For Stanyan and Mitford, like most other British writers, Homer gave transparent and direct access to the age that had existed before the city-states. Mitford accepted a ninth-century date for Homer, following Herodotus (2.53), but disingenuously asserted that no ancient writer gave a date for the fall of Troy itself. Passing over in silence not only Eratosthenes' precise date of 1184/3 BCE but also Thucydides' placing of Homer 'much later' than the Trojan war (1.3.3), Mitford argued that Homer had in fact lived before the return of the sons of Heracles, and therefore less than eighty years after the war (Mitford 1784: 228–35). Homer thus became almost a primary source, believable even on details. Mitford's only real criticism of the legends is revealing: he was prepared to concede that Agamemnon's sacrifice of Iphigenia never happened, but only because Homer did not mention it (ibid.: 77). He defended Homer at length against 'some grave writers of late' who dared to assert that the Trojan war was merely a story (ibid.: 81–84).

Mitford's discussion of early Greece was for many years the most influential in England. A century later, Freeman (1880: 127, n.) was to call him 'a bad scholar, a bad historian, a bad writer of English', but at the same time 'the first writer of any note who found out that Grecian history was a living thing with a practical bearing'. But even while Mitford's volumes were still appearing, a radically different approach to early Greece very suddenly won prominence in Germany, in the form of more rigorous philological analysis. This is best known through Wolf's *Prolegomena ad Homerum* [1795], although many of Wolf's theories seem to have been common currency in German academic circles for some years. Heyne, Wolf's teacher, complained bitterly that Wolf had in fact stolen his ideas (Grafton *et al.* 1985: 12–15, 25–26). Wolf argued that Homer had stitched the *Iliad* together from older folk lays. Mitford (1784: 85) had suggested that Homer was at his best as a guide to 'the manners and principles of his age'. Wolf himself did not comment directly on questions of historical interpretation, but his theory was widely used in the nineteenth century to support arguments that the *Iliad* was useful *only* as a source for the general ethos of Homer's time, taken to be long after the Trojan war.

Wolf's success defined the terms of the so-called 'Homeric Question' for the next 150 years. On one side were the Wolfian analysts (also known by their critics as separatists or disintegrationists), usually arguing either that Homer was the author of a short Ur-*Iliad*, around which other poems slowly coalesced, eventually forming the inconsistent and flawed text we know as the *Iliad;* or alternatively that Homer was a mere redactor who stitched together earlier short folk lays to form a huge poem. On the other side were the unitarians, who argued that Homer was a lone and inspired bard who composed the *Iliad* as a single great poem, in more or less the form we have it. Few nineteenth-century Homerists could reasonably be called pure analysts or unitarians, but the furious rhetoric on both sides often gives the impression of two radically opposed schools of thought in early Greek poetics and history.

Two further factors contributed to this sense of polarization. The first was nationalism: the unitarian position was generally felt to be typically British, and the analyst position, German. But these stereotypes were at best only partly true. Analysis steadily gained ground in Britain, while as late as 1857 Ernst Curtius could devote forty-five pages of his *Griechische Geschichte* to a detailed retelling of myth as early Greek history. But the nationalist debate also fed a second stereotype, which was that the German philological approach to Homer was merely one dimension of a more serious German aberration, the higher criticism of the Bible. Blackie (1866: 245) argued,

> Those who believe in a great poem cannot avoid feeling that the Wolfians are engaged in a perverse attempt, closely analogous to the meagre method of explaining the world without a god, in which certain incomplete intellects in all ages found an unnatural delight.

But this view was no more monolithic than the nationalist stereotype: in the same year, the Reverend Paley could rebuke unitarians as 'persons who prefer sentiment to truth' (1866: xvi).

The nationalist and religious tone of the Homeric Question may have done much to discourage scholars in other countries from taking part. Diderot had translated Stanyan into French as early as 1743, but on the whole, Greek history remained less popular in France than Roman (Momigliano 1952: 5).

When French writers did deal with pre-archaic Greece in the early nineteenth century, they tended to take much the same line as the British. Clavier, for instance, insisted that Homer and the Epic Cycle were primary sources which allowed a continuous history to be written from Inachus to archaic times (1809: preface, 11–12), and engaged in chronological debates with Newton (ibid.: preface, 25–40). Fauvel, upon excavating Late Geometric graves at Athens in 1812, simply followed Thucydides (1.8.1; cf. Herodotus 1.105, 2.44, 6.47) in assuming that they must be Phoenician (cited in Poulsen 1905: 10). But by the middle of the century, French writers tended to ignore the entire Anglo-German debate. The most remarkable text is Fustel de Coulanges' *La Cité antique* (1864). Fustel was a leading light in the reactionary Catholic circle around the empress Eugénie. Ferociously anti-German, he rejected all methods pioneered by the philologists across the Rhine and wrote a polemical tract that ignored contemporary classical scholarship (Momigliano 1977: 325–43, Momigliano and Humphreys 1980). He argued that all Indo-European societies were founded on ancestor cults, and that these cults, which focused on a tomb outside the house, had caused Greek and Roman society to be based on agnatic descent. Classical history became for Fustel the story of the struggle between this kinship principle and emerging political forces. This periodically came to a head in revolution, which, Fustel argued, was always bad. Humphreys observes (1993: 79) that the book 'has had, for a thoroughly self-contradictory argument, a remarkably successful career'; it was translated into English in 1873, and long remained central to French interpretations of early Greece.

Early Greece was as heavily implicated in political debates within nation-states as in rivalries between them. One admiring reviewer of Mitford wrote in the Tory *Blackwood's Magazine* in 1819 that Mitford looked at 'everything in the bright PAST of antiquity with an eye cooled and calmed by the reflection and experience of the troubled PRESENT in which himself [sic] had lived' (quoted in Turner 1981: 203). As has often been pointed out (e.g., Turner 1981: 192–204, Roberts 1994: 204–05), Mitford watched as the events of the American and French Revolutions unfolded before his horrified eyes, and strove to incorporate into his text warnings drawn from history about the dangers of any form of republicanism. He argued from Homer that

> absolute MONARCHY ... was unknown among the Greeks as a legal constitution. The title of KING therefore implied with them, as with us, not a Right of Absolute Power, but a Legal Superiority of Dignity and Authority in One person above all others of the state, and for their benefit.
>
> (Mitford 1784: 250)

He drew an explicit analogy between the Homeric kings and those of contemporary Britain, for 'Monarchy with us perfectly accords with the Grecian idea of Kingly government' (ibid.: 255). By taking Homer as a faithful recorder of early times, Mitford argued that in the Heroic Age monarchies of this kind had flourished, only to be replaced in archaic times by various forms of republican government. His main peculiarity was to insist that Sparta, as a republic, was every bit as unpleasant as Athens. The implication throughout was that if England was to avoid the mob rule of the Grecian republics, it had better make sure that its monarchy did not go the way of the Homeric royal families.

Mitford's political message was perfectly clear to his contemporaries. George Grote complained in the Whig *Westminster Review* (1826: 331) that this model of Greek history was 'eminently agreeable to the reigning interests in England', and that the greatest blow anyone could strike for liberalism would be to write 'a good history of Greece'. By 'good', Grote meant a history informed by liberal principles and German philology. He was one of the first British practitioners of the rigorous new methods, feeling 'painfully sensible of the difference between the real knowledge of the ancient world possessed or inquired for by a German public, and the appearance of knowledge which suffices here' (Grote 1826: 281).

Grote himself was too busy at the time to write such a history, since he was not only a prominent banker but also a leading figure in the radical wing of the Liberal party, heavily involved in the reform movement. Fortunately, his old school friend Connop Thirlwall did have time to write an eight-volume *History of Greece*. Turner (1981: 211) calls Thirlwall 'the first British historian to bring the vast accomplishments of German classical scholarship into the service of Greek history', but as Mahaffy noted (1890: 13), Thirlwall tended to bend the rules of source criticism to suit himself, and drew heavily on legends. In his account of the origins of the Greeks, for instance, Thirlwall struck a stern theoretical position on evidence, suggesting at one point that 'if no such person as Hellen had ever existed, his name would sooner or later have been invented' (1835: 80); but he then immediately went on to accept almost the whole genealogy. On reaching the Trojan war, while arguing that 'the poet . . . did not suffer himself to be fettered by his knowledge of the facts' (ibid.: 157), Thirlwall nevertheless concluded, 'According to the rules of sound criticism, very cogent arguments ought to be required to induce us to reject as mere fiction a tradition so ancient, so universally received, so definite, and so interwoven with the whole mass of the national recollections, as that of the Trojan war' (ibid.: 151). Thirlwall was unlike Mitford in constantly emphasizing the problems of using Homer as a source, but his position that Homer did tell us about the Trojan war while simultaneously being an even better source for contemporary manners was much closer to Mitford than to Wolf. And, again like Mitford, Thirlwall made Homer's portrait of the Heroic Age cover a single, homogeneous, pre-lyric poetry period:

> What he represents most truly is the state of Grecian society near to his
> own day; but if we make due allowance for the effects of imperceptible

changes, and for poetical colouring, we are in no danger of falling into any material error, in extending his descriptions to the whole period which we term the Heroic.

(Thirlwall 1835: 159)

Grote's political programme collapsed in the 1841 election. He then turned to write his own twelve-volume *History of Greece,* published between 1846 and 1856. He explained in his preface that he had initially wanted to refute Mitford, but that Thirlwall had already done this. Grote then insisted, almost certainly in order to avoid causing offence to his old friend (Turner 1981: 212), that he only went ahead with his own book because he was already far advanced with it when Thirlwall's work appeared (Grote 1846a: iii–iv). But in spite of the lavish praise he heaped on Thirlwall, Grote disagreed with him almost completely over his model of a Heroic Age.

Grote favoured a compromise between the analyst and unitarian Homers, seeing books 1, 8, and 11–22 of the *Iliad* as a core *Achilleis* (1846b: 118–209), but argued at length that no serious history could be based on mythology (Grote 1843). Grote did not deny that legends could include factual information, but felt that there was no way to distinguish between genuine stories and plausible fictions. He concluded that the Trojan war was

essentially a legend and nothing more. If we are asked whether it be not a legend embodying portions of historical material, and raised upon a basis of truth ... whether there was not really some such historical Trojan war as this, our answer must be, that as the possibility of it cannot be denied, so neither can the reality of it be affirmed ... Whoever therefore ventures to dissect Homer, Arktinus and Lesches, and to pick out certain portions as matters of fact, while he sets aside the rest as fiction, must do so in full reliance on his own powers of historical divination, without any means either of proving or verifying his conclusions.

(Grote 1846a: 321)

Mitford and Thirlwall had already argued that Homer was most valuable as a source for contemporary manners; but Grote was more consistent than his predecessors, insisting that Homer was useful for historians *only* in this role. He held that 'the very same circumstances, which divest [the epics'] composers of all credibility as historians, render them so much the more valuable as unconscious expositors of their own contemporary society' (1846b: 57). Grote spent seventy-two pages reconstructing the customs of Homer's own day, which he placed around 800. He spoke of 'intermediate darkness' between the world evoked in the legends and the beginning of real history (1846b: 1), but does not seem to have proposed this as a serious historical periodization. For Grote, history began in 776, with the first Olympiad.

Before this, there was nothing, and all the chronological studies of earlier events, going back to Newton and Ussher, were worthless (1846b: 34–57).

Grote's vision was highly controversial. Many readers clearly felt that such agnosticism was merely the mark of a pedestrian mind. John Stuart Mill, for instance, wrote to Carlyle in 1833 that Grote 'is a man of good, but not first rate intellect, hard and mechanical, not at all quick; with less subtlety than any able and instructed man I ever knew' (quoted in Momigliano 1952: 11). So far as Blackie was concerned, Grote 'declares war against all literary, all poetic instinct, and all the common sense of common men in the matter of Homeric poetry' (Blackie 1866: 247); while for Lang, Grote was 'an excellent banker, but no great poetic critic' (Lang 1910: 234). Yet to Geddes, Grote's reading of Homer was the only one that was 'scientifically tenable' (Geddes 1878: iv). By the 1860s this latter view was gaining favour, and Grote had won over most British and German readers (Momigliano 1952: 13). Grote's philological skills were indisputably technically superior to those of his rivals, and even when a politically more conservative mood set in after 1870, there was no way historians could go back to a pre-Grotean view of the relationship of Homer to later Greek history. There was growing consensus that we could know virtually nothing about Greek history before the eighth century, and that even then, knowledge was restricted to cultural history.

PHASE II. INVENTING THE DARK AGE, 1870–1939

Schliemann's Heroic Age

A new era began with Heinrich Schliemann's work at Troy. Schliemann had abandoned his education in 1836, at the age of 14, only to resume his reading of Homer in 1866. By then, his obsession with proving that Troy had really existed, and that it had been at Hissarlik rather than at Burnabashi, marked him as an old-fashioned crank. But his finds gradually changed this, particularly after 1874, when he moved to Mycenae.

Schliemann's interpretation of his discoveries required a totally new vision of early Greece. He claimed that there really had been a Heroic Age, and that it was associated with the Mycenaean palaces, for which Homer was a reliable source. At some point the palaces were destroyed and the Heroic Age had ended. This point had to be earlier than the seventh century, but at first could not be dated any more precisely. This flew in the face of the modified analyst scholarly orthodoxy, which held that Homer was only relevant to the values of the beginning of the archaic period, and that nothing could be known about earlier times.

Institutional developments in these years gave the controversy a particularly sharp edge. A massive transformation of scholarly activity was under way, as a new class of professional academics emerged, employed in university departments, and priding themselves on their scientific standards as compared to earlier generations of clergymen or politically motivated men of letters (Heyck 1982). Classical philologists made particularly strong claims for the rigour of their scholarship, and classical archaeologists were eager to assimilate themselves to these standards (I. Morris 1994: 27–29). Schliemann's lack of professional training, destructive methods, and frequent changes of mind about the dating of the cities at Troy left him open to charges that he was no scientist. In America, Stillman vigorously opposed him, but Schliemann won public opinion over to his side (Chambers 1990). In Britain, the first generation of professional classicists generally lined up against Schliemann, who once again sought popular support. Here he was in a peculiar position; the German excavator's discoveries seemed to support the older pre-professional and British unitarian model of Homer as a faithful recorder of a Heroic Age. Schliemann marketed his own views skilfully, approaching Gladstone to write a preface for his new book *Mycenae* (Vaio 1990: 419). Gladstone at first hesitated, feeling that Schliemann should have asked Charles Newton, then the best-known professional British classical archaeologist, but Schliemann was insistent, and Gladstone relented (Gladstone 1878). Newton, it turned out, had serious doubts about some of Schliemann's ideas, and Evans was later to suggest that Newton was in fact hostile to the whole notion of Aegean prehistory (Newton 1880: 246–50, MacDonald and Thomas 1990: 67).

Overall, Schliemann's arguments carried the day, and by 1914 most Hellenists were arguing or assuming that Homer described a Heroic Age which was in most regards similar to the way of life of the royal families of Mycenaean times. The decisive factor was of course the spectacular finds made precisely where Homer said they should be. Classicists were keen to be seen as scientific, and all of them, to the best of their abilities, paid scrupulous attention to the new evidence. The analyst consensus of the 1860s about early Greek history – that the Heroic Age was a legend and that Homer could only tell us about eighth-century culture – collapsed. But while enthusiasm for Bronze Age archaeology transformed historical scholarship, it had less impact on broader philological agendas. In 1914, Homeric scholarship was still dominated by the old Homeric Question. For twentieth-century unitarians, Homer was a Bronze Age poet, whose works were passed down to archaic times intact; for analysts, he was usually a ninth- or eighth-century editor of Bronze Age lays. The scholars' ability to reject the historical implications of Grote's position while preserving his philological framework is perhaps the most revealing lesson in the history of the periodization of early Greece, and I will return to it later in this chapter. While treating the evidence with all due respect and being prepared to change their views in the light of new finds, scholars have consistently allowed broader disciplinary forces to shape the importance of that evidence and the periods they construct around it.

Nilsson (1933: 21) went so far as to claim that Homerists in fact 'cared but little' about squaring their readings with the finds in detail, but the level of debates in the 1880s suggests otherwise, particularly in Britain. Here, Homer's ideological significance had increased throughout the nineteenth century. The one Homeric issue over which Gladstone (1857: 1–56) and Jebb (1907: 565–67) seem to have agreed was that the poems should be central to the education of élite British schoolboys. The debate between them was to some extent over whether such an ideologically central field of learning was to be dominated by amateurs like Schliemann and Gladstone or by professionals like Jebb. Jebb argued against Schliemann's claims more fiercely than anyone. He claimed that since 'the Homeric Greek exhibits all the essential characteristics and aptitudes which distinguish his descendant of the classical age' (Jebb 1887: 38), he could not possibly belong to an incredibly distant prehistoric world. The newly founded *Journal of Hellenic Studies,* the major mouthpiece of the emerging classical profession in Britain, was the forum for a series of debates over the relationship between Bronze Age archaeology and Homer. For Jebb, Homer summed up many of the attitudes of Greeks at the dawn of the historical era, and could not possibly be describing some lost Heroic Age, let alone one rooted in the barbaric splendour of Schliemann's finds. He insisted that Hissarlik was not Troy, and that Mycenae and Tiryns were in fact Byzantine fortresses (Jebb 1881, 1882, 1886, Sayce and Jebb 1883). Other scholars, including Mahaffy (1882), Gardner (1882), and Leaf (1883a, 1883b, 1884), sided with public opinion against Jebb's authority. By the late 1880s opinion was tipping in Schliemann's favour. Even in Germany, an entrenched analyst like Schuchhardt was able to admit that 'for certain parts of his descriptions, Homer can have had no other models before him but those of Mycenaean art and civilisation' (1891: 313).

The debate had equally strong ideological implications for Greek intellectuals, who were developing their own models of their past, which often resisted foreigners' attempts to appropriate a 'classical' period and to argue that Western Europeans were descended more directly from this than were the 'Byzantinized' Greeks. One way in which Greek archaeologists opposed this was to argue for a single Greek *Zeitgeist,* as present in Mycenae and modern Greece as in classical Athens (I. Morris 1994: 22–23, 33–34). After initial suspicions about Schliemann, the Archaeological Service opened its own excavations at Mycenae in 1886–88, uncovering the palace. Tsountas blended Schliemann's interpretation of early Greece with claims about an unchanging Hellenic *Zeitgeist,* suggesting that

> Mycenaean culture in Greece belongs to the Greeks: this view is daily gaining ground. True, people of other stocks were drawn within the sphere of its influence; but in the Peloponnesus and on the adjoining Mainland, and for the most part in the Islands too, this civilisation was Greek, and cultivated y Greeks.
>
> (Tsountas and Manatt 1897: 272)

By 1914 Homer was firmly linked to the palaces. Few writers, if any, openly denied this, though some continued to feel that the position needed extended defence (e.g. Seymour 1908: 17–44). The commonest form of dissent was to phrase the issues ambiguously. Albert Keller, for instance, insisted that 'the *Iliad* and *Odyssey* give the impression of spontaneity and an entire freedom from artificiality of historical "reconstruction"' (Keller 1902: 5), but refused to locate the 'time of Homer' at any specific point. It may be significant that the title page of the book describes Keller as 'Instructor in Social Science at Yale University'; standing outside the classical profession, he perhaps saw little profit in taking sides. But Gilbert Murray's famous *Rise of the Greek Epic* (1907) was equally vague. Murray emphasized post-Mycenaean times in the formation of what he called Homer's 'traditional book', but, as Nilsson noted (1933: 25), 'Murray leaves us in the dark in regard to the times when the traditional book came into existence.' Similarly, in his widely read *Hellenic History*, George Botsford only cited Homer once in a twenty-three-page account of the Bronze Age, and in an ambiguously worded passage suggested that Homer

> may have composed both the *Iliad* and *Odyssey*, not by incorporating earlier lays or by merely adding to an existing epic, but by totally new creations, yet from tradition contained in extant songs ... The life he pictures is not homogeneous but a mingling of the traditional and the ideal with contemporary facts.
> (Botsford 1924: 43, cf. Botsford and Sihler 1915: 2–5)

But even this tactful evasion was a minority position. Mahaffy claimed that 'even the most trenchant of sceptics does not now deny that there must be some truth in legendary history' (1890: 18). Isham (1898: 3) simply stated that Schliemann had discovered 'the Mycenaean period, the life of which no one seriously doubts that the Homeric poems reflect'.

J.B. Bury's changing views across this period illustrate neatly the growing strength of Schliemann's position. In the first edition of his *History of Greece* (probably the most commonly used English-language textbook of the twentieth century), Bury took an analyst view. The original *Iliad* described the wrath of Achilles and death of Hector, and was expanded in the ninth century into something like our poem, while the *Odyssey* only took shape in the eighth century. Each poem had two historical layers. He agreed with Schliemann that 'the old Achaean poet, doubtless, reflected faithfully the form and feature of his time' (Bury 1900: 67), but also felt that the later redaction had a significant impact on the poems as history. Homeric society reflects the rise of the city-state, which he dates in a marginal comment on p. 72 to the tenth or ninth century; and the margin of p. 74 suggests that the Thersites episode was 'composed in the ninth century', as part of a royal reaction against the new spirit of citizenship. Bury's original picture was complex and multi-layered, more optimistic that we could learn about early

Greece than Grote, but lacking Schliemann's certainties. But by the time of the second edition, thirteen years later, Bury's doubts had largely evaporated. Bury simply states:

> Our earliest written record, the *Iliad* of Homer, refers to the peoples and civilisation of Greece in the thirteenth century ... the picture which Homer presents is a consistent picture, closely corresponding, in its main features and in remarkable details, to the evidence which has recently been recovered from the earth.
>
> (Bury 1913: 5, 50)

In writing an entry on 'Homer' for the *Cambridge Ancient History,* Bury was still more confident:

> Since the poems were not, on any theory, composed till about three centuries after the Trojan War, the natural place for considering them and questions associated with the name of Homer might seem to be not here but at a later stage of our history. There is, however, a good reason for anticipating chronology. The Homeric poems tell us almost nothing directly about the history of their own age. It is the civilization of the Mycenaean age they reflect.
>
> (Bury 1924: 498)

This orthodoxy had its own problems. In 1871 Palaiologos had found a cluster of rich graves outside the Dipylon Gate at Athens, which, when published by Brückner and Pernice in 1893, were seen as belonging to a post-Mycenaean *Dipylonzeit.* In the 1880s most archaeologists had put the end of the palaces as late as the tenth century, which made for a short *Dipylonzeit*; Schuchhardt (1891: 316) was fairly typical in placing the transition around 1000. If Homer was describing the world of the palaces, and that world had survived until 1000, then bridging the gap between the Bronze and archaic ages, and explaining how the ninth- or eighth-century editor could know so much about Mycenaean poetry, was not too difficult. However, in 1890 Petrie published Mycenaean pottery from Egyptian contexts of the Eighteenth and Nineteenth Dynasties, fixing the end of the Mycenaean world around 1200 BCE. Some archaeologists resisted the implications of his discoveries (see James *et al.* 1991: 15–18), and Tsountas and Manatt, while agreeing with Petrie, still felt a need to justify his dates (1897: 320–22); but a decade later, writers simply took them for granted.

As with Schliemann's finds twenty years before, Homerists were ready to face the evidence even when it complicated their theories. Andrew Lang vigorously defended Petrie's high daing (1893: 349–81), even while recognizing the problems this created for his own view that Homer accurately described the Mycenaean world. He made explicit what many other historians were probably assuming, arguing that the epics were composed before 1200 and then preserved in the Linear B script on papyrus rolls until the alphabet was invented, and at this point they were copied into the new script (Lang 1906: 315–19). Other historians took different lines. Bury insisted that analogies with medieval Germanic epics made it reasonable to think that oral poets could preserve historical facts; and further, that 'the immeasurable superiority of the Greeks in the art of poetry ... implies an intelligent, lucid, and discriminating method in grasping and handling the material' (1924: 512–13). Leaf (1915: 296) argued instead that Bronze Age poetry was the pride and joy of post-Mycenaean Ionian kings, and that

> under such conditions it need cause no surprise if the tradition of the Achaian age was religiously preserved intact ... The tradition was the hall-mark of the aristocratic poet, and it was all the more tenaciously maintained because he had to compete with other poets who were not aristocratic.

One way or another, by 1914 most Homerists agreed that the poems reached more or less the form in which we have them around 700 BCE, but described the Mycenaean world which had ended around 1200. Petrie's work was thus as important as Schliemann's for periodizing early Greek history: scholars now had to confront not a brief transitional phase between palaces and city-states, but a major epoch about which almost nothing was known.

Inventing the Dark Age

Between 1870 and 1914, then, the periodization of early Greece had changed beyond all recognition. The older disputes about the reality of a Heroic Age, growing out of the Homeric Question, had come to seem rather old-fashioned, and historians were now busy reconstructing the years before 700 as two periods – a Mycenaean age, which Homer described and which could cast further light on the poems; and a post-Mycenaean world, which, by general agreement, Homer did not describe, and which could not be particularly useful in filling out the poems' background. It was clear enough that scholars' knowledge of this 500-year period was woefully inadequate. Gilbert Murray (1907: 29) summed up the model – 'perhaps a shade prematurely', as Snodgrass (1971: 21) puts it – by saying, 'There is a far-off island of knowledge; then darkness; then the beginnings of continuous history.' It was also clear that archaeology would be the only way to fill the gap (e.g. Leaf 1915: 35). Yet very few archaeologists were interested in doing this.

On the face of it, there were at least three good reasons why historians and archaeologists between 1890 and 1939 ought to have been interested in the post-Mycenaean period. The first, and most powerful, was that many felt that the coming of the Dorians at its beginning perfected the racial mix of classical Greece. 'Scientific racism' was a major force in the prehistory of most parts of the world in those years (Trigger 1989: 110–206). There could be no better illustration than Virchow's reaction to the discovery of a group of skeletons at Troy in 1878. He was disappointed by the cranial indices which he measured; 'But', he added, 'if besides the skull index we take into consideration the entire formation of the head and face of the dolichocephalic skulls, the idea that those men were members of the Aryan race is highly pleasing' (in Schliemann 1881: 511). When skeletons were available from post-Mycenaean deposits, skulls were earnestly measured to find out whether the Dorians were Aryans, most determinedly at the Kerameikos cemetery in Athens (Breitinger 1939); when human remains were not available, heated debates grew up over whether particular styles of vase-painting were Dorian. These arguments were particularly popular in Germany (e.g. Miltner 1934, Wirth 1938, Kraiker 1939), but had plenty of adherents in other countries (for Britain alone, see Droop 1906a: 60–62, 1906b: 92, Wace and Thompson 1912: 29, Payne 1929: 229–30, Heurtley and Skeat 1931: 35, Skeat 1932).

A second reason to be interested in the newly defined period was the general agreement that the origins of Greek art lay here (e.g. Kroker 1886, Rayet and Collignon 1888: 19–38, Waldstein 1900). Nottbohm (1943) likened the eighth-century Dipylon Master to Giotto, seeing both painters as stimulating an artistic renaissance. A few archaeologists in the 1890s also argued that even if Homer's Heroic Age did largely reproduce the Mycenaean world, since he had probably lived in the eighth century, the ship scenes on Late Geometric pottery could illuminate the *Odyssey* (e.g. Afsmann 1886, Pernice 1892, 1900, Graef 1896). Excavations produced a growing body of post-Mycenaean pottery, and art historians set about cataloguing this, identifying regional styles, and fixing its chronology. But only one published monograph was devoted exclusively to Iron Age art before the Second World War (Schweitzer 1917). Kahane completed a full-length study of Attic Geometric in the late 1930s, but this was never published.[2]

Archaeologists seem to have agreed that their energies would be better spent on the art of other periods. Beazley covered the period between 1200 and 750 in a single sentence for the *Cambridge Ancient History:* 'Between the flourishing of the Creto-Mycenaean civilization, and the geometric period proper, there lies a long period which has been named, not very happily, the proto-geometric: a period of cultural decay, doubtless of invasions and incessant conflict' (Beazley and Robertson 1926: 580). Certainly, less artwork survived for study than from archaic Greece, but Beazley seems to be very clear that the perceived cultural decline of these times means that its materials have no interest.

A third reason for interest was the consensus that the origins of Greek religion also belonged between 1200 and 700. This did inspire some fieldwork aimed specifically at eleventh- to ninth-century deposits. The British School began digging at the temple of Artemis Orthia at Sparta in 1906, pressing directly down to the earliest layers, and publishing them promptly; in Macmillan's opinion (1911: xx, xxii), this, rather than Knossos, was the School's most important project. At Olympia, Curtius found much redeposited

Iron Age material between 1875 and 1881, quickly published by Furtwängler (1879). On other sites, though, the early phases of worship were less appealing to excavators. In France, Schliemann's discoveries had had much less impact on scholarship than in most other Western countries; the new periodization was generally accommodated to Fustel's evolutionary scheme without disturbing it much (e.g. Francotte 1907, Glotz 1929). Duruy simply avoided the Homeric Question and Schliemann's finds altogether, arguing that since the Greeks had believed their legends, historians should study them in accordance with the same principles (1887: 45, cf. Mahaffy 1890: 30). R. Cohen (1939: 35–56) similarly avoided the debates, and in one of the main textbooks of these years, Francotte (1922: 3–8) ignored pre-archaic Greece almost totally. French archaeologists were equally unexcited. Excavations began at Delos in 1873, but no significant soundings were made to the Geometric levels until 1904, and the first major publication of early pottery came only in 1934. Picard sketched a synthesis of the early deposits in an unpublished lecture in 1947, but it was not until 1958 that Gallet de Santerre published a monograph on the pre-archaic sanctuary (see Plassart 1973).

The example of Olympia is particularly telling. Even here, where the Iron Age remains were published with the greatest speed, they were not discovered by excavators who had been particularly interested in finding them; rather, they had been an unintended side effect of attempts to investigate the classical sanctuary. Similarly, the excavation in the Kerameikos cemetery at Athens, which has produced some of the most important Dark Age evidence, was not aimed specifically at the graves of this date. Excavations of fourth-century tombs began in 1863, but it was only in 1927 that the Dark Age graves received systematic attention. The same story can be told for Delphi, Knossos, the Athenian Agora, and numerous other projects. Classical archaeology was text-driven throughout this period, a subdiscipline structured around illuminating philology, not challenging it (I. Morris 1994: 23–35).

Despite contemporary interest in the origins of race, art, and religion in ancient Greece, the post-Mycenaean period remained a backwater. The reason seems obvious: Schliemann's spectacular finds had not moved the centre of interest from texts to archaeology. Rather, they had made the Bronze Age interesting by showing that it was relevant to Homer, one of the canonical texts of Western culture. The post-Mycenaean period was significant mainly as an annoying gap in the record. Nilsson explains that Homer

> stands in the morning twilight of Greek history and looks back to a preceding age, which according to him was an age of much more brilliant glory and valiant men than the age in which he himself lived. The question is whether Homer can help us to bridge over the gulf of the dark ages which separate the historical and the Mycenaean age of Greece.
>
> (1933: 1)

For Nilsson, this was 'the poorest and darkest epoch in all Greek history except for the Stone Age' (1933: 246). The concept of a Dark Age rapidly took hold (e.g. G. Murray 1907: 29, Bury 1913: 57), or, for some authors, a Greek 'Middle Age' (e.g. Botsford 1924: 31–51, R. Cohen 1939: 45. Snodgrass (1971: 22, n. 2) suggests that the expression was coined by Meyer in 1893). Tsountas and Manatt combined both terms, arguing that 'the Dorian migration marks the beginning of long dark ages, the medieval epoch of Greece' (1897: 365). Murray saw the era as

> a chaos in which an old civilization is shattered into fragments, its laws set at naught, and that intricate web of normal expectation which forms the very essence of human society torn so often and so utterly by continued disappointment that at last there ceases to be any normal expectation at all.
>
> (1907: 55)

This was not an attractive period to study.

Excavations aimed at other periods had, by the outbreak of the Second World War, generated significant quantities of Iron Age finds. But for classical archaeologists, subordinated to a more prestigious literary discipline, there was no good reason to concentrate on this Dark Age, and little chance of building a career on it. For the stories classicists wanted to tell in the 1870s–1930s, it was just not very important, and very few archaeologists working in Greece were eager to take their research goals from the less prestigious field of European prehistory. In Snodgrass's words (1971: vii), the Dark Age appeared as 'an unsatisfactory interlude, interrupting any pattern of continuous development, yet not providing the positive evidence needed to demonstrate a fundamental change in direction'.

Probably nothing illustrates the marginality of the Iron Age better than the partial feminization of its study. Beard (1994) has recently stressed that women achieved more prominence in classical field archaeology in these years than in classical philology, perhaps because working in the Mediterranean made their perceived racial superiority over the locals count for more than their perceived sexual inferiority within the academy. But as in more recent periods and other areas of the world, a pronounced sexual division of labour in archaeology is also clear, with men dominating fieldwork, and particularly the excavation of whatever type of site is currently considered to be the most important (see Gero 1983, 1985, Walde and Willows 1991: 177–232, Victor and Beaudry 1992, Claasen 1994). Women were noticeably more prominent in directing excavations at Dark Age sites than at sites of other periods. Two of the earliest purely Dark Age excavations were carried out on Crete by Harriet Boyd Hawes (1901) and Edith Hall (1914), even though both were interested mainly in the Cretan Bronze Age (Allsebrook 1992, Bolger 1994). This division of labour was by no means complete. Some men did excavate

Iron Age sites in Crete, and Boyd Hawes (1908) did dig Bronze Age sites; but even her major Bronze Age project, at the village site of Gournia, was itself a rather peripheral event at a time when the leading archaeologists were digging up palaces and archives. It remained until recently the only large-scale excavation of a Minoan village.

The most exciting kind of pre-archaic archaeology was to excavate a palace which could be linked with a Homeric hero, as Schliemann did for Priam at Troy and Agamemnon at Mycenae. Other archaeologists eagerly tried to repeat this. The most elusive palace was Odysseus' on Ithaca. Schliemann had briefly dug in search of it, and Dörpfeld spent thirteen years on nearby Lefkas in the belief that this had been the Mycenaean Ithaca. In 1931, Lord Rennell of Rodd (1933) instituted a new British project on Ithaca, with William Heurtley as its director. This series of campaigns also failed to locate a Mycenaean palace, but did find important Iron Age deposits. Heurtley published much of this, but considerable responsibility also passed into the hands of Hilda Lorimer (Heurtley and Lorimer 1933) and Sylvia Benton (1935, 1939).

PHASE III. REVALUING THE DARK AGE, 1945–1980

The new Heroic Age

If the years between 1875 and 1900 saw the definition of the Mycenaean world as an exciting Heroic Age and the post-Mycenaean world as an uninteresting Dark Age, those between 1945 and 1980 saw a redefinition, in which both text-based historians and archaeologists assigned new prominence to the post-Mycenaean period. On the philological side, two developments were particularly important. The first was a gradual change. Before the war, Milman Parry (1971 [1928–37]) had argued on the basis of fieldwork in Serbia that Homer was an oral poet. Then in 1945 Rhys Carpenter, in his Sather lectures at Berkeley (Carpenter 1946), combined Parry's insights with folklore studies to reject completely the historical readings of Homer which had dominated the field since the 1880s. A series of studies published by Parry's former assistant Albert Lord spread understanding of the implications of orality, which made older arguments like Bury's or Leaf's about the transmission of Achaean poetry across the Dark Age harder to sustain (e.g. Lord 1948, 1953, 1960). However, the pre-war models still had their champions, and in the 1957 Sathers, Denys Page (1959) forcefully restated the older view. In his chapter on 'The Homeric poems as history' for the second edition of the *Cambridge Ancient History*, Geoffrey Kirk (1975; first published as an independent fascicle in 1964) found a middle ground, preserving the unitarian idea of an early monumental composer whose poems were then passed down by memory, but placing him early in the Dark Age, and seeing few survivals from Mycenaean times. Kirk was less radical than Carpenter and many other Parryans, and when in October 1963 Moses Finley took a Grotean position of agnosticism about the Trojan war in a BBC radio broadcast, Kirk joined a group of senior scholars in defending the war's historicity (Finley *et al.* 1964). But Kirk's chapter nevertheless contrasts sharply with Bury's interpretation of Homer and history for the first edition of the *CAH*.

A second development was more abrupt: in 1952, Michael Ventris deciphered the Linear B script, which meant that there could no longer be any doubt that the economic basis of the Mycenaean palaces was completely different from that of Homer's heroic society. Finley (1981 [1957–6]: 199–232) argued that the Mycenaean palaces now seemed to have more in common with those of the Near East than with Homer. Finley offered a new periodization in terms of what he called a 'highly schematic model of the history of ancient society. It moved from a society in which status ran along a continuum towards one in which statuses were bunched at the two ends, the slave and the free' (1981 [1964]: 132). Finley was unusual among ancient historians. As a research assistant at the Institut für Sozialforschung in New York, he had cut his teeth in the 1930s on the Frankfurt School's critique of Marxism, and in 1948–53 he worked with Karl Polanyi's economic history seminar at Columbia University (B. Shaw and Saller 1981). Unlike most of his contemporaries in Classics, debates among social and economic historians of other periods counted for more in his research programme than did relevance to the canon of Greek authors. His major interest was in the economic and social structure of classical Athens. In his first book, on the structure of credit in fourth-century Athens, he adapted Polanyi's model of reciprocity, arguing that loans expressed the civic egalitarianism which bound together the Athenian citizen group (Finley 1952). In the next five years, Finley tried to explain how this socio-economic formation, a complex economy in which markets and money were important but which could in no way be called capitalist, had come into being. Most classicists continued to periodize the past (and thus to attach importance to different parts of it) according to the potential they saw for historical analysis to contribute to the study of Greek literature. Finley's radical politics gave him completely different grounds for periodization. Borrowing another of Polanyi's models, he suggested that in contrast to classical civic reciprocity, the Mycenaean palaces were a redistributive economic system, and that the key to understanding classical Athens lay in these changes in the broader economic system. For this, the Dark Age was the decisive period.

Borrowing also from Mauss, Finley argued in *The World of Odysseus* (1954, but begun even before Ventris's decipherment) that the Homeric economy was based on gift exchange, which both created and expressed hierarchy among the heroes. Drawing on Parry and making explicit analogies between Homer and medieval epics such as the *Song of Roland,* Finley also argued that the *Iliad* and *Odyssey* reflected neither the Mycenaean world nor

Homer's own time, but memories of an intermediate point, which he located in the tenth or ninth century (1954: 48). He seems to have been influenced by contemporary anthropology; in a recent seminal book, Radin (1949) had similarly argued that since Winnebago oral poetry did not seem to describe contemporary conditions, it probably preserved memories of the poets' grandfathers' days. In Finley's vision, the Mycenaean redistributive economies collapsed around 1200, being replaced by Homeric-style gift economies. At some point between the ninth century and the sixth, these systems of graded statuses were further transformed into a world where a free and equal citizen population practised reciprocal exchange. In 1959, Finley published the first of a series of papers giving his explanation for the transformation: slavery. Archaic social revolutions such as that leading to Solon's reforms at Athens in 594 swept away the Homeric spectrum of statuses, replacing it with a situation in which men (women are conspicuously absent from Finley's story) were polarized into two groups, one made up of free citizens practising reciprocal exchange, alienating exploitation on to the second group, of chattel slaves (Finley 1981 [1959–65]: 97–195, 1980: 11–92).

The World of Odysseus played an important part in separating Homer from the Bronze Age. By the mid-1960s the post-Mycenaean Homeric society was firmly established in the most influential new syntheses (e.g. Forrest 1966: 45–66; Andrewes 1967: 32–55), and in the preface to a revised edition of *The World of Odysseus*, Finley explained that his only major changes had been to delete sections attacking the Mycenaean model, because 'today it is no longer seriously maintained ... that the *Iliad* and *Odyssey* reflect Mycenaean society' (1979: 10). Some historians writing in the wake of Finley argued that Homer reflected his own eighth-century world more than that of the tenth or ninth century, but linking Homeric society with the Bronze Age was increasingly defined as eccentric. Yet Finley stimulated little further research along the same lines until the late 1970s. In part, this may have been because few ancient historians shared his political commitments: like Grote in the late nineteenth century, his reasoning might persuade them, but his sense of the seriousness of Homeric history need not. Further, Finley himself largely abandoned the period. He seems to have felt that he had settled the main problems, and after 1958 never again wrote specifically about Homeric society, moving instead on to the later phases of his 'schematic model'.

But *The World of Odysseus* contributed to a new periodization. The eleventh to ninth centuries were no longer to be seen as a Dark Age of little relevance. Finley redefined the Bronze Age as a Near Eastern palatial society, and the post-Mycenaean period as a hierarchical and complex world of heroes. These were calculating supermen struggling against common enemies and each other in a Hobbesian war of all against all, forming a complex web of political alliances, gifts, and counter-gifts where might was right and the price of weakness was destruction. For the first time, the post-Mycenaean period was important within a larger historical narrative.

The new Dark Age art history

The post-Mycenaean period enjoyed an even more striking revival among archaeologists. Like the influence of Parry's work on Homeric philology, the new interest had pre-war roots, and Gray (Myres and Gray 1958: 240) suggested that in fact it should be seen chiefly as a 1930s phenomenon (although the examples she mentions are more concerned with archaic archaeology than the Dark Age). The British had begun excavating on Ithaca and at Karphi, and Vincent Desborough began his studies of Protogeometric pottery as a student at the British School at Athens in 1937–39 (Desborough 1952: vii). However, it was only after 1945 that major monographs on the period began to appear. The post-1945 archaeology differed sharply from its pre-war antecedents in focusing almost exclusively on art history. A few archaeologists, particularly in eastern Europe (e.g. Milojcic 1948/49), continued to focus on waves of intruders, but as early as the 1950s scholars were trying to reconstruct the Dark Age without the aid of invasion models (e.g. Andronikos 1954).

One obvious factor in this development was the amount of evidence that had accumulated, but had never received thorough analysis. Thus Verdelis (1958) systematized the masses of Protogeometric pottery from many years of excavations in Thessaly; Gallet de Santerre (1958) put in order the complex early remains on Delos; and Courbin (1966) classified the Geometric pottery from French work at Argos. But the most influential Dark Age archaeologists were British. Hilda Lorimer's *Homer and the Monuments* (1950) was the most systematic study of Homeric archaeology since the 1880s, and was the first to treat the Iron Age as seriously as the Bronze Age. But Vincent Desborough's *Protogeometric Pottery* (1952) was still more significant, revolutionizing the study of the Dark Age by making it possible to compare regions on a systematic basis; and from 1957–60 Coldstream, like Desborough as a student at the British School at Athens, extended a similar kind of treatment to the end of the Dark Age in a dissertation which was published as *Greek Geometric Pottery* (1968).

It is not easy to explain why British archaeologists working on the Iron Age were more numerous than those of other countries, nor why the British interest tended toward Panhellenic systematizations rather than publishing the finds from their own excavations. The British School had certainly produced a wealth of Iron Age pottery, from older digs at Knossos as well as from the 1948–51 work at Smyrna; but if this were the main criterion, we might expect Tübingen to have been the centre of the post-war revival of interest, since, as Desborough (1948: 260) pointed out, the Kerameikos at Athens long remained the most important single site. The publication of the Kerameikos finds (Kraiker and Kübler 1939, Kübler 1943) was the major enabling factor for this new Dark Age archaeology, but even this cannot be made the sole explanation, for Lorimer (190: viii) mentions that *Kerameikos*

IV only became available in Britain in 1949, too late for her to use it in *Homer and the Monuments* (Desborough presumably saw it in Athens during a second stint at the British School in 1947–48).

There is little in the archaeologists' own writings to explain the new interest among British researchers. Desborough (1952: xv) went no further than to say that his aim was to study the interrelations of the Protogeometric styles; other evidence, such as the graves themselves, were only drawn in 'to support this general picture'. Similarly, Coldstream described his work as 'being concerned exclusively with style and chronology' (1968: 3). The main impression these books create is that the study of a large body of poorly known material was such an obvious thing to do that it needed no explanation: as Coldstream put it (1968: 1), 'for the art historian, the study of Geometric pottery is an end in itself' (cf. Courbin 1966: 1).

The one factor that is conspicuous by its absence in these books is the new philological interest in the Iron Age. Desborough described his *The Last Mycenaeans and Their Successors* as a historical enquiry into the period down to about 1000 BCE, but at no point mentioned the new approaches to Homer; Finley's *World of Odysseus* did not even appear in his bibliography (1964: 274). Desborough explained that 'I intend to use the archaeological evidence as the basic material, at the same time assuming as true the existence of major movements of population as given by the [literary] tradition' (1964: xvii).

This split between archaeology and history was a new development in the 1950s and 1960s. Within a decade of starting to dig at Mycenae, Schliemann had claimed that there was a professional gap between archaeological and textual studies; he felt he could simply state that 'no courtesy on my part can save Professor Jebb from the fate on which an eminent classical scholar rushes when he mingles in an archaeological debate in ignorance of the first principles of archaeology' (Schliemann 1884: 237). But this was not really true, and at least until the Second World War Homerists and Bronze Age archaeologists were expected to have a basic grasp of each other's fields. Lorimer's *Homer and the Monuments* (1950) remains the most impressive of these studies. Lorimer (1950: viii) explained that Parry's demonstration of the great antiquity of some formulae showed the need for a book like hers, collecting all the archaeological evidence, from the coming of the Greeks to Homer's own day. Lorimer's goal was radically different from Desborough's; she closed her book not with a formal analysis of the material evidence but with a long account of what the archaeology could tell us about the Homeric Question (ibid.: 462–528).

Myres and Gray's *Homer and His Critics* (1958) and Wace and Stubbings' *Companion to Homer* (1962) share similar aims, but – like *Homer and the Monuments* – both these books owed much to the pre-war period. Myres' had begun in a series of lectures at Bangor in 1931, had been revised as more lectures at Harvard in 1937–38, delayed by the war, and completed by Gray after Myres' death in 1954; while Wace had planned the *Companion* before the war, and (like some of the contributors) died well beore Stubbings (himself the second assistant editor to work on the project) could complete the book. Some of the contributions to the *Companion* (particularly Wace's own chapters) clung to the old model placing Homeric society in the Mycenaean palaces, while Myres, Gray, and Lorimer all preferred a composite picture, stressing the mix of Mycenaean and Iron Age material culture in the poems (see Myres and Gray 1958: 244 on the evolution of Myres' thought from the 1920s to the 1950s). All these books struggled to bring together texts and archaeology in a single picture, always structured around the old assumption that interest in Homer must precede interest in archaeology. Stubbings (1962: vi) made this clear by explaining that the *Companion* was intended for people reading Homer in Greek, particularly those doing so for the first time.

By the 1960s, the aims of these books must have seemed distinctly old-fashioned. The new social historians of Homer and the new art historians of the Dark Age seem to have felt that they had little to gain from close study of one another's work, and the massive systematizations of *Protogeometric Pottery* and *Greek Geometric Pottery* may have done more to divide the groups of scholars than to unite them. Although each of these books included a section of 'historical conclusions', neither was what the social historians recognized as a historical synthesis. Desborough (1948: 260) was particularly insistent that 'Protogeometric must be the name given to a *style* of pottery, and not to a Period' – i.e., that ceramic typology was not the same thing as historical periodization; but the two concepts tended to merge. The pottery all too easily became the period, with history being reduced to aesthetic principles. Whitley (1987, 1991: 13–23) shows how Desborough and Coldstream drew on a long tradition of German idealist art history, which had few points of contact with the questions of the social historians.

The first social archaeologies

The first serious effort to connect the material record to the social historian's questions came from Chester Starr, in his seminal *The Origins of Greek Civilization* (1961). Starr had previously worked mainly on imperial Roman and modern history, but had combined textual evidence with visual materials in original ways, and in 1953 decided to apply similar techniques to the beginning of classical civilization. He accepted some of Finley's views on Homeric society (1961: 123–38), but was not primarily influenced by *The World of Odysseus*. Instead, he based most of his argument on the newly published pottery from the Kerameikos, and on study of museum collections in 1959–60.[3] He explained that:

> The historian ... will use this pottery with due circumscription. He may – indeed must – go beyond the limited range of most modern studies

of the material, for specialists restrict themselves to descriptive or morphological classification with the aim of setting the chronology of evolution and the interrelationships between the different fabrics. This is a highly useful and necessary foundation which reduces the masses of scattered finds to orderly terms; but it is not all the story. On the other hand, the careful student will not be able to follow in their details the overly subtle, at times virtually mystical interpretations of early Greek pottery which have occasionally been advanced.

(Starr 1961: 101)

Origins had its own share of idealism and racial theorizing, but Starr's concern with social questions was very different from Desborough's connoisseurship. Starr (1974) perceptively argued that Desborough's approach was not just unhistorical, but anti-historical. Starr wanted to go beyond the pottery to construct a totalizing model, and this required a new periodization. He identified two major discontinuities. The first meant that 'the pattern of civilization which we call Greek emerged in basic outline in the eleventh century BC'; the second, that 'the age of revolution, 750–650, was the most dramatic development in all Greek history ... Swiftly, with simple but sharp strokes, the Greeks erected a coherent, interlocked system politically, economically, and culturally, which endured throughout the rest of their independent life' (1961: 99, 190). Desborough had anticipated Starr's first argument, suggesting that late eleventh-century Athens saw 'certain innovations which were to affect almost the whole Aegean, and [which] can be considered the starting-point from which developed later Greek civilization' (1952: 298); and the idea of an eighth-century renaissance was well established. But Starr's book was none the less strikingly original. Instead of dividing post-Mycenaean Greece into two aesthetic eras, as Desborough had done, or equating it with a static 'Homeric society', as Finley had been forced to do by limiting himself to written sources, Starr constructed a dynamic model, emphasizing change through time and regional contrasts.

But for all its importance, Starr's contribution had no more impact on most archaeologists than had Finley's. At roughly the same time, archaeologists operating within the art-historical tradition were also experimenting with social archaeologies of early Greece. John Boardman was successfully blending Beazleyan connoisseurship with ancient history, to produce a new understanding of Greek colonization (Boardman 1964), but his doctoral student Anthony Snodgrass was moving still further away from the art-historical tradition. Snodgrass differed from most Dark Age archaeologists in that he concentrated on iron weapons, which could not easily be integrated into an art-historical narrative.

The motivations for this work came from outside the new Dark Age art history. The first source of inspiration was archaic Greek social history. It was widely held that there was a major change in arms, armour, and tactics in the seventh century, the so-called 'hoplite reform', which ushered in a social revolution. Lorimer (1947) had already used artefacts to illuminate this problem, but Snodgrass (1964) put the archaeological evidence on a firmer footing by carefully cataloguing all the finds, quantifying them to demolish earlier impressionistic accounts of the shift from bronze to iron weapons. This allowed him to tackle social change in much more direct ways than his predecessors had done (e.g. Snodgrass 1965a). His work was more widely cited by historians than that of the pottery experts, and was taken by Finley (1975: 99) as a model of the kind of bridge that was needed to link archaeology and history. This was unusual enough; but Snodgrass's second major source of questions and problems came from archaeologists working on the Iron Ages of other parts of Europe, whom he also directly addressed (Snodgrass 1965b, 1971: viii–ix).

The archaeological syntheses

In the 1970s, each of the three major British Dark Age archaeologists produced a synthesis of the scattered excavation reports and forbidding specialists' monographs (Snodgrass 1971, Desborough 1972, Coldstream 1977). These efforts were preceded by Bouzek's *Homerisches Griechenland* (1969), but this had relatively little impact outside German-language scholarship. It was less detailed than the British studies, and focused on connections with central Europe, which seem to have lost much of their interest among Western classicists with the decline of racial archaeology.

Within the English-language world, the British syntheses were massively influential, shaping the field for the next twenty years. The new periodization made the twelfth century an abrupt break, with the Mycenaean heritage almost entirely disappearing. Desborough and Snodgrass agreed (with Starr before them) that there was also a major change in the eleventh century, sending the Aegean on a course very different from the rest of the Mediterranean. Snodgrass (1971: 237–49) linked this to a collapse in long-distance trade around 1025: the Aegean lost contact with the outside world, and shifted over to an iron-based economy. In this process, regionalism became much more pronounced, and an 'advanced' area in the central Aegean began to take shape (ibid.: 374–76). The general agreement that the Dark Age ended in a major revival in the eighth century also continued. Snodgrass (1971: 378–80, 1987: 188–210) saw economic changes underpinning the history of the period, with a shift towards nomadic pastoralism around 1100, and back towards sedentary agriculture after 800. He went on to argue for a massive population explosion in the eighth century, at Athens reaching 4 per cent per annum, as fast as human populations had ever been known to grow. This stimulated political centralization and state formation (Snodgrass 1977, 1980: 15–84).

Taken together, the three syntheses constituted an archaeological vision of a Dark Age which stood in sharp contrast to the Finleyan, text-based model of a post-Mycenaean Heroic Age. Snodgrass (1993: 35) has recently summed this up by suggesting

> there is a long-standing division of opinion between those who believe that Greek society of the Early Iron Age was in general rather egalitarian, and those who on the contrary hold that it was markedly stratified. Broadly speaking, archaeologists have tended to make up the former group and historians . . . the latter.

For Finley (1970: 93), it made little sense to speak of a 'Dark Age' at all: 'In the sense . . . that *we* grope in the dark, and in that sense only, is it legitimate to employ the convention of calling the long period in Greek history from 1200 to 800 a "dark age".' Starr (1977: 47), on the other hand, preferred a vision recalling Gilbert Murray's: 'During the Dark Ages . . . men struggled to survive and to hold together the tissue of society.' The pre-war temporal distinction between a Mycenaean Heroic Age and a post-Mycenaean Dark Age had been replaced by a methodological distinction between a text-based model of the 500 years after the destruction of the palaces as a Heroic Age and an artefact-based model of it as a Dark Age.

At this point we might expect to find an academic debate to rival the fury of that of the 1880s, but nothing of the kind happened. Finley (1979: 155) did argue that Snodgrass's rejection of his own theories rested on a 'confusion between objects and institutions', while Snodgrass (1974) ingeniously drew on comparative anthropology to renew Lorimer's arguments against treating Homer as reflecting the social structure of any single period. But such direct confrontations were the exception rather than the rule. Instead, there was a classic example of a paradigm shift (Kuhn 1970): with hardly any sustained debate in print, the archaeological model quietly swept the field. Within Britain itself, the clearest evidence is institutional. During the 1970s, Dark Age archaeologists won a disproportionate share of the most prestigious British university positions. Coldstream and Snodgrass took the chairs in classical archaeology at London and Cambridge respectively, and Desborough returned to Oxford, where in 1981 Boardman was elected to the Lincoln professorship. Outside Britain, the published versions of the three major international conferences on Greece between 1200 and 700 also suggest that in the 1980s the British scholars' archaeological model, and particularly Snodgrass's version, was simply taken for granted by most linguists and philologists, as well as by archaeologists (Hägg 1983, Deger-Jalkotzy 1983, Musti *et al.* 1991). The first chapter of Oswyn Murray's *Early Greece*, one of the most successful textbooks of the 1980s, presents the archaeological model of the Dark Age without any serious questions (O. Murray 1980: 13–20).

Paradoxically, the success of the archaeological syntheses did much to revive interest among Homerists in Finley's questions. Qviller (1981), Donlan (1981, 1982, 1985, 1989a, 1989b, 1994, Donlan and Thomas 1993), and Redfield (1983, 1986) combined Polanyian economics with the archaeological syntheses (see Tandy and Neale 1994: 15–20). Abandoning Finley's claims that Homer described a functioning society of the tenth or ninth century, their periodization provides a compromise: the years from roughly 1100 to 800 were after all a Dark Age, while the eighth century was more like the Heroic Age of Homer, which could then be connected to the archaeological model via Snodgrass's eighth-century population explosion and political centralization. Nagy also addresses the contrast between the archaeological evidence for regional variation and the homogeneity of Homeric society, linking Snodgrass's model of eighth-century state formation with a broader process of the formation of a Panhellenic culture. He argues that 'this poetic tradition synthesizes the diverse local tradition of each major city-state into a unified Panhellenic model that suits most city-states but corresponds exactly to none' (Nagy 1979: 7).

This extraordinary success demands explanation. Bernal (1987: 9) would account for it by what he calls '"archaeological positivism" . . . the fallacy that dealing with "objects" makes one "objective"; the belief that interpretations of archaeological evidence are as solid as the archaeological finds themselves.' But archaeological evidence had been around long before the 1970s; it was something about the syntheses, rather than the evidence itself, which made the difference. It seems to me that the crucial factor was that the archaeologists simply produced fuller and more dynamic pictures than the philologists. Until the end of the 1960s most archaeological energy had gone into producing what seemed to outsiders to be a rather narrow form of art history, and the results were generally hidden in dense technical monographs on pottery; but the 1970s syntheses, especially Snodgrass's, with its relevance for the questions in social history raised by Starr a decade earlier, changed this. The archaeological models incorporated regional variation and changes from century to century, while older visions derived from Homer, such as Finley's, provided a single, static model of early Greek society. In providing a bigger picture and linking the period to compelling questions about social evolution, the archaeologists could claim to have produced a *better* account than had previously been available.

But we should not exaggerate the unity of the archaeological vision of the period. Snodgrass's social archaeology moved steadily away from the older art history. His was the only synthesis to refer to Starr's *Origins* as a major source of inspiration (Snodgrass 1971: viii); and in an unusually explicit methodological statement, Snodgrass defined a major difference between his own approach to the evidence and that of the other Dark Age scholars. He said that his aim was

> to examine the whole period in chronological sequence, scrutinizing the evidence as it comes, assembling the facts and endeavouring to face them. This sounds banal enough, but in this instance it involves abandoning the normal priorities of the historian, the literary scholar

or the Classical archaeologist ... This method also entails an almost obsessional insistence on chronology. Much of the material that is available is trivial in itself and ambiguous as to the conclusions that can be drawn from it; yet this same material has some security as a basis for broader understanding of the period, in a sense in which no inference or analogy from better-known periods or regions can be secure.

(Snodgrass 1971: vii–viii)

This inductivist, positivist method might be seen as setting Snodgrass apart from contemporary developments in processual archaeology (see particularly Binford 1972), but his interest in so-called 'trivial' data and totalizing questions about social change nevertheless made him sympathetic to debates among prehistorians and to the kind of questions they were putting to the archaeological record. He drew on Renfrew's models of the multiplier effect and peer–polity interaction to explain the take-off at the end of the Dark Age (1980: 54–55, 1986), and went over some of the same ground as the neo-evolutionists in his Cambridge inaugural lecture on *Archaeology and the Rise of the Greek State* (1977). He subsequently embraced intensive surface survey as a tool (Snodgrass 1982, 1987: 99–131, 1990, 1991). Survey data are even more difficult to accommodate in an art-historical framework than iron weapons, and Dark Age archaeologists who continue to operate within the art-historical tradition have been critical of some of Snodgrass's claims for survey (e.g. Boardman 1988: 796; Popham 1990).

PHASE IV. BEYOND SYNTHESIS: SINCE 1980

In some respects, the dominance of the 1970s archaeological model seems stronger than ever after twenty years. A recent pair of papers by Snodgrass (1993) and Raaflaub (1993) discussing the relative contributions of archaeological and written sources to understanding the rise of the polis illustrates this well. Snodgrass emphasizes the conflict between the Heroic and Dark Age models, and argues for the superiority of the latter; while Raaflaub accepts without comment the Dark Age model and treats the literary sources as taking off from the end of that period. Increasingly, the society of the poems is being treated as more of a heroic culture than a Heroic Age, a set of beliefs about what the world had once been like rather than a window on to a real society (e.g. I. Morris 1986; van Wees 1992).

But in other respects, there have already been significant shifts in the definition of these periods. I see two major changes. The first is in the disciplinary structures and agendas which give meaning to the discussion of the period. Since 1980, there has been a widespread sense of 'crisis' among classicists (see Culham *et al.* 1989), often perceived as a struggle between older practitioners of empirical research, and younger champions of explicit theory. This self-doubt is typical of most fields within the humanities and social sciences, and classical archaeology has been caught up in it in complex ways (I. Morris 1994). One of the main results has been an acceleration of the process already clear in Snodgrass's work since the 1960s: archaeologists no longer look so automatically to classical philology to define their goals. Instead, ancient social history and various forms of non-classical archaeology provide alternative frameworks. A second important change, in some ways related to the first, has been a move towards more gradualist models, de-emphasizing the importance of changes in the eleventh and eighth centuries, most often in conjunction with increased emphasis on the role of Near Eastern influences on Greek culture. New archaeological finds have played a big part in these developments, but it is hard to see them as actually *causing* the changes.

One of the most striking developments is the apparent end of the century-long lack of interest in the Dark Age among French scholars. In the early 1960s, Jean-Pierre Vernant published a series of important articles examining Hesiod's poetry as an expression of early Greek values, drawing on Dumézil, Lévi-Strauss, and Meyerson (collected and translated in Vernant 1983). This was the first application of anthropological structuralism to early Greek studies; and twenty years later, François de Polignac succeeded in combining Vernant's structuralism with a Snodgrassian concern for social archaeology in his influential *Naissance de la cité grecque* (1984). De Polignac supported Snodgrass's argument for seeing a religious revolution in the eighth century as a central element in the rise of the polis by looking at the construction of extra-urban sanctuaries as a way in which formative states defined their boundaries.

De Polignac's powerful blend of structuralism and positivist archaeology was a timely one, coinciding with a general turn towards religious history all across the humanities. His book has played a large part in inspiring a revival of interest in early Greek religion (e.g. Hägg, Marinatos and Nordquist 1988, Morgan 1990, Marinatos and Hägg 1993, Alcock and Osborne 1994), and also coincided with a new wave of interest in early Greek religion among field archaeologists. Some of the new finds in fact ran counter to de Polignac's emphasis on the eighth century as a time of profound change. By insisting on sound stratigraphic criteria for identifying religious continuity across the Dark Age, Snodgrass (1971: 394–401) had done much to demolish unfounded claims, but digs in the 1980s produced good evidence for ritual activity and even religious buildings going back to at least 900 at several sites. At Kalapodi, there may be genuine stratigraphic evidence for continuous cult from the twelfth century on (Felsch *et al.* 1980, 1987), and at Kato Symi Viannou on Crete there can be no doubt of this (Kanta 1991). De Polignac (1994, forthcoming) has subsequently modified some of his views about the abruptness of changes in the eighth century.

Snodgrass's social archaeology has also been developed further by his own students, sometimes in ways that challenge his interpretations. With both

Finley and Snodgrass holding chairs at Cambridge in the late 1970s, it was perhaps predictable that this would become a centre for British Dark Age studies, to an extent that Papadopoulos (1993: 196–97) calls the Dark Age 'a phantom that has haunted the "musty confines of Cambridge" for too long.' This perhaps exaggerates the longevity of the period's prominence there, but in the 1980s Cambridge was a particularly suitable place for a new social archaeology of the period. Cambridge was one of the major centres for processual and post-processual archaeology (see Hodder 1991, 1993). Snodgrass's students followed his lead in combining the methods and goals of other fields of prehistory with questions which had become important in ancient social history. This led to a series of attempts to move beyond the methods of the post-war Dark Age archaeology by focusing on smaller bodies of material, which could be analysed in great detail in terms of more explicit theoretical models drawn from other archaeologies, while remaining at least partly wedded to traditional questions about the Dark Age as a period. Some of these dissertations have been published as books, concentrating in different ways on social evolution, ideology, class conflict, and the symbolic construction of meaning (I. Morris 1987, Morgan 1990, Whitley 1991). Whitley (1991) and Shanks (1992) even brought post-processual arguments and complex quantitative methods to bear on the most traditional field of all, vase-painting.

Snodgrass (1993: 35) notes that some members of this 'group of the younger archaeologists' have moved back towards Finley's arguments for a more hierarchical vision of Greek societies between 1100 and 800, challenging the 1970s consensus about periodization; but other archaeologists would go much further, effacing the whole concept of a Dark Age. Papadopoulos (1993: 195) suggests that the concept of a Dark Age which I employ in my own work is 'a period that has no pedigree, a period which appears out of nowhere', an inappropriate periodization resting on 'the assumption – approaching religious belief – that the demise of the Mycenaean way of life heralds a clean, almost surgical break'. He suggests that social archaeologists have exaggerated the scale of discontinuity in the twelfth and eighth centuries, and blames the misunderstanding on 'the guiding hand of . . . Anthony Snodgrass, the guru of the Greek Dark Age' (ibid.: 194). Sarah Morris is still more explicit in linking the concept of a Dark Age to social archaeology:

> It may be time for a reform of our current adulation of 'the state' in early Greece, a spectre which has acquired a monolithic, nearly totalitarian set of powers over contemporary scholarship. In my view, community-by-consensus evolved slowly, gradually, and continuously since the Late Bronze Age . . . without the 'explosion' or 'renaissance' attached to the 8th century.
>
> (S.P. Morris 1992a: xvii)

She links the theme of continuity from the Bronze Age with that of influence from the East: 'it is the Orient which can liberate Greece from the strait-jacket of the polis as a form of community which sprang full-blown in all its democratic armour in the 8th century' (ibid.: xviii).

This implies a very different periodization, going back to a model of gradual evolution, and Sarah Morris (1989a) has also tried to revive pre-Finleyan positions on the relationship between the Homeric poems and Bronze Age culture (see Starr's [1992] response). To some extent this model is based on new finds, particularly at Lefkandi. Sarah Morris suggests, 'Recent archaeology on Euboia has dispelled Greece's "Dark Age"' (1992b: 140). It is certainly true that the 'heroon' excavated at Lefkandi Toumba in the 1980s (Popham *et al.* 1993) is not easy to fit into earlier views of the Dark Age, but neither do the new finds compel a new periodization. Snodgrass, Desborough, and Coldstream had all insisted in the 1970s that Greece became more involved with the wider world in the mid-tenth century, with an 'awakening' by 850. The new evidence from Lefkandi and the strong evidence for a ninth-century Phoenician shrine at Kommos on Crete (J. Shaw 1989) make equal sense within the older model, so long as we follow Snodgrass's demand for an 'almost obsessional insistence on chronology' (1971: vii). Snodgrass (1994) even argues that, if anything, the Mediterranean imports in the Lefkandi graves from *c.* 950–825 reinforce the same picture of an insular Aegean Dark Age between 1100 and 950 followed by expansion after 950 which he drew in *The Dark Age of Greece*.

Recent attempts by non-classical archaeologists to situate Iron Age Greece within a broader Mediterranean context seem to point in the same direction. The speakers at an international congress on the twelfth century in 1990 generally argued that the idea of a general crisis around 1200 BCE had been much exaggerated, but most of them sought to replace it not with a model of long-term continuities between the Bronze and Iron Ages, but with one of a drawn-out series of problems and opportunities which radically transformed the east Mediterranean between 1200 and 1000 (Ward and Joukowsky 1992). And in a pair of widely read papers, Sherratt and Sherratt (1991, 1993) have proposed a broader model of Mediterranean economies in the early first millennium, stressing core–periphery relationships between the Levant and other regions. Their periodization operates independently of the concerns of classical archaeologists, but follows more or less the same lines, seeing a major decline in the eleventh century, and rapid recovery and interregional integration beginning in the eighth.

The new periodization proposed by some Hellenists seems to me to be driven as much by the broader external forces which are causing many classicists to rethink their position within the academy as by new archaeological discoveries. Some years earlier Walter Burkert (1984) had argued that racial stereotypes had blinded classicists to the importance of the Near East in social change in Greece in the eighth and seventh centuries, urging a broader geographical approach. Martin Bernal (1987, 1991) was subsequently to link these issues to serious questions concerning the classical profession as a whole, suggesting that since the early nineteenth century, Western scholars had determinedly denied strong evidence for massive Egyptian and Near Eastern influence on Greece in the Bronze Age, in an effort to make classical Greece the starting point for a pure tradition of Europeanness, strongly distinguished from the degenerate cultures of the East. Bernal (1991: 12–15) criticizes the influence of processualism, for discouraging classicists from looking outside a closed Aegean system for explanations of culture change. He further suggests (1991: 8) that speaking of a Dark Age encourages images of 'a clean break from the past', allowing classicists to concede strong links between the Aegean and Near Eastern palace systems, while denying that this had a significant impact on classical culture. Sarah Morris (1989b, 1990) has made clear the similarities and differences between her position and Bernal's.

CONCLUSIONS

In periodizing the past, scholars necessarily bring the data, as they perceive them, within systems of thought that are generated outside those data. There is nothing in the evidence itself to tell us what is important, nor to tell us what themes to group our facts around and to use as the basis for drawing lines through time. I have suggested that in trying to make sense of what happened in Greece in the years leading up to the appearance of our first literary sources, scholars have always responded in a serious and diligent way to new evidence and methods, but that their responses to the texts and artefacts have also been moulded primarily by disciplinary structures created in the late nineteenth century, and by professional goals defined within these communities.

By 1870, some degree of consensus had formed among the first generation of 'scientific' classicists that we could not know anything significant about the history of Greece before about 776, and that Homer could only tell us about the social mores of his own day. The violence of the response of classicists such as Stillman and Jebb to Schliemann's finds in the 1870s and 1880s cannot be explained wholly in terms of his own abrasive personality. That Schliemann could, by the lights of the times, prove correct a theory that seemed hopelessly old-fashioned and eccentric posed a serious challenge to the credibility of the professional scholars, who had supposedly already proven that there was nothing to the story of the Trojan war. But by the 1890s this challenge had been neutralized. Classicists found that they were able to keep Homer at the centre of early Greek studies by linking him firmly to a Heroic Age set before 1200, and declaring that the post-1200 period was a Dark Age of little significance. This position seems bizarre one hundred years on, but worked well at the time.

The Dark Age as the era of the Dorian invasion ought to have been a period of intense excitement for archaeologists at this time, when interest in race was running so high. But the perception of Classics as the study of the great literature of Greece and Rome, combined with the position most classical archaeologists favoured, of a subordinate field within Classics rather than as a part of a field of world archaeology, allowed disciplinary goals to overpower externalist forces. No prominent archaeologist before the 1940s built a career on the study of the Dark Age, even though most excavators who generated Dark Age remains did publish them reasonably promptly. The Bronze/ Heroic Age was important, because Homer illuminated it, and it illuminated Homer; the Iron/Dark Age was marginal, because it had nothing really to do with Homer.

This view changed rapidly after the Second World War. The pre-war chronological distinction between a Heroic Age and a Dark Age was transformed into a methodological distinction. Philologists and archaeologists could now all agree that the post-Mycenaean era was important, but for different reasons. Historians generally argued that Homer belonged somewhere between the tenth and the eighth century, and showed that the post-Mycenaean era was a Heroic Age. Archaeologists largely ignored this. The philologists' downdating of Homeric society by three to five centuries must have helped increase the credibility of Iron Age archaeology among classicists, but there are few hints of the parallel scholarship in the archaeologists' published writings, which consistently assert that the finds revealed a true Dark Age of poverty, simplicity, and isolation. The two positions were incompatible, but there was little discussion of this in the literature of either camp. By the 1970s, though, positivist archaeology showed that it was a more powerful methodology than poetic sociology, in the sense that it could incorporate a huge range of data and provide a model which accounted for regional and temporal variation. The three great syntheses of that decade won an extraordinary level of acceptance. Without much fanfare, by 1980 there had been a classic example of a paradigm shift, and the archaeological Dark Age had become the consensus view.

The tensions between philological and archaeological approaches since the war perhaps reveal the processes of periodization in Greek history better than the study of the historiography of better-documented periods could do. The story I have reconstructed is by no means one of the pursuit of pure knowledge, with periodization as merely a helpful step in ordering the data, and changing in the light of new evidence. Others' periodization always looks arbitrary and misleading. But what this study suggests is that when we draw lines through the past, there is a wide range of forces affecting our appreciation of continuity and change. These forces change as quickly as do the data themselves, and indeed play a major part in the collection of new data. In the last fifteen years, a growing sense that there is something wrong with classical scholarship as it had been practised during the previous century has had a huge impact on the forces shaping our periodizations. One result has been to make the questions and goals asked by social archaeologists working on other parts of the world count for as much as the traditional goals of elucidating the great texts of antiquity; another has been to inspire a search for continuities between the Bronze and Iron Ages, and for stronger cultural links between the Aegean and Near East. In different ways, both these trends have had a major impact on the concept of the Dark and/or Heroic Ages.

There is one final question: so what? Does it really matter how our periodizations have evolved? I suggest that it matters a great deal, and that we can best understand the importance of the issue by drawing on a distinction made by Foucault (1970: xi) between what he called the 'negative' and the 'positive unconscious' of thought. Ancient historians tend to think about the problems created by periodizing the past largely in terms of Foucault's negative unconscious, as 'that which resists [clear thought], deflects it or disturbs it' – an obstacle to be overcome. We can get further by thinking of the forces that shape the act of periodization as 'a positive unconscious of knowledge: a level that eludes the consciousness of the scientist and yet is part of the scientific discourse, instead of disputing its validity and seeking to diminish its scientific nature'. We cannot get by without periodization: it is a fundamental part of the job of doing history. But if we are to avoid a fetishization of the period into something which really does resist, deflect, and disturb clear thought, our periodization must be a reflexive exercise. And the only way to make it such is through historical analysis of the processes of writing history.

NOTES

1 I would like to thank Robert Cook, Mark Golden, Sarah Morris, John Papadopoulos, Anthony Snodgrass, and Chester Starr for their comments on earlier drafts of this chapter.
2 Robert Cook, pers. comm., May 1995.
3 Chester Starr, pers. comm., May 1995.

7

RECONSTRUCTING CHANGE: IDEOLOGY AND THE ELEUSINIAN MYSTERIES[1]

Christiane Sourvinou-Inwood

This chapter reconsiders the early history of the Eleusinian cult of Demeter and Persephone and its place in Athenian religion. The investigation will also offer one model for reconstructing change in ritual and ideology on the basis of archaeological and other evidence. The conclusions will further confirm the thesis that a significant change in the collective attitudes to death took place in the archaic period.

Though the scarcity and problematic nature of the evidence for early Greek history often make it virtually impossible to reach incontrovertible conclusions, it is desirable to attempt to reconstruct the ancient realities through systematic investigations; for otherwise the vacuum is implicitly filled by older orthodoxies and unexamined assumptions so subtly enmeshed into the scholarly discourse as to appear to be self-evidently correct – 'common sense'. The unfavourable circumstances make it imperative to base such attempts on a rigorous and neutral methodology. A strategy conducive to rigour is to pursue independently the different lines of investigation that pertain to different sets of evidence. This avoids cross-contamination from fallacious assumptions and unconscious adjustments to make the different parts of the evidence fit, and also permits some cross-checks: if the results of the independent lines converge, this provides some validation.[2] I will not centre my investigation on the previous scholarly discourse, for this would cast the data into preconceived moulds, structure them through that discourse, which entails making – conscious and/or unconscious – adjustments, highlighting some data and underprivileging others, to make them fit modern, culturally determined schemata. In order to follow the separate grids strategy, I shall consider the archaeological evidence of the Eleusinian sanctuary on its own, in isolation of the textual and epigraphical evidence which will then be considered independently.

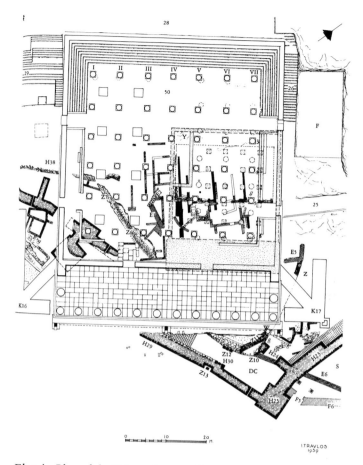

Eleusis: Plan of the Telesterion area (by J.N. Travlos, Mylonas
1961: Figure 6). Courtesy of Princeton University Press.

ARCHAEOLOGICAL EVIDENCE: EIGHTH AND
SEVENTH CENTURIES

The Eleusinian sanctuary of Demeter and Kore lies in the periphery of the
Athenian polis, near the frontier with Megara. Recent work has shown that
it began in the eighth century, and that the notion of a Mycenaean cult and
megaron surviving through the Dark Ages is a mirage.[3] The earliest votives
are of eighth-century date, as are the earliest Iron Age walls under the later
Telesteria: part of the retaining wall of the terrace and a curved wall belonging
to an apsidal temple.[4] To judge from the width of the surviving apsidal part
it would have been a temple of not insubstantial size (which would fit the
importance of the sanctuary), not narrow, and with not very much space in
front of it. The sanctuary had been inside the eighth-century city wall.

133

Between the latter and the east part of the retaining wall of the temple terrace
there was a space, the so-called external court, which was traversed by a N–
S paved road (cf. Mylonas and Travlos 1952: 54–56) and divided in two by a
cross wall between terrace and city wall, with a gate allowing the road through
(cf. Travlos 1983: 326, fig. 2; 1988, 110, fig. 115). It is surely not a culturally
determined judgement to think that the cross wall separated symbolically the
two areas; that (given Greek ritual logic and spatial articulation) it inevitably
created an 'inside' and an 'outside' space. A stairway at the southwest
(Mylonas 1961: 56) provided the main access to the temple terrace. In front
of the SW portion of the retaining wall and between it and the column base
III 6 of the Periclean Telesterion were found the remains of a cultic pyre, a
fill of ashes, terracotta figurines, pinakes and pottery (Mylonas 1961: 56–57;
Kokkou-Vyridi 1991: 5, 35–36, and *passim*). A well under the southeast
corner of the Periclean Telesterion, well W, was almost certainly in use
already in the eighth century; its religious significance is shown by the fact
that the Solonian retaining wall went round it, framed it in a carefully
constructed niche (Mylonas and Travlos 1952: 55–56, cf. also Mylonas 1961:
44–45, well at W of his fig. 6). Mylonas identifies it with the original
Kallichoron well, which, he thought, was subsequently replaced by the one
in front of the sanctuary's north entrance (Mylonas 1961: 44–47, Richardson
1974: 326–28, Ziro 1991: 20–21). The paved road went past well W, and part
of that road connected it to a court to the east, outside the east gate.[5] In the
seventh century a paved court outside the gate included cultic structures, an
altar and a podium, and was the locus of ritual. Below the floor of the court
that belonged with the seventh-century podium there was an older floor
belonging to an earlier court (Mylonas 1961: 71). Thus the rites that were
performed to the east of (and in connection with) the well in the seventh
century had been performed there also in the eighth.

According to Ziro (1991: 21), the fact that the eighth-century city wall had
separated well W (which was inside it) from the court outside tells against the
view that well W is the Kallichoron and can be associated with the rites in
the court with the seventh-century podium. However, given the road that
connects them, and given that there was in the eighth and seventh centuries
a gate at that point, if we abandon preconceived notions about what we ought
to expect, this state of affairs can be seen as duplicating the inside–outside
articulation of the ritual space. Thus, one basic articulation was 'outside city
wall–inside city wall'; but the latter was further articulated into 'inside city
wall and to the SW of the cross wall', that is, inside the sanctuary proper, and
'inside city wall and to the northeast of the cross wall', that is, outside the
sanctuary.[6] Well W is symbolically outside the sanctuary; the court was more
strongly outside in that it was outside the city wall. In the seventh century
the nexus outside the east gate included, besides the court, the following
elements. First, an altar, to the south of the southmost projection of the
Solonian terrace (Z 13 in Mylonas 1961, figs 6 and 23, cf. 70–71). (When the

Peisistratean wall was constructed, it went round this altar and enclosed it in a niche; when the wall was rebuilt after the Persian wars, the niche was repeated.) Second, a stepped podium, twenty-three metres to the east of the easternmost projection of the retaining wall. The altar, well W, the court, and the podium were part of a complex, the podium perhaps a stand for people to watch rites taking place in the court (Mylonas 1961: 72). In the Peisistratean period the city wall/peribolos was built across the court, which became unusable. This area, then, ceased to be the locus for ritual performances in the Peisistratean period at the latest, if it had not done so before, after the Solonian construction phase had surely put well W out of use.

Thus, significant cultic activities had taken place in the external court and immediately outside it from the beginning of the sanctuary until some time in the sixth century; another rite, involving cultic pyre A, on which offerings were thrown and burnt (cf. Kokkou-Vyridi 1991: 256–59 and *passim*), took place just beyond this nexus, immediately before the ascent to the temple terrace. The fact that the main access to the temple terrace was from the southwest does not entail that the entrance to the sanctuary had to be from the south. On the contrary, the north–south road, the cross wall with the gate, and the performance of rites in that area combine to suggest a ceremonial north–south route towards the temple, which went through the gate of the cross wall and to the entrance of the temple terrace to the southwest, a route that involved the performance of rites around well W and in the court outside the east gate, and at the cultic pyre. In other words, it suggests that, contrary to accepted opinion, from the beginning of the sanctuary the main, the ceremonial, entrance to the sanctuary area was from the north, where it was in later times, at the end of the Sacred Way.

There is another, independent, argument in favour of the thesis that the sanctuary's main entrance was at the north from the beginning. Part of an eighth-century apsidal temple was discovered underneath the later temple of Artemis Propylaea, outside the entrance to the sanctuary.[7] It would seem to have been very roughly on the same axis as that of Demeter,[8] only facing in opposite directions. This may conceivably suggest that the two were not unrelated, and that this arrangement was not without significance, especially since it entails that each would have been vaguely facing towards the direction of a northern access to the sanctuary: the temple under that of Artemis would be facing towards the last stretch of the Sacred Way that led from Athens to Eleusis, traces of the eighth-century phase of which were found under the southeast corner of the Little Propylaea;[9] the temple of Demeter would be facing roughly in the same direction. The fact that there was an eighth-century apsidal temple spatially not unrelated to that of Demeter under the later temple of Artemis Propylaea offers an argument in favour of the view that the privileged direction from which to enter the Demeter sanctuary was from the beginning from the north, as it was later.[10] That temples and sanctuaries could be related in this way in the eighth century can be seen in the comparable situation at Delphi. The sanctuary of Athena Pronaia was so named because it was situated before the sanctuary of Apollo when coming from the east, which was the privileged direction of access since the main entrance to the sanctuary of Apollo was from the east. Since the Pronaia sanctuary appears to have begun in the eighth century, in the form of a sacrificial area without a temple (Morgan 1990: 129–30, 138), the relationship between the two sanctuaries appears to have begun in the eighth century, despite the fact that much of the area of the later temenos of Apollo was then part of the settlement (cf. Amandry 1981, Themelis 1983: 246). In these circumstances, I suggest that the evidence on the ground strongly indicates that the privileged direction from which to approach the Eleusinian sanctuary was from the beginning, as it was later, from the north. If this is right, it removes the one argument put forward on the basis of archaeological evidence in favour of the thesis that Eleusis had been independent from Athens until the sixth century, that the main entrance to the sanctuary had been to the south, and had moved to the north, the direction of Athens, when Athens took it over; in fact, it offers an important argument in favour of the view that Eleusis and the Eleusinian sanctuary were part of the Athenian polis from the time of the latter's formation.

The apsidal form of the early temple of Demeter is significant: not only is it different from that of the later Telesteria, but also, most importantly, unlike the latter, it was one of the normal temple forms at that time, and was used in the same period at the same site for a temple of a non-Telesteric type, that under the temple of Artemis Propylaea. Such absence of differentiation suggests that the functions of the two temples were not perceived to have been radically different, as they would have been if the temple of Demeter was a Telesterion.

ARCHAEOLOGICAL EVIDENCE: THE 'SOLONIAN' PHASE

The next major phase, usually referred to as Solonian, at the end of the seventh, or, more likely, in the early sixth century,[11] brought considerable change. The eighth-century temple terrace was radically extended, to the east and south, so that the area immediately in front of the temple was considerably enlarged, and the apsidal temple was replaced by a building 24 metres long and 14 wide, the 'Solonian Telesterion', the entrance of which would appear to have been on its long east face, as in the subsequent Telesteria (Mylonas 1961: 68). The easternmost part of the Solonian temple terrace covered the 'external court', since on the south side of the eastern extremity of the terrace a fragment of a pre-Solonian archaic city wall (Z 12) was incorporated into the Solonian retaining wall.[12] At this point the peribolos of the Solonian sanctuary consisted of the upper part of the retaining wall.

Thus the north–south ceremonial route was disrupted, and in any case deprived of the crucial feature that had been well W. The court with the podium may also have gone out of use at this time. This state of affairs[13] can be seen to be correlative with the fact that the main access to the temple terrace is now on the north,[14] accompanied by a new cultic pyre Γ, outside the north retaining wall near this access. Pyre A had been covered up by the extension of the temple terrace and was replaced by two new pyres: pyre B in a position adjacent, and corresponding in location, to that of pyre A, near the south entrance of the terrace (Kokkou-Vyridi 1991: 7); and pyre Γ, outside the new north retaining wall of the terrace and near the new main access to that terrace, that is, corresponding to pyre A with regard to its position in the ritual nexus, just before the main entrance to the terrace. Both pyres continued in use until the early fifth century (Kokkou-Vyridi 1991: 91, 238–39). This state of affairs, and perhaps also the erection of the temple in the Ploutonion, the cave precinct immediately to the west of the north entrance which had contained an entrance to the Underworld,[15] if it is Solonian rather than Peisistratean in date (Solonian: Travlos 1988: 115, fig. 125; Peisistratean: Mylonas 1961: 99–100), entailed that the whole area from inside the north gate became part of the sanctuary – inside space. The area's identity was stressed, at least in the Peisistratean period, through the erection of cross walls, *diateichismata*, that separated the sanctuary from the city.[16] This entails that the symbolically outside area now began at the north entrance, and this makes sense of the notion that well W was replaced by the well outside the north entrance known as the Kallichoron. It is now clear that the Kallichoron in its present form is the result of one building phase, to be dated between 490 and 480, and does not include Peisistratean elements (cf. the detailed study by Ziro 1991: 19–47); its earliest phase cannot be dated, but it predates the Peisistratean phase, since the Peisistratean city wall was at this point designed to take the position of the Kallichoron into account (Ziro 1991: 17). Thus it is a reasonable interpretation of the evidence to suggest that well W went out of use in the Solonian phase and was replaced by a well outside the north entrance when the whole area inside the city wall to the north and east of the temple became part of the sanctuary, symbolically 'inside'.

Since we do not know the dimensions of the eighth-century apsidal temple, we cannot compare its dimension with those of the Solonian Telesterion very precisely. But in so far as it is possible to judge, it does not look as though there was a very considerable increase, if any, in the size of the cult building. There was not in front of the eighth- and seventh-century temple sufficient space for anything that could be considered in any way comparable to that of the Solonian phase. Besides the radical enlargement of the area in front of the cult building, another thing that changed was the latter's position in relation to the terrace: from the Solonian phase onwards, the cult building's long axis is parallel to the long axis of the terrace. The result is that there was a large and relatively regular triangular space in front of the entrance of the Telesterion. A third change concerns the cult building, which changed from a 'normal' type, one of the common types of early Greek temple, paralleled in this very site, to something different. The superficial similarity between the elongated form of the Solonian cult building and traditional Greek temples is less important than the nature of the differences between the two and the former's essential similarity with its successor Telesteria. Nothing of the internal structure of the Solonian Telesterion has survived – though it is generally accepted that it had the inner structure identified as the Anaktoron in the later Telesteria[17] – and only a small part of its external walls. But no one has ever suggested that the evidence allows it to be reconstructed as one of the normal types of temple, in antis or prostyle, and this divergence goes together with the location of the entrance on the east long side, as in the Athenian Eleusinion, and facing the large area in front of it. Moreover, a comparison of the Solonian cult building with its successor, the Peisistratean Telesterion, shows that the fundamental difference between the two is size and monumentality. The orientation is the same and the building's relationship to the terrace is the same; the Peisistratean Telesterion has been created through, as it were, expansion in the area around that of the Solonian, which was demolished. The difference in form results from this increase in size in interaction with the choice to increase size not by elongating the building but by making it quadrangular, a choice clearly reflecting specific cultic needs, since it went against normal Greek temple tendencies. These choices created the need for column supports all over the internal space and transformed the building to a hypostyle hall.

Another choice, to add a front portico, adds monumentality to the building. Increase in the size of temples is a common phenomenon elsewhere in Greece at this time and later, and on its own is correlative with an increase in the size of worshipping group and/or an increase in the investment made in the sanctuary whether or not the size of the group had increased. When, as here, increase in size is combined with the introduction of or increase in monumentality, it is clear that whatever may have happened to the size of the group, there is certainly an increase in investment that is not motivated purely or mostly by pressures of space. Such an increase in investment reflects factors pertaining to the availability of resources and/or ideological factors affecting the proportion invested in ritual and ceremonial in general, and also pertaining to the place of the particular cult in this investment programme and in the relevant community. In this case an increase in the size of the worshipping group may be indicated by the fact that the specific choices made in the form of the enlargement of the building indicate specific cultic functions different from those catered for in 'ordinary' temples: the fact that these needs were reflected in this way may indicate that adequacy of space was one factor, and thus that an increase in the worshipping group is also likely. What the changes between the Solonian and the Peisistratean Telesteria do *not* suggest is a change in function. Indeed, the changes from the Solonian to the Peisistratean Telesterion are comparable to those between the Peisistratean and its successors, increasing size and splendour, not to those between the eighth-century and the Solonian cult buildings. Though we cannot, of course, be absolutely certain that other changes did not take place between the time of the Peisistratean Telesterion and that of the Periclean, we do know that the size of the worshipping group and the importance of the cult did increase. The building of the magnificent Periclean Telesterion[18] took place in the same context as the attempt to make Athens a major Panhellenic religious centre by turning the Eleusinian cult into a major Panhellenic cult: 'the First Fruits decree', invoking a Delphic oracle, orders the Athenians and their allies to bring *aparchai* to Eleusis and exhorts the other Greeks to do the same.[19] Thus, it is likely that the great increase in the size of the Peisistratean Telesterion reflects an increase in the size of the worshipping group.

Whatever the context in which this took place, the replacement of pyre A by two pyres, B and Γ, the duplication of the pyre ritual, also entailed a change. Moreover, if it is right that cult in the Ploutonion cave began or was upgraded in this period, with the construction of a temple, this would also involve a change. The major and certain changes between the eighth century and the Solonian cult phase and their significance – the great expansion of the temple terrace, the change in the temple's orientation, and in the relationship between temple and terrace and the change in the type of cult building – these must be considered together, since they form a system reflecting certain needs and practices, and it is this system and the needs and practices it reflects that we are trying to reconstruct. Attempting to make sense of each feature separately distorts this process by wrenching that feature from the system that ascribes it meaning. Though changes did take place in the spatial articulation of Greek sanctuaries at this time, I do not know of any parallel in another archaic Greek sanctuary where a combination of changes of this type took place. This entails that we cannot use parallels from other sanctuaries as eye-opening, let alone explanatory, models of this change; but it also suggests that something unusual may have taken place in this sanctuary at this point, something different from the things happening in other sanctuaries. This hypothesis would appear to converge with a tentative conclusion that may be drawn from the discussion of the cult buildings: that the changes between the eighth century and the Solonian cult building reflect changes in the function of this building and of the space outside it. The fact that it does not look as though there was much of an increase in the size of the building in the Solonian phase suggests that it was not an increase in the size of the worshipping group that motivated the enlargement of the area in front of the entrance, an interpretation that is also indicated by the fact that the whole nature of the relationship between cult building and area outside changed, and adds support to the view that what changed was the nature of the cultic needs and thus of the cult. Given that the earlier type appears to correspond to the normal type of temple, while the nexus beginning in the Solonian phase does not, and that the basic arrangement of the latter continues into the fifth century and beyond, which means that it reflects the cultic needs of the Mysteries as we know them, this state of affairs suggests strongly that the Eleusinian cult did not begin as a Mysteries cult but was transformed into one at the end of the seventh/beginning of the sixth century.[20]

I shall now step outside the archaeological evidence to consider whether we can know anything about the function of the area in front of the temple that can confirm or invalidate this hypothesis: that the radical changes in its size, shape, and relationship to the temple were an important element in the transformation of a normal temple into a Telesterion for the Mysteries. Mylonas (1961: 68) thought that the altars of the goddesses stood in the 'court' in front of the entrance of the Telesterion. Clinton (1988: 71–72) has argued that the altars of Demeter and Kore were not in front of the Telesterion but in the forecourt of the sanctuary, outside the main gate. Whatever may have been the case, the following fragments of evidence from later periods seem to indicate that the space in front of the entrance of the Telesterion played a significant role in the initiation ritual.

First, Aristophanes, *Clouds* 302–04, *hou sebas arrhêtôn hierôn, hina mystodokos domos en teletais hagiais anadeiknytai* ('where the not to be spoken of sacred rites are revered, where the initiates-receiving (cf. Schol. *ad loc.*) house is displayed by opening its gates') indicates that the rite of the Eleusinian Mysteries included a ceremonial opening of the gates of the Telesterion to display its interior to the *mystai* who will be received in it, and probably also that this was a significant moment in the initiation ceremony. A much later passage, Plutarch, *Moralia* 81DE, confirms that the space immediately outside the Telesterion played a role in the ceremony by making clear that the entrance of the initiates to the Telesterion took place at a specific ritual moment – presumably following the ceremonial opening. This text involves a complex simile in which being inducted in philosophy is compared to the ritual of the Mysteries. The initial noise and disorder of the initiates is contrasted with the silence and awe with which they watch the *dromena* and the *deiknymena*, and an analogy is made with the induction into philosophy, described in metaphorical terms derived from the Mysteries. The initial noise and disorder of the initiates in the first part corresponds in the second part to the noise and pushing *peri thyras* of those who enter philosophy; their silent attention corresponds to the silence and awe with which those who have been inside and seen light (as when the Anaktoron is opened) follow the philosophical argument. The reference to being inside and seeing the light when the Anaktoron is opened leaves no doubt as to the Mysteric reference, and thus makes clear that the noise and pushing by the initiates was *peri thyras* outside the Telesterion, with initiates pushing to get in. Thus, this complex simile is articulated by the knowledge that outside the Telesterion there was a crowd of people and a lot of noise, but when they entered they saw a great light when the Anaktoron opened up and they were silent and in awe watching the *dromena* and the *deiknymena*.

Another rite may also have taken place in the area in front of the Telesterion on the last day of the Mysteries, the day called Plemochoai, because two ritual vessels called *plêmochoai* were filled and then ritually upturned. Critias (*TrGF* 43 F 1) speaks of pouring the liquid from the *plêmochoai* into a *chthonion chasma*. This has been identified by Clinton as one or more of the pits or shafts that are attached to the front of the Telesterion (Clinton 1988: 78 and 74–75, figs 4–8, 1992: 74). The fragment is cited by Athenaeus (2. 496A), who adds that on the day called Plemochoai they filled up two *plêmochoai* and then upturned them, one facing to the east and one to the west.[21] The *mystai* may have done all this together, in which case only some would have actually poured their liquid into the *chasma*, and as with the rite of opening the doors, a lot of space would be needed in front of the Telesterion. Or they may have carried out the ritual one after the other, each presumably having to wait their turn, which would also require space in the same area. In either case, the area in front of the entrance of the Telesterion was an important ritual space in the Mysteries, and required considerable free space.

In these circumstances, the thesis that the radical changes in the cult building and its terrace in the Solonian phase of the sanctuary indicate the transformation of a normal temple into a Telesterion for the newly founded Mysteries gains considerable confirmation. If cult in the Ploutonion with its entrance to the Underworld had begun, or been upgraded, in this period, this would further confirm it. Such an entrance would undoubtedly have been implicated in the *dromena* of the Mysteries, so its beginning or symbolic upgrading would be correlative with, and indicate some change in, something to do with the Mysteries; the development of the Mysteries as an initiatory ritual out of a non-initiatory one provides a perfect correlative for such change.

To sum up the results of this investigation of the archaeological evidence. First, the sanctuary of Demeter and Persephone at Eleusis began in the late eighth century in the context of the formation, and as part, of the Athenian polis. Second, the nature of the cult practised in the sanctuary changed some time around the end of the seventh century or, more probably, the beginning of the sixth, from what one may loosely call a cult of a 'normal' type to a cult focused on Mysteric initiation. Finally, during Peisistratus' rule the size of the worshipping group, as well as the investment in the sanctuary, may have increased very considerably.

MYTHS LINKING ATHENS AND ELEUSIS

The important ritual links between the Eleusinian sanctuary and the centre of Athens, which will be discussed below, have mythological correlatives, myths which say – among other things – that important cults in the centre were instituted as a result of a war between Athens and Eleusis which ended with the defeat and incorporation of Eleusis into the Athenian polis.[22] Euripides' *Erechtheus* explicitly places this war at the centre of the constitution of Athens and of its poliad cults in their 'present' form. In this tragedy the Eleusinians with an army of Thracians led by Eumolpus, son of Poseidon, were threatening Athens. Eumolpus wanted to replace Athena with his father Poseidon as the poliad divinity of Athens. On the oracle's advice Erechtheus, the Athenian king, sacrificed his eldest daughter to Persephone; two more daughters sacrificed themselves. The enemy was defeated, Erechtheus killed Eumolpus and was himself killed by Poseidon. Athena appeared at the end of the play and instituted the cults of Erechtheus' daughters as Hyacinthides and of Poseidon Erechtheus;[23] the latter was closely associated with that of Athena Polias, of which Athena now makes Erechtheus' wife Praxithea the first priestess, thus instituting the cult in the form in which it was practised in the fifth-century audience's time. This war, then, was connected with the constitution of the most central polis cults and of the polis. In the very fragmentary verses 102ff., Athena continues with a prophecy about the Eleusinian Mysteries, which will be founded by Eumolpus, the descendant of the Thracian Eumolpus. Thus in the Euripidean version, the Mysteries were founded while Eleusis was already part of the Athenian polis. In other versions, pre-existing Mysteries were incorporated in a polis that was constituting itself and its central cults. According to one (Marmor Parium *FGrH* 239 F 12, 14–15), Erechtheus was king in Athens when Demeter came and when Eumolpus the son of Musaeus founded the Eleusinian Mysteries.[24] According to another (Apollodorus 3.14.7), Demeter was received by Celeus, king of Eleusis, when Pandion was king in Athens, which means in the generation before Erechtheus.[25]

The fact that in all the myths the integration of Eleusis into the Athenian polis is placed in the very early stages of the latter's history, and connected with the constitution of Athens, means that in the Athenian perceptions of the past articulated in and articulating this myth, the integration of Eleusis in the Athenian polis and the constitution of the Athenian polis in its present form happened together. Far from suggesting that Eleusis had been independent until the early sixth century, as modern interpreters until quite recently assumed, these myths place Eleusis at the very centre of the emergence of the Athenian polis in its 'present' form. Thus, if a historical correlative had indeed existed, which is itself an *a priori* assumption, it would have to be situated at the 'point' of the emergence of the Athenian polis, not later; in the eighth century, not the early sixth. But for the ancient audiences the myth of the Athenian–Eleusinian war was, among other things, about origins, of cults as well as of political configurations: origins that were located in the heroic past. The heroic nature of that past is central to the myth, one of the meanings of which is that it anchors the cults in question more securely in a world in which gods spoke to men and helped them institute cults. The fact that these myths place the incorporation of Eleusis in the Athenian polis specifically in the period in which the Athenian polis as it 'now' is was being constituted and its most important cults instituted, indicates that, far from reflecting historical events of a few generations ago, these myths were perceived to be about the formation of the Athenian polis.

The notion that the mythological wars between Athens and Eleusis reflect first-millennium history relies on a particular approach to myth that not only begins with the presumption that it reflects history, but also implicitly underprivileges elements that do not fit the particular historical interpretation chosen as the historical correlative of the myth. I have argued against this approach to myths elsewhere (Sourvinou-Inwood 1991: 191, 217–43); here I will only point out how distortion operates in this case. The implicit presumption that the myth reflects historical reality led to a search for a time when Eleusis was independent. It was part of Athens in the sixth century, but Athens' absence from the *Homeric Hymn to Demeter* was taken to entail that Eleusis was independent at the time of the hymn's composition, in the late seventh or early sixth century; consequently, Eleusis was taken over by Athens some time since then.[26] Thus, the presumption of the historicity of myth and another invalid argument, the use of the hymn as historical evidence pertaining to the time of its production, mutually support each other, in a context of an unspoken rationalizing privileging the political dimension over the religious, and construct a coherent and superficially convincing picture.[27] For this use of the *Homeric Hymn* is also fallacious.[28] It relies on a reading that takes no account of the terms of the hymn's discourse,[29] of the fact that it is a religious poem about a divine withdrawal and return, catastrophe averted, a divine epiphany, and the foundation of a cult by a deity at a time when in the archaic mythological landscape Eleusis was not part of Athens (cf. a similar view in Foley 1994: 174). The notion that the depiction of the heroic past would have been shaped by the present privileges the political and underplays the religious. But even the political dimension is crudely perceived in such a theory, which relies implicitly on a construct of a centralized Athenian state, underplaying the tensions among the élites competing for power and influence within the polis and the local priesthood's concern to stress its special credentials for controlling this important cult. If there was a political dimension to the choice to present Eleusis of the Heroic Age in the hymn as it was perceived to have been in the mythological world of archaic Greece and to exclude Athens, its motivating force would have been élite competition between *genê*, each with their own power base within the polis.

There are basically two versions of the foundation of the Mysteries. In the first, in the *Homeric Hymn to Demeter*, the Mysteries had been revealed by Demeter to Eleusinian heroes of the heroic past, including an Eleusinian Eumolpus (*Hom. Hymn. Dem.* 475–82). This version stresses the divine authority of the rite, its revealed nature. In the second, they were founded by someone connected with Thrace or Orphic poetry or both, a Eumolpus of Thracian origin or his homonymous descendant;[30] a somewhat later tradition makes Orpheus the founder.[31] This version connects the Mysteries with

Thrace, Orpheus, and Musaeus (on one tradition Eumolpus' father), to whom was attributed Eleusinian eschatological poetry.[32]

The myth that Heracles and the Dioscouroi were adopted by Athenians so that they could be initiated in the Eleusinian Mysteries (Apollodorus 2.5.12, Plutarch, *Theseus* 33) articulates, and is articulated by, the perception that to begin with only Athenians could be initiated. A comparable perception is articulated in Xenophon, *Hellenica* 6.3.6, which says the first *xenoi* initiated in the Mysteries were Heracles and the Dioscouroi, and reflected in Euripides, *Ion* 1074ff., referring to a heroic past in which only Athenians were initiated. This perception need not, of course, reflect historical reality. Let us investigate. Given that one of the modalities of operation of Greek myths was as legitimating paradigms, one of the meanings of this Heracles myth in ancient eyes was inevitably that of mythological paradigm for the initiation of non-Athenians. Thus one possible context for its generation is the time when the Mysteries became open to non-Athenians. Unfortunately, we do not know the date of the first appearance of the myth. It has been suggested that it appears around or just after the mid-sixth century.[33] Whether or not this is right, we do not in any case know whether the earliest version had included the mytheme that Heracles had to be adopted before he could be initiated. If the Mysteries had been restricted to Athenians alone at an early stage they were certainly accessible to all Greeks by the earlier part of the fifth century, as is shown by Herodotus 8.65 and the existence at *c.* 460 (Sokolowski 1962: no.3) of the Sacred Truce, correlative with a Panhellenic dimension of the Mysteries. I shall return to this.

ELEUSIS AND ATHENIAN RELIGION

I will now investigate the Eleusinian cult and its relationship to Athenian religion. The Eleusinian sanctuary was connected to the centre of the Athenian polis through ritual movements, processions. The most important nexus of such movements is that of the festival of the Mysteries. I will summarize the parts that pertain to the relationship between Eleusis and Athens.[34] First the *hiera* were brought from Eleusis to the Eleusinion in Athens, accompanied by the priests and priestesses of the Eleusinian cult and escorted by ephebes. When they arrived the *phaidyntês*, a minor Eleusinian official, went to the Acropolis and notified the priestess of Athena Polias of their arrival. On the first day of the festival proper there was a proclamation by Eleusinian officials in the Agora, inviting those who wanted to be initiated and setting out the criteria of eligibility (they should speak Greek and have pure hands). On the second day the *mystai* were purified in the sea at Phaleron.[35] On the third took place the main sacrifices for Demeter and Kore located in Athens. On the fourth the *mystai* stayed indoors.[36] On the fifth day the procession from Athens to Eleusis took place. It has been argued convincingly[37] that there were in fact two processions, on 19 Boedromion the *pompê* proper, escorting the *hiera* with religious personnel, ephebes and magistrates, and on 20 Boedromion a procession in which Iacchus led the initiates and other participants, met by the ephebes who marched out of Eleusis and escorted them part of the way to Eleusis. It seems that in the procession to Eleusis, priests and priestesses of important Athenian central polis cults took part and walked together with the Eleusinian priesthood, most notably, the priestess of Athena seems to have walked side by side with the priestess of Demeter and Kore (Clinton 1974: 35–36), a ritual enactment of the intimate relationship between the most important central polis cult and the most important periphery cult of the polis. All Greeks, including slaves, could participate in the Mysteries – from which barbarians and those who had impure hands were excluded (cf. Isocrates 4.157, Herodotus 8.65; Mylonas 1961: 247–48).

That the Mysteries are part of Athenian polis religion is shown by (a) the fact that it was the polis which regulated them and had authority over them, (b) the place of the Mysteries in the calendar, (c) the role of the ephebes,[38] and (d) above all, the fact that the *archôn basileus* was responsible for their conduct (cf. Aristotle, *Ath. Pol.* 57.1; Rhodes 1981: 636 *ad loc.*) and was involved in the imposition of sanctions for any *asebeia* or cultic irregularity. On the return from Eleusis he reported to the prytaneis and then the *boulê* sat at the Eleusinion on the day after the Mysteries and debated the issues in accordance with a law that Andocides ascribes to Solon (Andocides 1.110–12). The *basileus* also said prayers and performed sacrifices both at the Eleusinion in Athens and at the sanctuary at Eleusis on behalf of, and for the well-being of, the polis ([Lysias] 6.4). But the Eleusinian Mysteries were also a restricted cult, accessible through individual initiation by individual choice, which led to membership of a category *mystai* to which both Athenians and non-Athenians had access. The category 'Athenian *mystai*' was recognized in the political articulation of the polis; it interacted with 'political' polis groupings to create the category: 'those among the X who are initiates'.[39] However, in the person of the *pais aph' hestias*,[40] the whole polis was symbolically initiated.[41] It is now certain that the *hestia* meant in the Eleusinian Mysteries was that in the prytaneion, standing for the centre of the polis and the polis as a unit: a fourth-century law (Clinton 1974: 264 ll.41–42, 285) tells us that the *basileus* – who also stood symbolically for both the centre and the whole polis, especially in the older rituals that were under his control – was involved in the selection of this *pais*. Thus, since the latter derived 'authority' from, and expressed, the *koinê hestia* of the polis, his initiation – which, among other things, may have pertained to the Eleusinian cult's kourotrophic aspects – also represents the symbolic initiation of the whole polis. This stresses the central polis aspect of the cult and 'reconciles' the Eleusinian Mysteries' character as a central polis cult with their nature as a restricted cult accessible through individual initiation by individual choice.

The Eleusinion in Athens, where the *hiera* were brought from Eleusis, is the permanent physical manifestation of the presence of the Eleusinian cult at the centre of Athens, articulating the close link between the Eleusinian sanctuary and the centre and also the Eleusinian cult's identity as a central polis cult. This Eleusinion is not the same as the local Eleusinia in the demes. First, because its very location at the centre of the polis differentiates it radically by placing it in the central polis cult, as opposed to the deme cult system; second, because it could take on the role of housing the *hiera*, of a short-term alternative to the Eleusis Telesterion, and in general had a crucial role in the articulation of the close relationship between Eleusis and the centre of Athens, as, for example, when the *bouleutai* met there to discuss the conduct of the Mysteries. There are no traces of the earliest temple of the Eleusinion, which vanished without a trace when quarrying operations levelled off that part of the slope.[42] The date of the peribolos seems to be the mid-sixth century. If there is no earlier material, if that was indeed the date of the foundation of the Eleusinion, we must assume that the law attributed to Solon by Andocides was post-Solonian. If the shrine can go back to Solon's time (for this possibility see Clinton 1974: 121, n. 6) its foundation would be contemporary, and thus inevitably in some way correlative, with the changes at the Eleusinian sanctuary.

The involvement of Eleusinian religious personnel in other central polis cults constitutes another important modality of intertwining between the Mysteries and central polis cults. Thus, for example, the hierophants and *dadouchoi* took part in the procession at the Thargelia[43] and Eleusinian religious personnel participated in the Pyanopsia.[44] The central position of the Eleusinian cult at the centre of the polis is symbolically articulated in the fact that the hierophant is among those who had the privilege of *sitêsis* at the prytaneion.[45] Because the Mysteries were an important part of central polis religion, they could become the ritual locus for the introduction of a new cult. The cult of Asclepius[46] was established in Athens at 420 in some ways under the auspices of the Eleusinian cult, and more specifically of the Mysteries, since the god is said (in *IG* 2² 4960, the Telemachos monument) to have arrived at the centre of Athens from Zea during the Mysteries and was taken to the Eleusinion. In addition, one of the god's two Athenian festivals, the Epidauria, was celebrated during the Myster-ies, on the day when the *mystai* stayed at home.

A very important modality of relationship between the centre of the polis, and the central polis cults, with Eleusis, is that of the Proerosia. The fact that for the Proerosia, the 'Before ploughing' offering which was a festival celebrated in the demes and not in the Athenian centre,[47] the hierophant and the *kêryx* issued a proclamation (Sokolowski 1969: no. 7 A 4–7) at the City Eleusinion (Dow and Healey 1965: 14–15) inviting the Athenians to attend the Eleusinian Proerosia suggests that, for this festival, Eleusis and the Eleusinian cult of Demeter functioned as a second, alternative, central nexus, correlatively with the fact that the Eleusinian cult of Demeter was a most important central polis cult concerned with agriculture. As in the case of the Mysteries, the proclamation was one modality of articulating the central polis aspect of a ritual located in the periphery. A festival with an agricultural facet which was held at Eleusis and nowhere else was the Haloa.[48] In this case, then, Eleusis totally replaced the centre as the locus for the celebration of a central polis cult.

At the Skira or Skirophoria[49] a procession to Skiron took place, during which the priest of Poseidon Erechtheus and the priestess of Athena Polias[50] walked out under a canopy. Their destination was a temple, almost certainly that of Demeter and Kore, though Athena and Poseidon were probably worshipped there as well. It seems that in the deme of Paiania at least the Skira were celebrated at the local Eleusinion. Skiron has associations with the mythological war between Athens and Eleusis (cf. Pausanias 1.36.4) and modern scholars generally take it to have been the old frontier between Athens and Eleusis. As we saw, the cults of Poseidon Erechtheus and of Athena Polias were perceived to be connected with that mythological war and with the constitution of the Athenian polis as it 'now' is. But we should not assume that this was all that Skiron signified in Athenian perceptions, that its role in the mythological past neutralized any role it may have had in 'present-day perceptions' of territory; rather, we should consider whether any perceived role of the locality in the mythological past was not shaped out of the meanings it had 'in the present' and at the time when the religious system was set in place. Calame (1990: 359) was right to consider that the significance of Skiron cannot be divorced from that of Phaleron, where the sanctuary of Athena Skiras was located. He was also right to locate (implicitly) the significance of Skiron in a conceptual rather than a faithfully geographical map. He takes Phaleron to be on the border of *chôra* and sea (Calame 1990: 359, 361), and he understands Skiron to have been on the border of the *chôra*, cultivated territory on the one hand, and undifferentiated outside territory, fallow land on the other. I would like to suggest a modification to his interpretation, for, in my view, this is too distanced from the inevitably lived and perceived reality of the Athenians to be a possible refraction of it. Given its location, Skiron could not have been perceived as the border of un-differentiated outside territory, fallow land. What it could have been per-ceived as is the border between the 'urban' part of the polis and the in-between, the not-*asty* and not-border/periphery segment of the polis. Of course, in certain contexts the in-between space and the periphery could be subsumed into a category not-*asty*, and Skiron could symbolically drift into the role of border between centre and periphery – hence the notion that it had been at the border between Athens and Eleusis. I shall return to this.

Another rite that took place at Skiron was the sacred ploughing, the *hieros arotos*. According to Plutarch (*Moralia* 144A) the Athenians had three *hieroi arotoi*: one at Skiron, one in the Rharian plain at Eleusis and one below the Acropolis, this last called Bouzygios.[51] I hope to have shown elsewhere (Sourvinou-Inwood 1988b: 143–45) that all the *hieroi arotoi*, including the Bouzygios, belonged to the cult of Demeter. The three places where *hieroi arotoi* took place were the centre of Athens, Eleusis, the most hallowed place of Demeter's cult, instituted by the goddess herself and located at the (most symbolically charged) periphery, and Skiron, the place symbolically at the interface of the two. Thus, the three sacred ploughings articulate the Athenian territory, punctuate its tripartite articulation with a ritual pertaining to agriculture, the activity central to its function, and so symbolically 'cover' the whole territory with the protection of the goddess in whose honour the rite is performed.

This interpretation – with its notion of symbolic covering of the territory articulated as periphery, represented by Eleusis, centre, and in-between represented by Skiron – may perhaps be supported by the existence of a phenomenon that indicates a desire for symbolic coverage in another way, the distribution of the known local Eleusinia. Four out of the five are in east Attica, that is on the other side of the centre from Eleusis and the Eleusis–Athens space, and so may have been felt to be less strongly covered by this ritual articulation and more in need of strengthening: Paiania, Tetrapolis, Phrearioi, Thorikos (cf. Osborne 1985: 177 for references). Is it thus possible that these local Eleusinia were local foundations generated by the desire to reinforce symbolically the Eleusinian dimension, and thus Demeter's blessings, on their territory, through local versions of the periphery Demeter sanctuary *par excellence*, thus strengthening symbolically or at least giving material expression and a ritual focus to, Demeter's protection in a part of the periphery not as directly covered by the ritual movements focused on the Athens–Skiron–Eleusis axis? The fifth local Eleusinion is in Phaleron, but it differs from the other four in that it appears with the shrine at Eleusis and at Athens in *IG* 1³ 32.22–28, which puts all their finances under the same board of *logistai*. Phaleron, we saw, also plays a role in the Mysteries: it was one of the poles of the ritual movement that took place between the opening movement from Eleusis to Athens and the procession from Athens to Eleusis – the centre of Athens being the other. At Phaleron the sea is nearest to the centre of Athens. The ritual formula '*halade mystai*' makes clear that this is the facet of its persona that determined its role as the locality of this purification rite, that it was perceived as the place at the interface of an extended centre and the sea. Thus Phaleron, on the west coast, on the other side of the Peiraeus from Eleusis, could be seen as on a symbolic frontier of an extended centre; indeed the segment Phaleron to Halimous (where the central polis Thesmophoria began) could be seen as at the edges of the *asty*, at the frontier between an extended centre and a non-centre that included periphery and in-between and covered the coast to Sounion, shading into its hinterland. That this segment of the coast was, indeed, in ancient perceptions part of an extended centre is shown by the fact that Phaleron and Halimous after the Cleisthenic reforms belonged to city *trittyes*, Phaleron that of Aiantis, Halimous of Leontis. Phaleron, then, at the border of an extended centre and an extended periphery comprising both the in-between and the periphery proper, is comparable to Skiron, to which it is, in some ways, ritually correlative.[52] Inevitably, given the special place of Phaleron in the celebration of the Mysteries, the significance of the Eleusinion at Phaleron was different from that of the other local Eleusinia, and in some ways comparable to that of Eleusis and Athens, as is also indicated by the financial arrangements reflected in *IG* 1³ 32. In these circumstances, I submit that the location of those other Eleusinia may confirm the hypothesis that the ritual movements involving the Eleusinian nexus pertained, among other things, to the notion of symbolically covering territory.

The procession to Skiron shows again that there was a close connection in cult – as well as in myth – between the Eleusinian cult and the cults of Athena Polias and Poseidon Erechtheus. There is also a close connection between the Eleusinian cult and the other Athenian poliad deity, Zeus Polieus, who, to begin with, formed the important poliadic pair with Athena Polias and was subsequently overshadowed by the pair Athena Polias and Poseidon Erechtheus. The inclusion of Zeus Polieus in a list of Eleusinian sacrifices inscribed on two monuments, possibly altars, erected *c.* 510–480 in the Eleusinion in Athens (Jeffery 1948: 86–111, cf. especially 96) involves the Eleusinian cult with Zeus Polieus. Another connection between the two cults consists in the fact that the Ceryces, one of the two most important priestly *genê* of the Eleusinian cult, took part in the Dipoleia.[53] Burkert (1983: 146–47) sees the Bouphonia, the most important part of the Dipoleia, as a continuation, supplement, and inversion of the Skira, which took place just before the Dipoleia, and as one more incidence of the close connection between Athens and Eleusis. Certainly the Bouphonia are related to ploughing and agriculture by the fact that the 'resurrected' ox is yoked to a plough (cf. Parke 1977: 166). Thus, the Bouphonia were intimately connected with ploughing, and so also with the *hieros arotos* and the cult of Demeter, which entails also an intimate connection between Zeus Polieus and agriculture, especially the part of its ritual cycle which became the focus for the ritual representation of the relationship between Demeter and a polis articulated into centre, periphery, and in-between. Thus, the involvement of the Ceryces at the Bouphonia is part of a nexus at the centre which involved the poliadic deities, agriculture, and the relationship between centre and periphery. All these concerns were of primary importance at the formation of a polis, especially one with an extensive fertile territory. I suggest that this nexus of intertwined poliadic and agricultural central polis cults located at the centre, the periphery, and in-between, was set in place during the process of polis formation and is not the result of later ('politically motivated' or not) insertions.

The combination of the agricultural and the poliadic in the ritual movements and other cultic relationships connecting Athens and Eleusis is one element in a nexus that is also observed in other Greek poleis. Another element is the position of Eleusis in the Athenian territory, the fact that this sanctuary was located near the frontier with Megara: a live frontier, in the sense that it was disputed after the emergence of the Athenian polis and before the crystallization of this frontier during the sixth century. A third element is the myths that relate the incorporation of Eleusis into the Athenian polis to the constitution of that polis in the early heroic past. A fourth element is the date of the sanctuary's foundation, the late eighth century, the time of the formation of the Athenian polis. I have discussed elsewhere[54] what was and what was not new concerning sanctuaries in the eighth century. One of the changes was the great increase in their number in the context of circumstances, of which the most important was the emergence of the polis, which put religion at its centre and forged its identity through it. One result was the foundation of more sanctuaries to serve specific functions, for example to 'sanctify' a frontier, a particular version of a polis-defining sanctuary. The nexus described corresponds to de Polignac's model of a peripheral sanctuary ritually and mythologically connected with the centre of the polis, and with the constitution of the polis, a bipolar model which de Polignac himself thought did not apply to Athens.[55] Whether or not Demeter had a cult at Eleusis before the foundation of the sanctuary in the late eighth century – and it is very likely that she had – the fact that Eleusis was in an especially fertile area and at the live frontier of the Athenian polis constituted a strong parameter of selection for the role of frontier-sanctifying, agriculture-protecting sanctuary and thus the second, peripheral, pole of the Athenian polis during the process of its formation.[56] In these circumstances there are very good reasons for concluding that the Eleusinian sanctuary also started in the context of the formation of the Athenian polis. The notion that Eleusis and its cult were part of the Athenian polis from the beginning fits the fact that the intertwining between the Eleusinian cult and central polis religion discussed above is too intimate to have been an epiphenomenon and suggests that it was generated when the central polis cult nucleus was first being set in place at the formation of the polis.

THE INTRODUCTION OF THE 'MYSTERIC' INTO THE MYSTERIES

The festival of the Mysteries, we saw, had two important loci – the most important at Eleusis, the other at the centre – and also minor loci, such as Phaleron; the two poles were connected with ritual movements comparable to those relating Eleusis and the centre in other festivals. The bipolarity acted out in the spatial articulation of the Great Mysteries is in a way duplicated across ritual time: initiation at the Lesser Mysteries at Agrai in Athens was a necessary preliminary to initiation at Eleusis, and this can be said not only to reinforce the strength of the Mysteric cult component in the *asty*, but also to place the *asty* as the starting point of a bigger, spatio-temporal articulation of the mysteric initiation. The temporal articulation increases the symbolic strength of the initiation and thus goes with the grain of the ritual logic of rites of this kind. But there is an aspect of its spatial articulation which appears to be less in harmony with that logic. Much of the Mysteries, all but the last (major) stage inside the Eleusinian sanctuary, took place in spaces that were not secret, but open to all. In its basic lines, the spatial articulation of the Mysteries corresponds to the schema 'procession to outlying sanctuary', with the territorial/poliadic and agricultural dimensions of signification we discussed. The 'Mysteric' facet seems not to have significantly helped shape the articulation of the Mysteries, which only in its last stage reflects the cult's secrecy and its accessibility by individual initiation.

There is, then, a certain dissonance between the schema 'procession to outlying sanctuary' and the Mysteric facet of the cult. There is another facet to this dissonance. As we saw, the intimate connection between Eleusis and the centre was of fundamental importance in Athenian religion with regard to its crucial agricultural and poliadic spheres and relevant cults. The fact that the procession of the Mysteries was the most important ritual movement connecting Eleusis with the centre of Athens makes it extremely unlikely that this main procession was created at the formation of the polis as other than a polis procession; it is thus extremely unlikely that a procession carrying such meanings was limited to the *mystai* among the Athenian citizens and open to *xenoi*. One possible interpretation of this dissonance is to consider the Mysteric facet of the Mysteries to be a later transformation, a rereading in the light of new preoccupations of an originally agricultural periphery cult, which would also have entailed that a procession to an outlying sanctuary was transformed into something more complex. If it is right (cf. Clinton 1988: 70) that there were two processions – the *pompê* proper, escorting the *hiera* with religious personnel, ephebes, and magistrates, and on the next day a procession in which Iacchus led the initiates – this would add some support to the view that the procession began as an ordinary procession to an outlying sanctuary, and that when the cult's Mysteric facet developed, part of it was modelled on, and added to, that procession. This interpretation may be culturally determined. But other considerations also point in the same direction.

The *pais aph' hestias*, in whose person the whole of the Athenian polis was symbolically initiated to the Mysteries, reconciled, then, the character of the Mysteries as a central polis cult with their nature as a restricted cult accessible through individual initiation by individual choice. The *pais* was the symbolic locus of resolution of what may be considered a dissonance, the double nature of the cult, corresponding to the two main areas the cult is focused upon, namely agriculture and eschatology. Agriculture is everywhere in the Greek world a main concern of central polis and other subdivision cults, while eschatological concerns involving the hope of a happy afterlife were – at least in the archaic period – catered for in cultic manifestations articulated by the model of individual initiation through individual choice. Since, contrary to earlier orthodoxies, the basic cult unit in polis religion was the individual (cf. Sourvinou-Inwood 1988a: 264–67), and since the polis encompassed and legitimated all religious activities of its members (cf. Sourvinou-Inwood

151

1988a: 270–73, 1990: 297–300), the individual choice component in the Mysteries is not in conflict with the basic modalities of Greek religion. But the combination of the importance of the Mysteries as a central polis cult and its individual choice component makes it unique. Its nature as a cult that includes a strong soteriological element and is accessible through individual initiation by individual choice leads to membership of a category *mystai*, to which both Athenians and non-Athenians had access, and which interacted with 'political' polis groupings to create a strange category: within an Athenian polis grouping, those who are and those who are not *mystai*.

But the optionality of participation for Athenians was very ambiguous, since, if the *pais aph' hestias* did represent symbolically the whole polis, all Athenians were symbolically initiated under that heading. Certainly all Athenians were obliged to participate in the Eleusinian cult in so far as they were obliged to offer *aparchai* by the First Fruits decree (to be collected by the demarchs), whatever may have been the case before that.[57] The fact that the allies were also obliged to offer *aparchai* is correlative with their comparable participation in other Athenian central polis cults, the Panathenaea and the City Dionysia. The attempt to have other Greeks do the same involves an attempt to stress, increase, and express symbolically the cult's Panhellenic dimension. Isocrates (4.28–33) presents the Athenians as benefactors of humanity for making available to all the two gifts that Demeter bestowed on them, namely the fruits of the earth and the Mysteries which give hope for the afterlife, and brings as proof the fact that Athens receives *aparchai* from other cities every year in memory of the ancient benefaction; the Pythia admonishes any defaulters, and thus lends the authority of the Delphic oracle to the Panhellenic dimension of the Mysteries. That all Greeks, including slaves, could participate in the Eleusinian Mysteries makes this a polarized example of modalities encountered elsewhere. Slaves and *xenoi* also took part in other polis cults but on different terms from citizens.[58] The Panhellenic sanctuary model, as at Delphi and Olympia, involved Panhellenic participation in a cult centred on the model of a polis cult at which others are admitted to worship as *xenoi* (Sourvinou-Inwood 1990: 297–99). The fact that the Eleusinian cult is structured by such a combination, and modifications, of different Greek cultic modalities and schemata suggests that it developed through bricolage to serve different needs out of, and through, established Greek religious schemata. It can be seen as one particular version of a 'polis-become-Panhellenic cult', as the point of greatest opening, a case limit in the polis religious system. It is the cult's double nature, and the dissonances set out above, that we need to make sense of. I submit that my interpretation of the Eleusinian Mysteries – that they were the result of a transformation of a central polis cult of an agricultural type, in which the integration of the periphery aspect was important, into an initiatory soteriological one based on individual choice and promising a happy afterlife – can explain them and show that this cult is in harmony with Greek religious modalities.

The conclusion of the cultic investigation – that the Eleusinian cult was part of the Athenian polis religion from the latter's formation – converges with the tentative conclusions to that effect based on the one hand on the investigation of the archaeological evidence of the sanctuary and on the other on the analysis of the myths. The three investigations were independent. For while I brought in some aspects of the mythological and archaeological evidence in the attempt to assess the results of the analysis of some aspects of the cult, these aspects did not pertain to what the analyses of the archaeological evidence indicated with regard to the sanctuary's relationship to Athens, only to the date of its foundation. From the myths I brought in simply the fact that they connect the wars with Eleusis to the constitution of the early form of the Athenian polis; and I did not use any cultic evidence in the other analyses. Consequently, this convergence suggests that the conclusion is valid.

The tentative conclusion that there was a change in the nature of the Eleusinian cult which became Mysteric at a subsequent stage also converges with the conclusion of the archaeological investigation that at the end of the seventh, or more likely the beginning of the sixth, century the nature of the cult practised there changed, from a cult of what we may loosely call a 'normal' type to one that was different and which can be identified as the same cult as was practised in the classical period, and thus as the Mysteries. This convergence suggests that the conclusion is valid. This would involve a post-'Solonian' date for the *Homeric Hymn to Demeter*. I see no problem with that. As I understand it, there are no internal grounds for placing the poem at any particular time in the century between *c*. 650 and *c*. 550.

The conclusion that the Mysteries began as a cult restricted to Athenians and were subsequently opened up to all Greeks coincides with the tentative conclusion of the study of the archaeological evidence – that the Peisistratean phase of the sanctuary suggests that perhaps an enlargement of the worshipping group had taken place – and also with the Athenian perception, articulated in myths and elsewhere, that to begin with the Mysteries were not open to non-Athenians. The Peisistratean date tentatively suggested by the archaeological investigation coincides with the hypothesis cited above: that the pattern of appearance of the myth of Heracles' initiation suggests that it was under Peisistratus that the opening may have taken place.

CHANGING ATTITUDES TO DEATH AND THE ELEUSINIAN MYSTERIES

There is yet another convergence, between these conclusions and those of another set of analyses which I conducted elsewhere, where I argued (1981, 1983, 1995) that in the course of the archaic period a partial shift took place in collective attitudes towards death: from an attitude of acceptance towards a familiar death which was hateful but not frightening, to one of greater anxiety and greater concern for the survival of one's memory, a more individual perception of one's death. This was correlative with a changed eschatology, one of the new elements of which was the possibility of a happy afterlife for ordinary mortals. The conclusion that the Mysteries, which were accessible through individual initiation and which had an eschatological dimension promising a happy afterlife, were the result of a transformation of the Eleusinian cult that took place at the end of the seventh or the beginning of the sixth century, converges with the results of those analyses that the notion of a happy afterlife was generated in the archaic period in the context of a shift in the collective attitudes towards death.

I submit that the fact that the results of all the independently conducted analyses converge offers validation to the conclusions presented here. The likely locus of resistance is a perceptual cast shaped by the unconscious presumption that the established orthodoxy (often corresponding to modern conceptions of the 'plausible') is correct unless its invalidity is demonstrated beyond reasonable doubt, though hardly anything can be for early Greece. In the circumstances, which include our severe limitations of access to early Athenian history, it is not necessary for the validity of these conclusions that I show that there were circumstances conducive to the change in the nature of the cult that I have reconstructed. But in fact I will do so, and in the process produce some further, independent evidence to show that such a change took place.

The archaeological evidence placed the change in the nature of the Eleusinian cult at the end of the seventh century/beginning of the sixth. A tradition in our sources claims that at that time Solon passed laws pertaining to the Eleusinian Mysteries (cf. Andocides 1.111). The fact that classical tradition ascribed laws pertaining to the Eleusinian cult to Solon does not necessarily mean that they were Solonian, all it means is that they were perceived to be ancient;[59] nor does legislative activity entail that there had been change, let alone change in the nature of the cult. But it may not be totally without interest that later Athenian perception located an important phase in the history of the Eleusinian cult at about the same time as it is shown by the archaeological evidence that something important happened at this sanctuary pertaining to this cult. More significantly, there is a historical tradition which tells us that at the time that I argued the change took place, in the period from the late seventh to early sixth century, circumstances obtained in Athens that were conducive to changes of precisely this kind and which also speaks of religious reforms that took place in response to those circumstances. The circumstances in question are those described in Plutarch's *Solon* and alluded to elsewhere, a crisis of anomic terror and superstition, of a city filled with fear, and of external defeat by the Megarians, who captured Nisaea and Salamis. This defeat, incidentally, and other evidence of hostility with the Megarians ascribed to Solon's lifetime, inevitably activated the symbolic significance of Eleusis, the important sanctuary sanctifying this now clearly danger-charged frontier.

This crisis began with a political event, but was itself above all ideological/ religious, what in anachronistic terms might be called a kind of moral panic, anomic terror, crystallized into the concept of *Kyloneion agos*,[60] a pollution perceived to have been generated as a result of the sacrilegious killing of the supporters of the aspiring tyrant Cylon after the failure of his coup. The Megarian dimension is present here also: Cylon had been married to the daughter of Theagenes, tyrant of Megara. One of the results of the *agos* was the expulsion of the Alcmaeonids, who were considered responsible for it. After that expulsion the city was purified by Epimenides.[61] Epimenides was a poet, purifier, and miracle worker who had supernatural characteristics. He was said to be the son of a Nymph and was called *Kourês neos* by his contemporaries (Plutarch, *Solon* 12.4e), *FGrH* 457 T 1). He slept in a cave for fifty-seven years and lived an abnormally long time. He believed in metempsychosis; according to some, the Cretans sacrificed to him as to a god; he made prophecies that came true (*FGrH* 457 T 1, Theopompus *FGrH* 115 F 67–69, cf. Plato, *Laws* 642D). He conducted purifications.[62] In one tradition he purified Attica with human blood (Neanthes *FGrH* 84 F 16, Athenaeus 12.602CD). A recurrent motif is that he founded cults, including cults he founded in Athens as part of the purification (*FGrH* 457 T 1, cf. Plutarch, *Solon* 12.5). That the *agos* had created religious anxiety is clear; it is only later that it became an inherited disgrace (Parker 1983: 16–17). The fact that it could be subsequently reactivated and deployed for political purposes against the Alcmaeonids is precisely because of the potency of the memory of the ancient crisis. Also, very significantly, the persona of the individual associated with the response to the crisis, Epimenides, confirms that, at least in the perceptions of subsequent generations – which is all we have to go by – the crisis was, above all, religious and generally ideological.[63]

Some of the problems about the dating of these events as between the late seventh and the early sixth century (on which cf. Hornblower 1991: 204–05) would disappear if we see them as making up a protracted crisis which eventually led to the purification and religious reforms which in tradition crystallized into the activities of Epimenides and Solon. Plutarch (*Solon* 12) compresses the events into one nexus he attaches to Solon, but his account is suggestive of a long-drawn-out crisis involving the events following the killing of the Cylonians, the eventual expulsion of the Alcmaeonids, the Megarians' capture of Nisaea and Salamis, the anomic terror,[64] Epimenides' summons and arrival and his religious reforms, which, Plutarch says, paved the way (*Solon* 12.4) for Solon's legislation. Plutarch speaks of reforms in two stages. The first, Epimenides' (*Solon* 12.4–6), was part of the process of purification and restoration of order. Epimenides lowered the high emotional tone of the death ritual and removed its harsher aspects which until then had been practised by women. Also, most importantly, through rites of expiation, purifications, and sacred foundations, he initiated the city in secret rites (*katorgiasas*) and purified it and brought it to be observant of justice and more easily inclined to concord. The second stage is Solon's legislation, which includes his funerary legislation (*Solon* 21.4–5), presented in terms similar to those used for Epimenides' reforms, but this time with concrete details given. The duplication of the funerary legislation supports Plutarch's claim that Epimenides paved the way for Solon's legislation, which, in its turn, is one of the things that binds the two figures and their associated reforms into one nexus. This binding and conflation may, but need not, correspond to the ancient realities.

But were there any ancient realities, or was the whole thing an invention? Clearly, the *agos* and the purification were not invented, for the *agos* could be reactivated as a live reality in sixth- and fifth-century Athens and deployed against the Alcmaeonids. That the response to the crisis included reforms and foundations of cult is well rooted in the tradition and shaped the form of purification said to have been practised by Epimenides. This is not surprising in a context in which the notion of purification involved the elimination of various evils by various means,[65] brought about by an offence involving violation of divine rights (cf. Parker 1983: 271–77). But the story that Epimenides the miracle worker with a supernatural facet and ambivalently divine connotations founded cults in Athens is significantly comparable to the mythological schema 'cult founded by heroes in the heroic past': in both, the founder figures are distanced from normality and closer to the divine world, which helps to anchor symbolically, and guarantee the validity of, the cult. It is especially comparable to the later myth that Orpheus founded the Eleusinian Mysteries, in the nature of the founder figures and the eschatological/sectarian nature of the poetry ascribed to them, as to Musaeus, who was also connected with the foundation of the Mysteries through his son Eumolpos, and to whom was attributed Eleusinian eschatological poetry.[66]

Since the events of the *agos* and purification were not a myth, were they historical events that were mythologized? There should not be an *a priori* presumption in favour of such a reading of a myth that presents itself as history. But in this case, this interpretation is compelling because of the combination of the facts: we know the central events had taken place; we can identify the mythological schema that guarantees symbolically the validity of the religious response to the crisis through the supernaturalization of the founder/purifier; and finally, we know of mythologizing activity shaping the story in Athens in the 420s, when the mytheme was generated that it had been a Nicias, son of Niceratus, who had fetched Epimenides from Crete in Solon's time – thus connecting Epimenides' activities with the contemporary general and politician Nicias, son of Niceratus, and the contemporary purification of Delos (Diogenes Laertius 1.110 = *FGrH* 457 T 1, West 1983: 50–51). If it is correct that Plutarch's account is based on Androtion (cf. Jacoby, *FGrH* IIIB, p. 318), this would be the earliest account known to us of the crisis of anomic terror resolved by Epimenides. It is at any rate clear that Epimenides' role as a purifier was current in Athens in the 420s, when this mythologizing activity involving Nicias took place. This is as far as we can go in determining dates.

The fact that the Herodotean and Thucydidean references to the *agos* do not mention Epimenides or dwell on the responses to the crisis cannot be taken to entail anything, since their discourse and agenda were not, in any case, conducive to the selection of these elements.

It is not important for my argument whether there had really been a Cretan religious expert who came to Athens and was responsible for the purification and the reforms,[67] and who had, or accreted, the reputation of a miracle worker, and who was the same as the poet and religious expert Epimenides, or who had become identified with a real or invented poet and religious expert Epimenides. Nor is it important for my argument whether Athenian mythopoeia had ascribed authority to the things that happened in response to the crisis by associating them with such a religious expert and miracle worker, a figure with certain ambivalent connotations of higher-than-human status, thus aligning them as much as possible with the schema that validates and gives authority to cults in Greek religion, 'the cult founded by a heroic figure from a time when gods walked with men with or without the direct help of a divinity'. What is clear is that there was a perceived match between the nexus 'Epimenides' and the purification of Athens and response to the crisis provoked by the *Kyloneion agos*. The connotations of the nexus 'Epimenides' in the ancient perceptions were the following: he came from Crete and was associated with the Cretan Zeus, with cult foundations, initiation, prophecy, purification, and with eschatology of a non-mainstream kind belonging to the same general type as that of Pythagoras, and with writing in prose and poetry comparable to the poems of Musaeus and Orpheus. This suggests that the crisis was perceived to have invoked a response that, among other things, may have had something to do with things perceived to be 'Orphic-like'. The one thing that was so perceived in Athenian polis cult was the Eleusinian Mysteries. This, therefore, may suggest that the 'Epimenidean' response had something to do with the Mysteries. But even without this conjecture, it is clear, I submit, that this nexus of events which crystallized in tradition into the figure of Epimenides, usually in association with Solon – the crisis provoked by the *Kyloneion agos*, and the response to it, which included cultic reforms and funerary legislation lowering the high emotional tone of the death ritual and thus testifying to a shift in the ritual and ideological nexus of death, indeed very probably a shift in the attitudes towards death – are circumstances most conducive to the change in the Eleusinian cult that I have reconstructed above. All the more since one part of the crisis had involved an external threat from Megara, which inevitably increased dramatically the symbolic importance of Eleusis and the Eleusinian sanctuary.

Furthermore, there is evidence connecting the Eleusinian cult with the response to the post-Cylonian crisis crystallized into the figure of Epimenides, evidence that links Epimenides with this cult. First, Plutarch used the word *katorgiasas* to refer to one of the important reforms of Epimenides (he *katôrgiase* and purified the city through rites of expiation, purifications, and sacred foundations). Unless he is using language loosely, which does not seem likely, he is saying that Epimenides initiated the city in secret rites. Thus, especially given that *orgia* is a word used for the Eleusinian Mysteries (cf. *Homeric Hymn to Demeter* 476–77), it is at the very least possible that Plutarch may be reporting a tradition that associated the foundation of the Eleusinian Mysteries with the response to the Cylonian crisis crystallized into the figure of Epimenides. It is interesting that Plutarch (*Solon* 12.4) says that Epimenides had *telestikên sophian*, skill and wisdom in matters pertaining to mystic rites. Elsewhere we are told (*FGrH* 457 T 2) that Epimenides wrote, among other things, purifications and mystic rites. Second, Epimenides was identified with Bouzyges,[68] the agricultural culture hero, who first yoked oxen to the plough. He and the Bouzygae were associated with the *hieros arotos* which belonged to the cult of Demeter and to the ritual activities that wove the centre of Athens to Eleusis most closely. Through the plough ox and the Bouzygian curses which cursed, among others, anyone who killed a ploughing ox,[69] Bouzyges was connected with the Bouphonia; this gives him another connection with the nexus connecting the Eleusinian cults with cults at the centre of Athens. Finally, the Bouzygae raised the sacred oxen that ploughed at Eleusis (Schol. Aelius Aristides 3.473). Thus, through this identification Epimenides became associated with the nexus weaving together the Eleusinian cults and those at the centre of Athens in an agricultural and poliadic context.

Finally, and most importantly, according to Pausanias (1.14.4) a seated statue of Epimenides stood in front of the Eleusinion in Athens, as did a statue of Triptolemus and of a *bous chalkous*, a bronze ox – as though being led to sacrifice, comments Pausanias. This shows that in Athenian mainstream cultic perceptions, Epimenides was associated with the Eleusinian cult of Demeter and Persephone, since the presence of Triptolemos' statue makes clear that 'a statue in front of the Eleusinion' involved important status in that cult. It is clear that the statue in front of the Eleusinion represented the Cretan religious expert and miracle worker, since Pausanias calls the Epimenides whose statue this was Knossian, and speaks of his miraculous long sleep, of his poetry and of his purification of Athens and of other cities. It is not legitimate to suppose that Pausanias was confused, especially since he was clearly an initiate.[70] Furthermore, and most importantly, the statue was seated, a schema much more appropriate for a poet and religious expert than for someone above all defined by his ploughing. This identification is strengthened by the proximity of the ox, which is described by Pausanias as sacrificial, not a ploughing ox; this fits Epimenides the sacrificer and religious expert and not Bouzyges. On the other hand, Epimenides would also have evoked Bouzyges, with whom he was identified, so that he might have been perceived as shown in his double persona, both as the hero Bouzyges (like Triptolemus represented next to him, a culture hero in the realm of agriculture), and, and dominantly, as the religious expert who could have been considered a culture hero in ritual matters, in so far as one account tells us that he was the first to have purified fields and houses (Diogenes Laertius 1.112 = *FGrH* 457 T 1). Be that as it may, it is clear that at some point in the history of the Eleusinian cult, Epimenides came to be inserted, as a figure whose nature was both quasi-heroic, in his own persona, and fully heroic in his identification with Bouzyges. The details of this insertion and identification, and of Epimenides' perceived role in the Eleusinian cult, are impossible even to try to reconstruct.[71] But the fact of the insertion of Epimenides into the cult indicates the perception that 'Epimenides' had been somehow involved in it. Given his perceived role in Athenian history, this entails a perception that the Eleusinian cult was one of the cults that had come into play in the course of the cultic foundations and reforms that constituted the response to the *Kyloneion agos* which crystall-ized into the figure of 'Epimenides'. This crystallization, we saw, may conceivably indicate a perception that that response had also brought into play things felt to be 'Orphic-like'. Since one thing that was so perceived in Athenian polis cult was the Eleusinian Mysteries, this, if right, may suggest that in the tradition, the 'Epimenidean' cult reforms had involved the Mysteries. Such a perception would seem correlative with the mythologizing process that eventually generated the myth that the Mysteries had been founded by Orpheus, and before that, that they had been founded by Eumolpus, the son of Musaeus, another Orpheus- and Epimenides-like figure, to whom was attributed Eleusinian eschatological poetry.

However, as I hope is clear, the validity of my central conclusions does not depend on the validity of this hypothesis. What I hope to have shown (which is not, in itself, necessary for the validity of the main thrust of my case, which depends on the sets of independently conducted analyses, the results of which converge) is that there were circumstances most conducive to the generation of the cult change I reconstructed at the appropriate time and that there is not insignificant evidence connecting the Eleusinian cult with those circumstances.

The conclusion that there was a change in the Eleusinian cult in the late seventh or early sixth century which transformed an agricultural cult with poliadic content to one that included a significant eschatological/soterio-logical component offers further confirmation to the thesis that a significant change in attitudes to death and funerary ideology took place in the course of the archaic period. On this hypothesis, in Athens the soteriological religious discourse which developed as a result of anxieties and tensions which had emerged in the course of the archaic period was integrated into the religion of the polis and the polis institutions, enmeshed with its most central institutions, and constituted an important central polis cult.

NOTES

1 Some of the ideas set out here were first expressed in concise form in a paper delivered in Oxford and Nottingham in 1987. I am very grateful to Dr Robert

Parker for many discussions on Eleusis. I am also very grateful to Dr P. Papangeli, Epimeltria of Antiquities at Eleusis, who most kindly discussed the site with me. I would also like to thank Dr K. Kokkou-Vyridi, who kindly allowed me to read her as yet unpublished dissertation, *Proïmes pyres thysion sto Telesterion tis Eleusinas*, Athens 1991.

2   I have discussed the methodological difficulties of interpreting ancient Greek culture in general and the archaeological evidence in particular with a critique of model building as the governing paradigm in Sourvinou-Inwood 1991, 1993: 1–17, and 1994.

3   Darcque 1981, cf. also Le Roy 1984: 167. Travlos (1983: 329–30, 1988: 92) continued to believe in the Mycenaean megaron surviving into the eighth century, but did not offer arguments against the serious problems presented by this view.

4   Cf. Mylonas 1961: 56–63, Coldstream 1977: 332 (*pace* Travlos 1983: 330). Drerup (1969: 30) thinks that the radius is too big for an apsidal building and thinks the building was oval; but this relies on bold assumptions about the parameters of variability of early Greek architecture.

5   Cf. Mylonas and Travlos 1952: 55–56. The road discovered (Kourouniotis 1931–32: 16–17) along the internal side of the pre-Solonian archaic peribolos wall (on which cf. below) is clearly part of the (pre-Solonian) archaic north–south road inside the wall, which was covered up by the Solonian extension of the temple terrace (cf. below).

6   The fact that the Peisistratean wall, built after this ritual nexus had fallen into disuse, did not have an east gate may add support to the view that an important function of this gate was to provide communication between well W and the court outside.

7   Cf. Mylonas 1961: 60, Travlos 1988: 92. We cannot be totally certain that this apsidal building was a temple, but the fact that the temple of Artemis Propylaea was built over it, in combination with the fact that it was well constructed, makes this interpretation almost certain.

8   Since all that we have is a segment of the back wall in each case, we cannot put it any more precisely than this.

9   Cf. Kourouniotis 1931–32: 22–24, Ziro 1991: 13, n. 39, Kokkou-Vyridi 1991: 22, n. 20.

10 It would necessitate special pleading to argue that the temple had begun as something else and then was dedicated to Artemis Propylaea at a subsequent stage, especially since it did stand outside a gate. The fact that the temple was also dedicated to Poseidon Pater is not evidence of a change, since this is not an artificial grouping. First, both deities are significant in this position: Artemis because she is Propylaea and Poseidon because he is crucially involved in the Athens–Eleusis relationship in myth and cult (cf. below); then, Poseidon and Artemis appear side by side in an Eleusinian sacred law (*IG* 1^3 5; Clinton 1979: 1–4).

11 Cf. Kokkou-Vyridi 1991: 84, 237–38 on the date of pyre A's cessation, which she places soon after 600, perhaps 590–580.

12 On Z 12 cf. Mylonas 1961: 65, figs 6, 23, supra n. 5.

13 Which may not necessarily have happened in one go, but in stages, in response to needs becoming clear.

14 Cf. Travlos 1988: 125, fig. 115, though not as regards the east part of the terrace, for which cf. Mylonas 1961: fig. 23.

15 Clinton (1992: 18–27) rejects the identification of this precinct with the Ploutonion and identifies it with the Agelastos petra. Whatever the validity of this hypothesis, the view that this cave shrine was believed to have contained an entrance to the Underworld (Clinton 1992: 23–26) is extremely likely, and had been expressed by Mylonas (1961: 99–100) in connection with the Ploutonion identification.

16 Cf. Mylonas 1961: 96, Travlos 1988: 93–94. In the Peisistratean period the new wall did not coincide with the terrace wall and there was a new external court under the east part of the terrace.

17 Clinton (1992: 126–32) has argued that Anaktoron was a synonym of 'Telesterion'. I hope to offer a series of arguments against this identification elsewhere.

18 On the date and history of the Periclean Telesterion, cf. Clinton 1986; on the history of the Telesterion in the fifth century, cf. Clinton 1986, Shear 1982: 128–40.

19 On the date of the First Fruits decree, cf. Clinton 1986: 258–59, Meiggs and Lewis 1988: 222–23.

20 The hypothesis that the Eleusinian Mysteries did not begin as Mysteries but as a different type of cult which was then transformed into Mysteries has been put forward by others before; cf. e.g. Clinton 1993.

21 Cf. also Hesychius s.v. *plêmochoê*, Pollux 10.74, Brommer 1980.

22 On these myths cf. the excellent discussion by Parker 1987b.

23 She says that Erechtheus will take the name of his killer and be invoked in cult as Poseidon, one interpretation of the cult title Poseidon Erechtheus.

24 Cf. also Jeffery (1948: 95) on the association between Erechtheus and the Eleusinian cult. On Eumolpus as founder of the Mysteries, cf. also Richardson 1974: 198, Parker 1987b: 203–04, Kearns 1989: 163.

25 On Pandion, cf. Kron 1976: 104–19, Kearns 1989: 81, 191–92. On Celeus: Richardson 1974: 177–78, Kearns 1989: 176, Clinton 1992: 100, Foley 1994: 41, 142.

26 The notion that Herodotus 1.30.5 can be used as evidence of a war between Athens and Eleusis in Solon's lifetime is fallacious. The passage speaks of a war against neighbours in the territory of Eleusis (cf. How and Wells 1912: 67), which fits a war with Megara, with which we know Athens was engaged in serious hostilities at precisely that time. For the fact that there are no independent arguments in favour of the hypothesis that Eleusis became part of the Athenian polis later than other places, cf. Osborne 1985: 175, Parker 1987b: 204, Clinton 1993: 110–12. For the fallacy of the notion that the Ceryces were a non-Eleusinian genos, cf. Osborne 1985: 175.

27 And indeed the archaeological evidence was made to fit this model and was read in such a way as to appear to validate it. However, as I argued above, when read without any reference to alleged history, it clearly invalidates it.

28 Foley (1994: 172–75), who takes the view that the absence of Athens from the hymn does not constitute evidence for the view that Eleusis was independent from Athens at the time of its composition.

29 I accept the view put forward by Parker (1991: 1–17) that the hymn writer 'worked with Eleusinian themes, but put them into new combinations and gave them emphases that they had not received before' in the context of this particular genre of 'comparatively sophisticated carefully planned work'; and that the hymn was addressing potential initiates. Parker also (1991: 13) argued that the shaping of the hymn enacts in a sense the emotional experience of the initiation, the structure of the poem reflecting the structure of the Mysteries.

30 Cf. also, e.g. Istros *FGrH* 334 F 22; cf. Graf 1974: 17–18.

31 Cf. West 1983: 23–24, Parker 1987b: 203–04. Orpheus is first attested as the founder of the Eleusinian Mysteries in [Eur.] *Rhesus* 943ff.; on this, cf. Graf 1974: 23–39, West 1983: 23–24. On Musaeus and Eleusis, cf. West 1983: 23–24, 41–44. On the notion that an Egyptian Erechtheus had founded the Mysteries, cf. Graf 1974: 23–26.

32 Cf. Richardson 1974: 84–85, 198, Kearns 1989: 163. Another tradition makes Musaeus son of Eumolpus; Philochoros *FGrH* 328 F 208.

33 Cf. Lloyd-Jones 1967: 206–29 for an Orphic catabasis of *c*. 550, Boardman 1975: 7–10, Shapiro 1989: 76.

34 For a description of the Mysteries Mylonas 1961: 243–85, Deubner 1969: 69–91, Parke 1977: 55–72, Brumfield 1981: 192–222, Burkert 1983: 248–97, 1987.

35 Cf. Mylonas 1961: 249, Travlos 1971: 160 for the position of the Halade Gate through which the *mystai* passed to go to the sea.

36 After the introduction of the cult of Asclepius that was the day on which the Epidauria were celebrated.

37 Cf. Clinton 1988: 70, who cites an unpublished dissertation by J.M. Mansfield and offers further arguments.

38 Whenever this began, and whoever may have preceded them in the role of receiving the *hiera*.

39 Among jurors (Andocides 1. 28, 29, 31) and members of the Ecclesia (Andocides 1.12).

40 On which cf. Clinton 1974: 98–114, 1980: 285.

41 I take *aph' hestias* in a similar sense to that in which Aristotle uses it when he speaks of religious officials who *apo tês koinês hestias echousi tên timên* (*Politics* 1322b28).

42 Cf. Travlos 1971: 198. On the City Eleusinion, cf. also Thompson and Wycherley 1972: 150–52, Camp 1990: 152–55, Shapiro 1989: 69.

43 Sokolowski 1962: 14.34–36; cf. Dow and Healey 1965: 22.

44 Sokolowski 1969 no. 7: A 8–21; Dow and Healey 1965: 21–23. On the connection between the Proerosia at Eleusis and the Pyanopsia, cf. Dow and Healey 1965: 21.

45 Cf. Feaver 1957: 140–1; Schmitt-Pantel 1980: 58–59. This may or may not have been related to the myth that Celeus had 'invented' the prytaneion (Plutarch, *Moralia* 667D, cf. Burkert 1983: 147).

46 On the introduction of this cult, cf. Garland 1992: 115–35.

47 On the Proerosia (the name of which is attested in several variants), cf. Dow and Healey 1965: 14–20, Brumfield 1981: 54–69, Parker 1987a: 141.

48 Cf. Brumfield 1981: 116–17.

49 A festival which included a women-only ritual and which almost certainly belonged primarily to Demeter, though Athena clearly also had a role in it, cf. Deubner 1962: 40–50, Parke 1977: 156–62, Brumfield 1981: 156–81, Burkert 1983: 143–49, Calame 1990: 341–44.

50 According to Lysimachides *FGrH* 366 F 3, also the priest of Helios.

51 On *hieroi arotoi* cf. Jameson 1951: 53–61, Deubner 1962: 47, 250, Brumfield 1981: 63–65, 172–77.

52 On the relationship between Athena Skiras, Poseidon, Demeter, Phaleron, Skiron, and Eleusis with Salamis and the frontier wars with Megara, and as a particular model of the ways in which ritual articulates territory, cf. Calame 1990: 344–64.

53 Cf. Sokolowski 1962: 17 A b 8. This festival was considered old-fashioned in Aristophanes' *Clouds* (983–84). On the evidence for the Ceryces' involvement in the Dipoleia, cf. also Burkert 1983: 139–40, n. 17.

54 Sourvinou-Inwood 1993, where I set out my views on the emergence of early Greek sanctuaries and the way in which their development was affected by the emergence of the polis.

55 De Polignac 1984; cf. also on de Polignac's model and Athens and Eleusis the review by Malkin, in *Journal of Hellenic Studies* 97 (1987): 227. I had first put forward the suggestion that Athens fits de Polignac's bipolar model with Eleusis as the crucial peripheral sanctuary in a lecture in 1987. Since then Osborne (as cited by Foley 1994: 170–72) has argued in a detailed way on the basis of the material culture of the area from the Dark Ages onwards that Eleusis was part of the Athenian polis from an early stage and that the relationship between Athens and its extra-urban sanctuaries was not atypical by comparison to that of other

poleis. Cf. also Calame 1990: 361–62, 395, nn. 134–36 on de Polignac and the notion of bipolarity with reference to Athens.

56 I do not accept the view of Graf (1985: 274) that the age and spread of the cult of Demeter Eleusinia in Asia Minor entails that the Eleusinian cult predated the Ionian migration. For, as the cult of Apollo Pythius testifies, important cults have the tendency to radiate. In any case, the fact that the sanctuary began in the late eighth century and there is no continuity with an alleged Mycenaean cult building does not entail that Demeter had no cult at Eleusis before then. On the contrary, a pre-existing cult of the goddess of agriculture in this fertile frontier area was probably one of the parameters determining the selection of this locus for the creation of a major polis sanctuary.

57 On the association of the *aparchai* with the Eleusinian cult and the circumstances of their dedication, cf. Brumfield 1981: 61–62, 104, 108, 134–35, 148–49, 173–74, 185–86.

58 On openings and closures to outsiders in Greek polis religion, cf. Sourvinou-Inwood 1988a: 267–70.

59 On the *leges sacrae* of Athens, cf. Jeffery 1948: 106–11, Dow 1953–57.

60 On the *Kyloneion agos*, cf. Herodotus 5. 70–71 (also 1.61), Thucydides 1.126, and Jeffery 1976: 87–88, Rhodes 1981: 79–84, Parker 1983: 16–17, Hornblower 1991: 202–10.

61 Cf. *FGrH* 457 T 1, *Ath. Pol.* 1: Epimenides purified the city after the Alcmaeonids had been thrown out. The same order of events in Plutarch.

62 *FGrH* 457 T 1, 4. On Epimenides, cf. also Burkert 1972: 151–52, Parker 1983: 209–10, West 1983: 45–53.

63 Thus Seaford (1994: 79–83), who bases his discussion on Plutarch, *Solon* 12.1–5, is wrong to speak of the crisis as one of 'internal division and reciprocal violence' (82); the latter caused the events that led to the crisis, but the crisis as described in 123 had a metaphysical dimension which Seaford ignores when interpreting funerary legislation in primarily political terms, as aimed at curbing competition between kinship groups. In the same way, he takes no account of the difficulty for his interpretation caused by the fact that a phratry (the Labyadae) issued legislation of the same type. Most importantly, it is not correct that this passage shows (as Seaford 1994: 82 contends) that the funerary legislation was envisaged as contributing to political homonoia. Plutarch does not attribute the better conduciveness to homonoia to the funerary legislation part of Epimenides' reforms, but to the second part, which is specifically distinguished from the first: *To de megiston* refers to the purifications, sacred foundations and rites of expiation through which he purified and initiated the city and brought it to be observant of justice and more easily inclined to concord. In other words, through the removal of pollution expiations and institution of the appropriate rites, the polis became observant of justice and the circumstances conducive to homonoia. The right religious health and balance lead to the right political and social health and balance in the city. The passage does not support the type of direct rationalizing relationship between reform for political reasons and homonoia which Seaford suggests.

64 In *Solon* 12.3 fears derived from superstition and phasmata (strange apparitions) *kateiche* (were afflicting) the polis.

65 On the concept of purification involved in the *Kyloneian agos* and Epimenides' activities, cf. Parker 1983: 209–12.

66 On 'Epimenides' linking himself with Musaeus in the poems, cf. West 1983: 47–48.

67 Crete in the archaic world is a place of reputed ritual authority, and thus an excellent place of origin for the (real or constructed) foreign religious expert.

68 On Bouzyges, cf. West 1983: 45–46, Toeppfer 1889: 139–47, Kearns 1989: 152, Burkert 1990: 77–85. For the identification of Epimenides with Bouzyges: Aristophanes. fr. 342; Servius, *Georgics* 1.19; Hesychius s.v. *Bouzyges*.
69 On this Bouzygian curse, cf. Durand 1986: 175–77.
70 This is suggested by the fact that at 1.14.3 he has told us that a dream persuaded him to write only what is lawful for everyone to know about the Eleusinion.
71 Though it may be possible to speculate that, besides the possible relevance of the culture hero schema, one reason why Epimenides became identified with Bouzyges rather than any other Eleusinian figure may have been the similarity between aspects of the narrative pertaining to Epimenides and the mythico-ritual nexus of the Bouphonia and Bouzyges (cf. West 1983: 45–46).

8

THE PROBLEM OF PERIODIZATION: THE CASE OF THE PELOPONNESIAN WAR

Barry S. Strauss

Periodization is both the requisite framework and the false friend of all history-writing. Choosing one name or chronology for a period means not choosing another. The consequences are always political and often pivotal. For example, few can have ignored the recent debate, occasioned by the anniversary of 1492, as to whether Columbus discovered or contacted or conquered the human beings known variously as Indians or native Americans or indigenous people. In light of this debate, some may abjure the conventional name for the history of the Americas before 1492, that is, the pre-Columbian period. To take a more recent example from the history of the United States, the decade of the 1960s looks in retrospect considerably more similar to the 1950s than it did in, say, 1968. Such continuities as the Cold war, military action in East Asia, domestic prosperity, and political and cultural dominance by middle-class white males may outweigh such changes as the generation gap, black power, and the counter-culture. Interpreting the legacy of the 1960s is of no small moment in the American cultural politics of the 1990s.

Another example is what Americans call the Vietnam war, the putative lessons of which have often been invoked in political debate since 1974. To Vietnamese, however, it was the American war, and that war was merely an episode in an anti-colonial war that began against the French in 1945. A Vietnamese Thucydides might argue, with no little justification, that there was only one great war in Vietnam between 1945 and 1974. The difference is not merely semantic but affects both popular perception and policy debate.

The ancient historian likewise faces problems aplenty in periodization. Such terms as 'archaic' Greece or 'Late' Antiquity (or the French 'Bas' empire) may evoke negative connotation, as is notorious. The notion of the Hellenistic period is doubly problematic. One half of the term, -istic, suggests a mere derivative of the pure and original Hellenic; the other half, Hellen-, ignores the non-Greeks in the lands ruled by Alexander's successors, who

165

outnumbered and frequently ignored the conquerors and their descendants.[1] Indeed, the thesis of Droysen, that the centuries following Alexander's conquests should be considered the era of Hellenism in the ancient Mediterranean because they marked a fusion between Greek and Oriental culture, thereby paving the way for Christianity – that thesis is now in tatters, which tends to undercut the logic of the appellation (of many discussions, see Momigliano 1970 and Walbank 1991/92). Each of these periods, indeed any historical period, raises chronological difficulties. When, for example, did the Hellenistic period end? With the mission of Jesus c. 30 CE? Or earlier, in 30 BCE, with the death of Cleopatra, which event both marks the end of Macedonian monarchy in the eastern Mediterranean and symbolizes the foundation of the Roman principate by Augustus? Cleopatra's death also, incidentally, reminds the historian of another problem in periodization, that of Graeco-Roman Egypt: a term often invoked but lately criticized in favour of separate eras of Greek Egypt and Roman Egypt (Lewis 1970, 1984).

We reach firmer historical ground in turning to one of the more durable periods of the classical era, the Peloponnesian war of 431 to 404 BCE. Or do we? On closer inspection, the dates and nature of the war turn out to be artificial and fragile. The Peloponnesian war is an excellent case study of the paradoxes of periodization. The rest of this chapter examines that war as an example of a general problem in historiography.

Here is a story about classical Greece:[2] The Peloponnesian war (431–404 BCE) was the central conflict of classical Greece. It lasted longer (twenty-seven years) than any other of the various hegemonic wars of the city-states. It involved more states than did other wars, including Persia, Macedon, and the Greeks of Sicily. Its participants were at the peak of their power and readiness, which produced a most bloody and destructive conflict. The outcome of the war was decisive: the end of the Athenian empire. The war undermined the confidence of the Athenian literary élite, to judge from the works of Euripides, Plato, Sophocles, and Thucydides.

Here is another story about classical Greece: The Greek city-states around the Aegean, arranged in alliances, fought a series of hegemonic wars c. 460–338. In some wars other states – Persia, Macedon, the Thessalians, the Sicilian poleis – also took part. Some wars were inconclusive, others created or destroyed alliances. In the fifth century Athens and Sparta were the primary antagonists. Between 460 and 404 they fought at least three separate wars, punctuated by peace agreements that amounted to no more than extended truces: the so-called first Peloponnesian war (c. 460–446/445),[3] the Archidamian or Ten Years war (431–421); and the Iono-Decelean war (414–404). After another extended truce, the conflict continued, this time in the Corinthian war (395–387/386). Military success or failure is often echoed in Athenian literature throughout the classical period.

Several differences distinguish the two stories. The first story privileges the Peloponnesian war. The second story not only renders that war just another in a long series of classical Greek conflicts, but it questions the very existence of one Peloponnesian war. It sees instead two wars in the period 431–404, and ties them closely to wars in the years immediately before and afterward. The first story makes one war, the Peloponnesian war, into a focal event in classical Greek cultural history, while the second story imagines a long-term and diffuse process of interaction between the wars of the fifth and fourth centuries BCE and Athenian literature. To use the language of recent historiographical debate, the first story is a species of *l'histoire événementielle* while the second story, sceptical of the importance of any one event, focuses rather on *la longue durée*.

Consider two points at issue in the disagreement between the two versions. The general question is that of periodization, while the specific question is of 'the only begetter' of the Peloponnesian war, Thucydides. Thucydides not only 'composed a written account of the war' (*ksynegrapse ton polemon*: 1.1.1) as he tells us in the first sentence of his work, but he crystallized the idea that the many and varied conflicts of the years 431–404 were in fact all one war, separate from prior and later conflicts (see Loraux 1986, Edmunds 1993). Although the non-specialist is largely unaware of it, quite a few scholars have noted the polemical and provisional nature of Thucydides' unitary-war thesis.

Underlying the questions of periodization and of Thucydides is the larger question of war as an object of culture. The choice between one war or several will not change the cold, hard military facts. Sparta still will have conquered the Athenian fleet at Aegospotami in 405 whether we call the act an event in the Peloponnesian war or in the Iono-Decelean war, just as the Japanese will have attacked the US fleet in Pearl Harbor on 7 December 1941, whether we call that attack an event in the ongoing Second World War or the opening act in the Pacific war. What periodization will change, however, is perception. During wartime, perception affects the way belligerents proceed. After the war perception shapes memory, which in turn shapes behaviour in new conflicts: many a war, modern as well as ancient, has been fought according to the supposed lessons of the past. So there is more than just a name at stake in how we conceive of the Peloponnesian war.

After reviewing the details of Thucydides' thesis, this chapter attempts three tasks. First, it considers just how Thucydides' unitary-war theory may have coloured our understanding of the history of this era, and how fifth- and fourth-century perceptions may have differed. Second, it considers (briefly) the reasons why Thucydides argued for one instead of two or more Peloponnesian wars. Third, it considers the lessons of this case study for the larger problem of historical periodization. Note that for the sake of clarity (and to avoid clumsy periphrasis), this chapter will use the traditional term

'Peloponnesian war' to refer to the military and diplomatic conflicts of the Greek and Persian worlds in the period 431 to 404 BCE.[4]

Let us begin with what is an open secret among classicists and Greek historians. Those who fought or endured what we call the Peloponnesian war (431–404 BCE) perhaps never used the term (see de Ste Croix 1972: 294–95, whose fundamental discussion the rest of this paragraph follows; cf. Hornblower 1987: 7–8). To Thucydides it was the 'war of the Peloponnesians and Athenians' (1.1.1) or the 'war of the Athenians and Peloponnesians and the allies of each' (2.1.1). To his Athenians it was the 'war against the Peloponnesians' (e.g. 1.44.2; cf. Aristotle, *Ath. Pol.* 27.2) or the 'Dorian war' (2.54.2, 3). To his Peloponnesians it was the 'war against the Athenians' (e.g. 8.18.2) or the 'Attic war' (e.g. 5.28.2; cf. Cartledge 1987:34). Consider another important point: many, perhaps most contemporaries did not think of the 'Peloponnesian war' as one war at all. They thought, rather, of two or three wars. Nor did they see 431 and 404 as unique landmarks; they saw them instead as two among several monuments to a larger conflict that had begun around 460 and – to those who lived past 404 – continued into the fourth century (for the details on these points, see below). Well aware of what we sometimes forget today, that the notion of one 'war of the Athenians and Peloponnesians' was a debatable point, Thucydides argues vigorously on its behalf (1.1, 5.26).

Historians today recognize, as did Thucydides himself (see below), that the Peloponnesian war consisted of several distinct phases. Scholars commonly divide the war into phases such as: the Archidamian war or Ten Years war, that is, the Athenian–Peloponnesian conflict of 431–421; the so-called peace of Nicias, that is, the hot-and-cold war from 421 to 416; the Iono-Decelean war, that is, the Athenian invasion of Sicily of 415–413 and the free-for-all among Athenians, their rebellious allies, the Peloponnesians, and the Persian empire that ensued until 404 – and that broke out again in 395, the so-called Corinthian war (395–386).[5] In spite of such divisions, it is hard to resist the power of Thucydides' notion of one great war (see Cogan 1988: 288, n. 2) between two great powers, a paradigm that was only reinforced by our century's two world wars and the Cold war (see Henderson 1973, Connor 1977, Lebow and Strauss 1991, Roberts 1994: 260–61, 298).

Some of Thucydides' contemporaries too thought of the Peloponnesian war as one war, but only by an act of faith. From the start of the war, 'many people' prophesied that the war would last three times nine years (Thucydides 5.26.4). The actual conduct of military and political affairs, however, suggested two or three wars between 431 and 404. The earliest relevant source is Aristophanes' *Lysistrata* of 411. Lysistrata makes a distinction between the war in 411 and the 'earlier war' that was ended with a peace treaty inscribed on a stele (Aristophanes, *Lysistrata* 507, 513; Thucydides 5.18.2), referring presumably to the Archidamian war. In his *Atthis* Hellanicus spoke of two or three wars between 431 and 404, at least in Jacoby's judgement (Jacoby 1957: vol. 1: 19, vol. 2: 16, n. 147). Lysias spoke of the Archidamian war in his now-lost speech *Against Androtion*, though conceivably he saw it as a phase in the Peloponnesian war (Harpocration, s.v. *Arkhidameios polemos*). Several generations later, the orator Aeschines (2.175–76, 343 BCE) made a distinction between a war (presumably 431–421) provoked by Megara and a war provoked by Argos (presumably 414–404). Looking back on the Peloponnesian war a dozen years after its end (392 BCE), the orator Andocides, a participant in wartime Athenian debates, conceived of three wars: a war against Sparta 'on account of Megara' (3.8) – presumably, the war of 431–421: the war against Syracuse (3.30) – presumably, the Sicilian expedition of 415–413; and then a renewed war against Sparta 'at the instigation of Argos' (3.9, 3.31) – presumably the war of 414–404. For Andocides, moreover, the fourth-century Corinthian war is part of the same historical cycle as Athens' fifth-century wars against Sparta (3.28–29).

Plato's *Menexenus* surveys a panorama of Athenian wars, from Marathon to the Corinthian war (239D–46A). The work assigns two wars to the period 431–404: a conflict comprising 'much war' (242C), evidently the Archidamian war (242C–E); and a 'third war' corresponding to the Sicilian and Iono-Decelean wars (243A–D). These two wars are closely connected to a first war, a war – arguably forced on Athens – against the other Greeks, a conflict marked by the battles of Tanagra and Oenophyta (457), presumably the first Peloponnesian war (242A–C). (On these orators and Plato, see de Ste Croix 1972: 95.)

Thucydides himself tacitly concedes the frequency of the notion of two or three wars in his polemic against the belief that the treaty of 421 inaugurated a genuine peace; he argues, rather, that the so-called peace of Nicias was a time of war (Thucydides 5.26.2). Indeed, Thucydides recognizes three distinct phases in the Peloponnesian war. Ten years of war (5.26.3; cf. 'the first war', 5.20.3; 'the ten years war', 5.25.1; 'the earlier war', 7.18.2) preceded the 'uneasy suspension of fighting' of 421 (5.26.3, see Gomme *et al.* 1970: 15–17 on 5.26.6), while the 'later war' followed nearly seven years after the peace was sworn (5.25.2–3, 5.26.3; cf. 5.56.3): in 414, after an Athenian expedition, acting on Argos's behalf, ravaged Spartan territory (6.105, 7.18.2). Together, the three phases all added up to one long war (5.26.3). The two wars bracketing the uneasy peace of Nicias were thus each ten years long; as Rawlings shows, Thucydides draws rich and complex parallels between these two phases (Rawlings 1981: especially 5, 9, 45; see also Hunter 1973: 129–31, 145–48, 179–80; and, more generally, Connor 1984: 142–44).

Thucydides offers reasons, both philosophical and practical, to justify his decision to treat the phenomena which he is describing as one war, beginning in 431 and ending in 404. As Thucydides knew, the Athenians and Peloponnesians had fought before 431, and he may well have lived long enough after 404 to see a new conflict coming (see Hornblower 1987: 151–52, with references to scholarly literature). What made the Peloponnesian war unique in Thucydides' eyes, however, was its length (*toutou de polemou mêkos te mega proubê*, 1.23.1, cf. 7.87.5) and the enormity of sufferings that befell Greece within its twenty-seven years, a relatively short period of time to encompass the shedding of so much blood, the destruction of so many cities, and the sending of so many men into exile – not to mention earthquakes, eclipses of the sun, great droughts, famines, and the epidemic of the 420s, all of which disasters occurred in Greece during the war (1.23.1–3). Compared to the Peloponnesian war, even the greatest of previous conflicts, the Persian war, was brief (1.23.1).

Unfortunately, this statement begs the question, for it assumes the legitimacy of referring to one Peloponnesian war. Perhaps dramatic unity provided Thucydides with a better argument. In 431, he states, the two belligerent sides were at the peak of their power and preparations and endowed with allies as never before, hence promising a great and most noteworthy conflict (1.1.1, cf. 2.65.5). In 404 the Peloponnesians ended the Athenian empire and occupied the Long Walls and the Piraeus (5.26.1), thereby bringing the curtain down on the 'greatest motion' in the history of the Hellenes (1.1.1).

Yet Thucydides none the less might have begun the war *c.* 460 instead of in 431 had he been born earlier. That is, he might have considered the first Peloponnesian war (*c.* 460–446/445) and the Peloponnesian war (431–404) as one war (see de Ste Croix 1972: 50–51). The peace agreement of 446/445 lasted twice as long as the peace agreement of 421 (fourteen versus seven years) and was less violent, but only relatively: the 'peace' of 446/445–431 witnessed *inter alia* a war between Athens and Samos in which Sparta threatened to intervene, a war between Corinth and Corcyra in which Athens did intervene, and a war between Athens and Potidaea in which Corinthian 'volunteers' took part. Plato's *Menexenus* does not even bother to mention the peace agreements separating what we would call the first Peloponnesian war and the Peloponnesian war. The *Menexenus* would speak rather of two similar wars in which the other Greeks attacked Athens (242A, C). Yet even had Thucydides wanted to consider the war before the 'uneasy suspension of fighting' from 445 to 431 and the 'later war' beginning in 431 as one war, it would have been impractical to do so, for he considered it impossible to acquire clear information about earlier periods (1.1.2). By contrast, Thucydides both lived through the war years 431–404 and he was 'of an age to understand' them at the outset, that is, probably in his twenties (5.26.5, cf. Gomme *et al.* 1970: 12–15). For Thucydides, the war beginning in 431 was 'his war' in a way that the war beginning *c.* 460 was not.[6]

To sum up: according to Thucydides, 431 marks the acme of evenly matched power, 404 the nadir. The intervening war was the most disastrous in Hellenic history. Earlier conflicts were lesser events, and in any case Thucydides could not to his satisfaction acquire clear information about matters much before 431. Although several phases mark the fighting of the years from 431 to 404, the period was really one long war, the so-called agreement of 421 being in fact no more than an uneasy armistice. There was only one great war between the Athenians and the Peloponnesians, beginning in 431 and ending in 404.

However coherent or persuasive, the argument is also polemical and anachronistic, since most contemporaries, unless they took prophecy literally, were no more aware of living through one discrete Peloponnesian war than Monsieur Jourdain was aware of speaking prose. By envisioning several wars rather than one war, we may be better able to reconstruct contemporary perceptions.

Consider, for instance, the question of whether the war that began in 431 was inevitable. But which war? The Peloponnesian war? The Archidamian war? The war that had begun *c.* 460 and was now recommencing after an uneasy truce? It made a difference to the assembly-goers in Sparta and Athens in 432 whether the war they were asked to consider declaring was simply another swing of the pendulum, oscillating as it had between war and peace in Greece ever since the Persian wars (Thucydides 1.18.3), or a new and unprecedentedly ambitious venture. It makes a difference to the historian whether he is considering the outbreak of a conflict that lasted twenty-seven years and drew in Persia, or one that lasted ten years and involved primarily the city-states of the Greek peninsula and the Aegean. Likewise, it makes a difference whether he is examining a single war or one in a series. The two-war schema of Plato's *Menexenus* makes clear what the one-war model of Thucydides obscures, that while the Archidamian war was primarily an inter-Greek affair, the Sicelo-Iono-Decelean war represented something 'terrible and unexpected' because of the intervention of Persia (242F, 243B).[7]

In this context, consider the relative importance of the roles played by the non-hegemonic powers (Corinth, Corcyra, Thebes) in the origin of the war of 431. If that war was less a discrete conflict than an episode in a history of conflicts, then the two power blocs of the late 430s look considerably less stable than they might if the peace agreement of 445 marked a genuine caesura. For example, Corinth's threat at Sparta in 432 of defecting from the Peloponnesian alliance (Thucydides 1.71.4–6) seems less idle when one considers that Corinth (and Thebes) indeed switched alliance from Sparta to Athens in the 390s (and flirted with such a defection following the peace of Nicias).

Or consider questions about the years between 431 and 404. For example, was Athens' Sicilian expedition that was launched in 415 a violation of Pericles' dictum, delivered to the Athenian people, not to add to their empire during the war (Thucydides 2.65.7)? Thucydides thought so (2.65.7, 11), and Alcibiades, addressing the Athenian assembly in 415, rejects the implicitly Periclean policies of relative inactivity and imperial restraint in wartime (Thucydides 6.18.3, cf. 2.65.7). Technically, of course, Athens was at peace in 415. Thucydides underscores the fragility of that peace, but whether Pericles would have given the same advice in 415 that he had given before his death in 429 is an open question. To raise another question, was Athens' invasion of Sicily bad strategy or was it a good idea poorly executed (2.65.11)? The prospect of its success certainly frightened the Spartans into counter-action (Thucydides 6.90.2–4, 93.1–3). As a piece of military strategy, the Sicilian expedition must be judged in the context of 415 and not under the rubric of a larger war from 431 to 404.

Then there is the matter of peacemaking. What war did the belligerents imagine they were ending in 404: one that began in 431 or 415 or 414 or 460? Earlier, in 410 after the battle of Cyzicus, in 408/407, and perhaps again in 406 after the battle of Arginusae, Sparta had offered peace to Athens but Athens refused (for the ancient sources and scholarly debate, see Rhodes 1981: 424). The strategic situation in those years remains the same whether the Athenians imagined they were fighting a war that had begun in 431 or earlier or later, but the psychological situation might vary considerably in each case. The longer the war, the greater the war-weariness. When peace was finally established in 404, did the ending of the Athenian empire lend special gravity to the oaths of peace sworn, or did the peacemakers expect the promises of 404 to be no more decisive than those of 445 or 421?

Consider finally the way the Peloponnesian war was remembered in the fourth century, that is, not as one war but several. Charted on a graph, such history would appear to be a series of short waves rather than one long wave. For Andocides and Aeschines the lesson was clear. They believed that the frequent alternation of war and peace demonstrates the need to negotiate a lasting peace. Peace, they argued, was a great good, but they were self-interested, for in his own day each man was a peacemaker who had come under fire. Other fourth-century Athenians might draw different lessons from the past cycle of hegemonic wars. They might conclude that, since those wars had been generally short and indecisive, it was not terribly risky after all to undertake a new war. Or they might conclude that the most important lesson of Athens' recent past was not diachronic but structural. They might reason, that is, that making the polis great and free was less a matter of choosing the right time to go to war than of ensuring the support of a firm and loyal system of allies.

In the fifth century Athens' heavy-handed imperialism had alienated allies; when put to the test, they failed to stand by Athens. It appears that, a generation after the defeat of the Athenian empire, Athenians had learned from the past. Hence, Aristoteles' decree of 377 BCE (*IG* 2² 43), the charter, as it were, of the second Athenian confederacy, takes pains to guarantee the allies, among other things, freedom, autonomy, choice of their own constitution, and freedom from garrison, governor, tribute, or Athenian acquisition of property in allied territory. In short, the decree 'amounted to a thorough renunciation of the hated practices' of the fifth-century empire (Cargill 1981: 190). Finally, a fourth-century student of Athenian history might conclude that no matter how unified, a league of poleis was not to be the crucial factor in Hellenic strategy; that distinction, rather, might go to Persia: 413 (when Athens' Sicilian defeat moved Persia towards intervention) rather than 431 (when the Archidamian war began) arguably had proven to be the fatal date for the Athenian empire (on Persia's decisive intervention, see Kagan 1987: 28–35, 418–19, 423).

Such perceptions are neither as dramatic nor as clear as Thucydides' theoretical framework. They imagine a complex, indecisive, even chaotic world; but that notion perhaps better captures the outlook of the Athenian assembly than does Thucydides' vision of order.

Thucydides insisted that the wars from 431 to 404 were in fact one great Atheno-Peloponnesian war. His is a strong and formidable conclusion. During those twenty-seven years, one theme remained of central importance: the integrity of Athens' naval hegemony in the Aegean. By contrast, Athens' bid for a central Greek land empire dominated the first Peloponnesian war (c. 460–446/445), while the Corinthian war (395–387/386) ensued from the breakup of both the Athenian empire and the Peloponnesian league. Thucydides' unitary war theory, therefore, is acute and perceptive, but only in hindsight. The thesis obscures the commonsensical belief in two or three separate wars between 431 and 404, a belief predominant both among contemporaries and among their descendants over the next century. Why did Thucydides so insist, against the *communis opinio*, that the wars were really one war? The scholar begins to wonder if Thucydides did not have other reasons to define his subject as he does, reasons besides the acme of the two sides and the practicalities of gathering evidence. Thucydides was no chronicler but, as Cornford noted long ago, 'a great artist' (Cornford 1971 [1907]: vii). It is not merely useful, therefore, but necessary to take some notice of artistic considerations in Thucydides' work.

Thucydides' literary motives are complex, and to a considerable degree unknowable. Here I will merely suggest what certain of those motives may have been. First, the one Peloponnesian war makes an elegant contrast to the Trojan war of Homer and the Persian war of Herodotus, to which Thucydides explicitly or implicitly compares 'his' war (1.3, 9–11, 23.1; cf. Rawlings 1981: 10–12). Second, the unitary war thesis nicely frames Thucydides' exile from Athens, which began in 424, during what Andocides and Aeschines call war on account of Megara, and ended in 404, during what they call war at the instigation of Argos (see Strauss 1991). Perhaps the bitter pill of exile was easier to swallow if the exile was coterminous with one great war rather than with several smaller conflicts. Third, the notion of a two-power war, the 'war of the Peloponnesians and the Athenians' (1.1.1), may reflect nostalgia, in the complex and multi-polar world of the 390s, for a simpler world – however superficial that simplicity turns out to be on closer inspection, given the importance of such states as Corcyra, Corinth, Argos, Syracuse, and Persia in late fifth-century conflict. Fourth, the conceit of one war allows Thucydides to exalt Pericles. He becomes not just another politician who gambled wrongly on an indecisive ten-year conflict. Pericles becomes a unique genius whose wisdom remained valid over an epochal twenty-seven-year-long struggle (2.65.6). Had Athens followed Pericles' strategic advice and emulated his probity, Athens would not have lost the war (2.65.7; for a different view, see Kagan 1974: 350–62, 1991: 228–45). Thucydides' notion of the unity of the war, therefore, arguably has something to do not only with real but also with symbolic politics.

But why was it so important for Thucydides to exalt Pericles? Thucydides' admiration for Pericles' political and military leadership, explicit in the text (2.65.4–10), has received considerable scholarly comment (e.g. Finley 1942, McGregor 1956). Work on Sophocles suggests that Thucydides was also much taken with the tragic elements of hubris and nemesis in Pericles' last years (Ehrenberg 1954, Knox 1957). Here I would like merely to raise the possibility that, consciously or not, Thucydides admired Pericles as a father-figure.

I have argued elsewhere that both Thucydides and other fifth- and fourth-century Athenian texts from a variety of genres represent the Peloponnesian war by borrowing from the discourse of the family (Strauss 1993b). The texts structure politics and war by narratives of family relations, by 'family romances', to follow Lynn Hunt's appropriation of Freud (Hunt 1992a). In the family romance of the Peloponnesian war, Pericles is a strong father sternly ruling the Athenian people, whom he protects from a variety of enemies: from the Peloponnesians, from their own childishness, and from feminization. And, perhaps, Pericles is the father who might have protected Thucydides from the assembly that forced Thucydides into exile. It is not for nothing that in his funeral oration, Pericles presents the polis as a kind of surrogate oikos (Strauss 1993b: 212).

To have ended Pericles' war in 421 (or 429) and to have made the war of 414–404 into a separate war would have been to rob the story of its ending. The family romance of Athens is that of a family which refuses to obey a father's good advice and pays for it by the loss of its patrimony. The war between the Athenians and the Peloponnesians, therefore, cannot end before this terrible truth is revealed, any more than Sophocles' *Oedipus Tyrannus* can end before Oedipus' dreadful past is revealed.

Forays into Thucydides' psyche must, of necessity, be speculative. We know few details of his biography, let alone of his childhood. As for psychoanalytic hypotheses, we cannot put Thucydides on the couch and, even if we could, a couch constructed in bourgeois Vienna c. 1900 will be a Procrustean bed when moved to classical Greece. Yet one wonders.

But enough of speculation. We have seen that Thucydides may have had a variety of motives to argue for one war rather than several. Perhaps clear-sighted and hard-headed analysis, coupled with the pragmatic difficulties of evidence-gathering, were the sole determinants of his periodization. Perhaps literary, political, personal, or psychological motives also played a role.

Whatever the reader makes of Thucydides, he or she will be persuaded, it is hoped, that the notion of one Peloponnesian war (or, to be precise, Atheno-Peloponnesian war) is a Thucydidean invention – indeed, perhaps it is his masterpiece. Yet contemporaries, other than devotees of oracles, spoke rather of two or several wars. Today, when ancient historians speak of one Peloponnesian war, they use the term as a kind of abbreviation for a many-phased conflict. In so doing, they do justice to the underlying power realities of late fifth-century Greece, but they run the risk of obscuring questions of perception by contemporaries and by following generations.

The fragility of the notion of the Peloponnesian war offers food for thought. It does not mean that there is no such thing as a historical fact; it does not mean that historical facts are merely 'facts'. It does mean, however, that students of history should watch out for the assumptions and arguments underlying all schemes of appellation and periodization, whether of the 1960s or of the fifth century BCE.

The difference between imagining one great Peloponnesian war or a succession of smaller wars will have affected the perception and policy debates both of participants in the war(s) and of the following generations that struggled with the legacy of the conflict(s). To be sure, it is more unsettling today to question the periodization of classical antiquity than that of recent history, because the weight of two thousand years is not light. Yet, by the same token, perhaps such questioning can make an addition to the modern understanding of ancient culture. If this essay recalls Thucydides' disdain for mere contemporary perception, if it reminds the historian of the constant need to question Thucydidean categories, it also throws into relief the brilliance and originality of Thucydides' analysis.

NOTES

1 This is to say nothing of the term's failure to differentiate between Greeks and Macedonians.

2 I borrow this structure from J.H. Hexter's essay on the historiography of the English Civil War (Hexter 1961).

3 The First Peloponnesian war can be subdivided into a war of Athenian expansion (c. 460–c. 451), a peace (c. 451–c. 449) and a revolt against Athens (c. 449–446/445). Aeschines (2. 172–74) speaks of two such wars, as does Andocides' (error-filled) account (3.3–6).

4 One subject that I do not take up, however, is the question of composition. I follow the unitarian arguments of such scholars as de Romilly 1963 [1947] and Connor 1984; cf. Rawlings 1981: 250–54, Orwin 1994: 5–7.

5 Busolt 1967 [1904] offers probably the most thorough schema. His chapter titles for the years 431–404 refer to the Ten Years war, the uncertain peace and the Mantineian war, the Sicilian war, and the Decelean-Ionian-Hellespontine war.

6 Perhaps an additional consideration, as de Ste Croix notes (1972: 50–51), is the relative absence of Sparta from the first Peloponnesian war, most of the battles against Athens being fought rather by the Peloponnesian allies than by Sparta itself.

7 Note in this context that Davies (1993: 117) sagely and unconventionally makes 431–413 and 412–380 into two distinct periods.

9

CHANGE OR CONTINUITY? CHILDREN AND CHILDHOOD IN HELLENISTIC HISTORIOGRAPHY[1]

Mark Golden

Much about the Hellenistic period is open to discussion (Bichler 1983, Kassel 1987). When did it begin? With the close of the fifth century BCE? With the accession of Alexander the Great in 336? With his death, and those of his teacher Aristotle and his enemy Demosthenes in 323 and 322? With the battle of Ipsus in 301? The end date too is disputed. Though the prevailing practice is to set the terminus at the Battle of Actium and the end of the Ptolemaic dynasty in Egypt in 31 or 30, scholars have opted for a date as early as 146 or as late as the first centuries of the current era; for William Harris, 'Hellenistic' runs down to roughly the 70s BCE, 'by which date Rome's influence on the social order was being felt over most of the Greek world' (Harris 1989: 116, n. 2). Even the name itself has only become canonical since Wilamowitz took it from Droysen as part of his programme to re-evaluate the period's poetry. Before (as sometimes since) we find designations such as 'post-classical' or 'Alexandrian'.

But there is unanimity on one issue at least: the Hellenistic period is said to be marked by a change in the representation of children and childhood.

> The Hellenistic poets were the first to put children at centre stage, as they actually are and for their own sakes . . . and the art of that period swims with true depictions of real children, from whose amusing conduct Greeks of that time must have taken special pleasure.
>
> (Herter 1927: 251)

Herter's ideas still echo. We may read, in handbooks and surveys written some sixty years later, that the great poetry of the period 'delighted in scenes of emotion which it found in odd episodes of myth, in the child and the old, the housewife as well as the heroine' (Lane Fox 1986: 363) or that 'sculpture (and, we may infer, painting) displays a preoccupation with children' (Green 1990: 345, cf. 341, Pollitt 1986: 128). Nor is this new interest in children

176

thought to be confined to literature and the visual arts. Hellenistic medicine (we are told) developed a distinctive therapeutic regime for children – something unknown in the Hippocratic Corpus (Bertier 1990). Very young children gained admission to Dionysiac mysteries due to the 'sentimental love of children which begins in the Hellenistic Age and persists in the following centuries' (Nilsson 1957: 111, cf. Lambrechts 1957). Meanwhile the exposure of new-borns became morally problematic, as there developed a belief in the child's right to live (Deissmann-Merten 1984: 276–81). In fact, we seem to be engaged with just one manifestation of a fundamental shift in *mentalité*, based in far-reaching social and political transformations. Herter himself invoked a culture-weariness, a longing for simplicity and rest amidst the bustle of the great Hellenistic metropolises; this, along with the new political realities of a time when ministers ruled and mercenaries waged war, impelled a retreat to domestic life and a sentimental image of childhood (Herter 1927: 256, cf. Zahn 1970: 27, Rühfel 1984: 187, Green 1990: 359).

Particular elements of this picture invite debate, for example, on the relevance of depictions of the infant Dionysus for children's initiations into his mysteries (Matz 1960: 547) or on the ongoing attraction of the polis for individuals' interests (Gruen 1993, cf. L. Martin 1994). Perhaps the most instructive in the context of a book concerned with continuity and change is the question of the exposure of new-borns. Others have shared Deissmann-Merten's conviction that the Hellenistic period was a watershed in the history of exposure, but have differed with her on the nature and the implications of the change. So La Rue van Hook thought that Hellenistic Greeks exposed their children more often than in earlier periods, and termed this the repugnant practice of a decadent society (van Hook 1920: 144, cf. Rühfel 1984: 186). Robert Sallares accepts that there was indeed a change, argues that its extent was even greater, but denies that it had anything to do with decadence. In his great green book – as similar in size, intellectual vigour, and pugnacity to de Ste Croix's great red one as it is unlike in its understanding of human history (I think of it as *The Species Struggle in the Ancient Greek World*) – he asserts that the Greek population overshot the carrying capacity of the land in the late fourth century and early Hellenistic period; natural selection then favoured family limitation and, for the first time, Greeks practised exposure on a significant scale (Sallares 1991: 151–60). Still others, however, deny that this increase in exposure took place at all (Patterson 1985: 104, n. 3, Brulé 1992: 64).

Now it is certainly not beyond the power of scholarly ingenuity to reconcile at least some of these views – faced with the problem of supporting a growing population in a time of want (Sallares), the Greeks at first resisted ideologically (Deissmann-Merten) and then yielded to and even embraced necessity (van Hook). Nor need the conclusion that exposure was more frequent contradict the judgement that children were valued more highly. I have elsewhere explored the assumption that adults in high mortality populations do not care deeply for their children (Golden 1988); Mary Poppins' query – 'And what would happen to me, may I ask, if I loved all the children I said goodbye to?' – is ethnocentric. As far as motivation for change is concerned, we have Polybius' word for it (36.17.5) that his contemporaries limited the sizes of their families to ensure prosperity for those they chose to raise; in respect to effects, it is often argued that groups, both animal and human, who have fewer children, tend to invest more in individual offspring than do others. I think it is more useful, however, to consider some of the reasons that render agreement on this issue unlikely.

First, the nature of the evidence. There is simply no series of data which permits any reasonably reliable conclusion on the levels of exposure during the classical or the Hellenistic periods, let alone on variations between them. Arguments must be constructed on the basis of the distribution of the evidence over time, on quantitative data from particular places and times which need then to be generalized, and on scattered explicit statements of doubtful validity. But no one will feel confident about assuming that the preponderance of evidence on exposure from Hellenistic (and Roman) Greece corresponds to actual occurrence. (Similarly, any use of the incidence of inscriptions to track change over time must consider the fact that they themselves cluster at certain periods and try to explain it: MacMullen 1982, Meyer 1990.) As for the quantitative data, they consist of lists of new citizens in Hellenistic towns such as Miletus and Ilion (see Pomeroy 1983, Brulé 1990). Their severely skewed sex ratios have often been explained as a consequence of a high rate of exposure of girls, and their particular circumstances regarded as relevant to other parts of the Greek world. Even if this is so – and recent demographic research suggests that sex ratios may vary to a remarkable degree through such factors as the interrelationship of gender-based lifestyles and endemic diseases (Johansson 1991) and coital frequency (J. Martin 1994) – it reflects the treatment of one (admittedly large) class of new-borns only. It might therefore point to a change in gender relations rather than a new attitude towards children. In other words, the numbers of girls who were exposed may have increased at the same time as the overall rate of exposure remained constant or even dropped.

Finally, there is the famous passage of Polybius I referred to a moment ago. Here we find a statement about Polybius' own time, meant to be valid for all of Greece, that unwillingness to rear children was an important factor in the decrease in population. A class phenomenon? Perhaps – who else but the élite had wealth they could spend on children (Davies 1984: 268)? But even supposing that Polybius is accurately describing a phenomenon that affected people of every economic status throughout Greece, he is evidence for his own portion of the Hellenistic era only, around 150 BCE; that is, about 150 years after the plays of the New Comedy which provide Deissmann-Merten with the evidence for a child's right to live. We should be wary of eliding variation over a period as long as this. Nor should we assume that the variation was (in Peter Green's words) a 'linear, diachronic, evolutionary' development within the Hellenistic period (Green 1990: xvii–xviii). Polybius himself describes a state of disorder in the late third and early second centuries BCE, when a kind of mania overtook the Boeotians (20.6.5–6). The childless squandered their substance in parties and left nothing for their relatives; indeed, even those who had descendants (*geneas*) distributed much of their wealth among their dinner companions. There is no trace here of the desire to preserve property for posterity which led so soon thereafter, in Polybius' opinion, to depopulation throughout Greece. Perhaps it is safer, if not very satisfying, to suppose that the practice and rate of exposure varied with circumstances in different places and times, and that secular trends cannot at present be discerned (cf. Harris 1982: 115, Pomeroy 1986: 160–61, Kudlien 1989: 28, and, on regional and temporal variation in the archaeological record, Alcock 1994).

Another daunting difficulty in identifying change over time is genre – my focus in this chapter. Even those scholars who identify the Hellenistic period with a striking shift in attitudes towards children often observe that the literary and artistic evidence they adduce has earlier analogues. Rühfel notes that the characteristically Hellenistic portraits actually begin about 340 or 330 with the earliest free-standing statues and terracotta types of children (Rühfel 1984: 186, cf. Pollitt 1993: 97); Fowler finds real babies still earlier, on the Attic *choes* (Fowler 1989: 51, n. 12); for Zahn, the innocent children of *Medea* and *OT* are already focuses of adult pity and sentimentality (Zahn 1970: 26). It is noteworthy that Herter's last pronouncement on the subject, in an encyclopaedia article that appeared only after his death, also identifies 'Vorläufer' such as *choes*, Tanagra figurines, Pausias, Euripides (Herter 1993: 372). Now, no one supposes that the attitudes and assumptions of the classical period simply disappeared with (say) the deaths of Alexander, Aristotle, and Demosthenes; nor would it be easy to argue that allegedly Hellenistic characteristics were in all cases unknown to earlier Greeks. The differences between periods will often be matters of emphasis and degree, in the earlier years of a new epoch above all, rather than of sharp shifts and cleavages. What usually goes unnoticed, however, is how much of our impression of a change in attitudes towards childhood and children results from discontinuities in our evidence. To return to the comments of Rühfel, Fowler, and Zahn: we have no Hellenistic tragedies, and *choes* showing children were apparently a fashion that did not long survive the fifth century. On the other hand, the kinds of literature which supply much of the material for discussions of the new Hellenistic attitudes towards children – the hymns of Callimachus, Theocritean idylls – are unknown, or nearly so, in the classical period. As a result, what appears to be the consequence of a shift in *mentalité* over time may be mainly or even entirely an effect of genre. After all, genre bedevils many aspects of social history even within recognized periods: the forceful and effective women of the Attic stage are almost absent from classical courtrooms; the multi-generational family reconstructed from the Latin language and Roman law yields its place in letters and on tombstones to the nuclear family triad.

This is not to deny that genres themselves are historical artefacts. As Peter Rose has recently argued, 'The formal trajectory from epic formulas to choral lyric, trilogy, single play, philosophical dialogue is ... not intelligible on the basis of a purely internal Hegelian logic of forms' (Rose 1992: 372). Rose himself sees the genres he examines as products of class struggle. Other views flourish. But none supposes that literary forms are a consequence of conceptions of childhood and children, nor even that new attitudes towards children are among their most striking effects. The link between epyllion, say, and childhood is not so strong that the development of one need implicate the other.

Clearly, what we need to investigate change from one period to another is a body of evidence of the same genre. One likely set of candidates refers to a phenomenon attested for both classical and Hellenistic Greece: death. The archaeology of burial and the epigraphy of commemoration – both supply ample material for comparison, and indeed a number of studies exist of differences in the treatment of dead children and adults, of the designation of citizenship status on tombstones, of funerary epigrams and iconography. Unfortunately, these are less helpful than we would wish. Patterns of disposal of the dead vary widely in contemporary communities some fifty or one hundred miles apart; no one practice can safely be said to have any particular significance on its own; further generalization seems all but impossible (Musgrave 1990: 284, I. Morris 1992: 18–19). Athenian tombstones only rarely denote citizen boys by the addition of their demotics in the nominative case to their name. The practice becomes rather more common over time, especially in the Roman period – but the demotic might then be used as a surname, so the shift itself, let alone its significance, is problematic (Vestergaard *et al.* 1992). As for epigrams: Anne-Marie Vérilhac has discovered that the motif lamenting a young girl's death before marriage, common already in the archaic period, is applied to boys only in the Hellenistic (Vérilhac 1982: 157). But this, however valuable for our understanding of gender, cannot provide much help in illuminating attitudes towards children in general. And the development of iconography may run counter to prevailing preconceptions. 'The new reliefs' (the time is the third century) 'mostly abandon the intimate family emphasis – the seated women, the children in laps ... Children, if they are not the deceased, are accorded "miniature" status and are often indistinguishable from slaves' (R.R. Smith 1991: 188–89).

Among other literary genres, epic offers memorable glimpses of children – the *Iliad's* Astyanax, the 'cunning child' (*kerdaleon dê toion*, *Odyssey* 15.451) who can claim to be the first cute kid in Western literature; Eros, sassing his mother Aphrodite in *Argonautica* 3 – but none from the classical period. To compare Old and New Comedy poses a fundamental problem of categorization: does Menander belong at the end of the classical period or the start of the Hellenistic? (Even Wilamowitz wasn't sure: Kassel 1987: 16–17.) And where does Middle Comedy fit (see now Nesselrath 1990, with the comments of Csapo 1993)? On another front, the fifth-century biographer and gossip Stesimbrotus of Thasos 'evidently had a considerable amount to say about the youth and education of Themistocles, Cimon, and probably Pericles, not without a tinge of malice' (Pelling 1990: 215) – a lead that was not followed by later authors of politicians' lives. A promising clue, which the scarcity and scantiness of the evidence makes hard to pursue. I propose instead to examine the treatment of children and childhood in a related genre, namely history. I take my evidence in the first instance from Herodotus, Thucydides, Xenophon's *Hellenica* – all classical works – and from the great Hellenistic historian Polybius. I will take up two related hypotheses: (a) that interest in children and childhood increased during Polybius' time and (b) that attitudes towards children and childhood changed. The reader may regard what follows as a pendant to earlier reflections in which I accepted the fact, the inevitability, of social change in the ancient world at the same time as I underlined how very hard it can be to demonstrate (Golden 1990: 169–80, 1992). If my own work seems insufficiently inspiring, let me say that this case-study is written in the spirit of Gramsci, with pessimism of the intellect and optimism of the will. It also operates within two self-imposed restrictions, its focus on children and on literary genre. The first involves the disengagement of another group commonly joined with children in our sources and also often adjudged to have experienced changes in role, status, and regard in the Hellenistic period – women. The second in effect excludes institutional history, the development of public education above all. It is thus confessedly a very partial account, an exploration of one aspect of a complex reality only.

To return to my hypotheses: the first lends itself to a simple quantitative test. In Table 9.1, I set out the results of an investigation of the frequency of common words for 'child' in each of these four authors. The figures for Polybius derive from the first five books only; the rest of his work, extensive though it is, has been preserved through selections and chance allusions, and so may represent the concerns of later readers and excerptors rather than of Polybius himself. (For example, M, who collected the excerpts *de sententiis*, appears to have had no interest in geography and therefore omitted all of book 34.) The first column gives the numbers of words in the text of the *Thesaurus Linguae Graecae* (University of California, Irvine). The second, third and fourth provide the number of occurrences of *teknon*, of *pais*, and of *paidion*, *paidarion*, and *paidiskos/paidiskê*; the fifth the totals of these words. The sixth column calculates their frequency, reported as a ratio of the number of instances per one thousand words. The figures for Herodotus include only those instances of *pais* which Powell (1960) lists under 'boy' and 'girl' and those of *teknon* in which the word certainly or probably (in my judgement) refers to children under the age of majority; the figures for the other authors likewise mean to report uses for minor children only (and not for adult sons, daughters, slaves or *erômenoi*, or for the young of animals). There is obviously a danger that my own errors of judgement, as well as the use of criteria that may differ from Powell's, may distort the figures somewhat, and some minors who enter the narratives are not designated by any of the words in the table (e.g. at Xenophon, *Hellenica* 3.1.14). But the degree of error is unlikely to skew the results in any significant way. For these are clear enough.

Table 9.1 Frequency of words for child in four authors

	words	teknon	pais	paidion (etc.)	total	frequency per thousand words
Herodotus	189,489	15	77	47	139	0.73
Thucydides	153,292	–	28	–	28	0.18
Xenophon, *Hellenica*	67,939	–	14	2	16	0.24
Polybius 1–5	134,551	14	26	–	40	0.30

Herodotus refers to children much more often than the other three authors. Polybius comes second, but it is a distant second, much closer to Xenophon and Thucydides; in fact, the differences in their usage are not statistically significant. There is no evidence here, then, to support the hypothesis of a change in interest over time.

I now move on to the second hypothesis, the existence of a change in attitude. What kind of change should we be looking for? Authorities speak of a new realism at the same time as they identify a richer sentimentality: such labels may reveal most about those who apply them. It's safer, I think, to remain vague, and simply to say that the change involves emotional sensitivity, a stronger reaction to the mention or presentation of children in historical narrative, more joy or sorrow, more amusement or pity than before. Though stated in more or less quantitative terms, such a shift is less easy to demonstrate or rule out by statistics. It is certainly suggestive that only Herodotus and Polybius use *teknon*; the word has emotive connotations as early as Homer, connotations which persist in *koinê* (Golden 1985, Stanton 1988). Its absence from *Hellenica* may reflect Xenophon's self-conscious continuation of the history of Thucydides, since it occurs regularly in his other works (including a few times in *Anabasis*). Here again similarities cut across periods. But the implications of this finding for attitudes towards children should probably not be pressed: as Stanton remarks, *pais* and *teknon* often seem synonymous in Ptolemaic letters and wills (Stanton 1988: 469–70), and Polybius too can use them interchangeably (3.98.9, 10; 38.20.7, 8, cf. Thury 1988: 305, n. 9 on Euripides).

One final quantitative indicator sometimes appealed to in respect to attitudes is the order in which women and children are presented in phrases which group them alone or in longer lists. The earlier in order (runs the usual assumption), the higher the value (Wiedemann 1983: 164, Sealey 1990: 1–3), though it's not altogether easy to be convinced by this, given the inconsistencies of word order in passages such as Thucydides 2.6.4, 72.2 and 78.3 (on the women and children of the Plataeans) and 5.3.4, 32.1 and 116.4 (on the enslavement of the women and children of Torone, Scione, and Mende; cf. Harvey 1985: 78). At any rate, children are almost always mentioned before women in Herodotus (sixteen of nineteen times), in about two times in three (thirteen of nineteen) in Thucydides, and in both cases in *Hellenica*. In Polybius, however, the numbers are more nearly equal. Women and children (almost always *tekna*) appear together in some thirty-three passages in his histories. (Here I take my figures from the whole of Polybius' text on the grounds that the excerpts are as likely as other manuscripts to preserve his wording.) Children come first just over half the time, in nineteen places in all, the lowest proportion among the four historians. In some cases, it is tempting to explain the priority of women as exceptions to a general rule: so there is a tendency to mention a specific man's wife before his children (10.34.10, 35.2, 31.17.2, 38.16.10), and at least one passage (in which Chaeron despoils the sisters, wives, mothers, and children of Spartan exiles of their property (24.7.3)), seems to imply an ascending order of importance (cf. 28.14.4, Thucydides 7.69.2). It may also be true that passages where women go unnoticed – such as the description of the desperate men of Aegeira, fighting on behalf of their fatherland and their children (4.58.7, cf. 6.52.7) – are as significant as those in which they follow children. On the whole, however, it is best to leave such special pleading aside and to acknowledge that this evidence does not support the hypothesis that Polybius' work reflects more sensitivity to children than that of earlier historians, in comparison with women at least.

A quick survey of the presentations of children in these historians may be more revealing. Herodotus' text testifies to close observation. Anxious to learn which of the world's peoples is the oldest, king Psammetichus of Egypt shuts up two new-borns in an isolated hut and orders his principal investigator, a shepherd, to report on their first language; the research protocol carefully instructs him to wait until their meaningless babble has stopped (*apallakhthentôn tôn asêmôn knyzêmatôn*, 2.2; Golden 1995). Nor is it only baby speech which interests the historian. Among his 'rare but consistently positive presentations of children' (Lateiner 1989: 137), the advice of Gorgo, age 8 or 9, saves her royal father from yielding to the blandishments of Aristagoras and embroiling Sparta in the Ionian revolt (5.49–51). Here a child's intervention has an oracular force. (So too Cambyses offers his mother spirited and prophetic support at the age of about 10 (3.3).) Another child, the new-born Cypselus, smiles by divine chance (*theiêi tykhêi*) at the men who've come to kill him; in pity, they relent just long enough for his mother to hide him away and so begin the fulfilment of his prophesied greatness

(5.92γ). The infant is thus partly responsible for his own survival. But of course it is the murderers' response which is crucial, and in other places too Herodotus plays on the pathos of innocent and defenceless children. Most moving, perhaps, is the omen which presages the Chian defeat at the hands of Lesbos: a roof falls in at a local school, and all but one of 120 children are killed (6.27).

Thucydides does not link children with the gods in this way, though the fugitive Themistocles is shown taking the young son of the king of the Molossians and sitting with him at the hearth – the most potent form of supplication (1.136–37). The boy's role is akin to that of hostages (1.115.3, 5.77, cf. 2.72.2). Other children of wartime are objects of care or vengeance, sent away (1.89.3, 2.6.4, 78.3, 4.123.4) or taken within the walls (2.14.1) for protection, appealed to in exhortations to soldiers (7.68.2, 69.2, cf. 8.74.3), enslaved in the sack of cities (5.3.4, 32.1, 116.4, cf. 3.36.2). They often share the lot of women. Generally dispassionate, the narrative introduces a note of pathos in the account of the Thracian rampage at Mycalessus (7.29). The slaughter of schoolchildren is 'a disaster inferior to none that had ever befallen the city as a whole, and beyond any other unexpected and terrible', and its horror is accentuated by the detail that the children had just entered the school: they might easily have escaped the Thracians altogether. In one exceptional circumstance, children are allotted a more active role: Themistocles advises his fellow citizens to rebuild the walls of Athens – they themselves, their wives, and their children (1.90.3). The phrase is sometimes excised as an interpolation, but variations occur elsewhere as well, of the helots on Mount Ithome, the Aeginetans, and the Potidaeans, all in contexts of forced migration (1.103.3, 2.27.1, 70.3); and the return of women and children from their refuges is mentioned just before in the context of refortifying the city (1.89.3).

Xenophon is unsurprisingly similar. We find exhortation (2.4.17) and pathos, when Anaxilaus pleads that he helped betray Byzantium only because he saw children and women dying of hunger (1.3.19). To the horrifying deaths at Mycalessus we may compare the slaughter of the children of the Theban oligarchs, characterized by the intensive *kai* and the verb *apesphaksan* (5.4.12). The reference to small children's fear of bogeys, *mormones*, is in keeping with their defencelessness (4.4.17). Here too we find a child with unusual initiative, the son of Pharnabazus who makes Agesilaus his *ksenos* (4.1.39). The boy, we are told, is still beautiful, a reminder that Xenophon (unlike Thucydides in this) displays a lively interest in the attractions of young men and their effects (cf. 3.1.14, 4.1.6, 40, 5.4.25, 57, 6.4.37).

Polybius presents a more complex picture. In contrast to the great classical historians, he seems much concerned with the stages of life, their natures, and relationships. Consequently, he often notes exact ages (for examples, see de Foucault 1972: 103) and draws attention to what is appropriate (such as Artabazanes' fear, 5.55.10) and what is unexpected (Masinissa fathers a child in his mid-eighties, 36.16.5). These examples involve the old. Polybius is more interested, however, in the young (see Eckstein 1995: 140–50). Commanders' youth is remarked, and often needs explanation (1.8.3, 2.36.3, 3.71.6, 8.10.8, 18.12.5, cf. 24.6.5, on his own youth as an ambassador); sometimes it proves problematic, even disastrous (5.85.11, 9.17.9). No wonder, given the qualities Polybius ascribes to *neoi*, *neôteroi* and *neaniskoi*: lack of self-control, inexperience and indiscretion, naïvety, passion and savagery (2.8.9, 21.2, 4.3.5, 5.12.5, 75.4, 10.11.8, 15.25.31, 16.21.1, 34.6, 23.2.2, 31.11.7, 32.5.8). Youth excuses many faults (5.12.5, 7.13.3): so it is among Scipio's distinctions to show care and discretion even as a young man (10.6.10, 9.1, 40.6); among Philip's that he belies the low expectations inspired by his youth (4.22.5, 82.1, 5.16.2, 18.6, 26.4, 29.1). Yet young men can be vigorous too (21.29.11), and Polybius relates a number of events which highlight their initiative and daring (if not necessarily their judgement): *neoi* and *neaniskoi* murder members of the pro-Macedon party at Sparta (4.22, 34–35), denounce Apelles to Aratus (4.76.8), try to break into king Philip's quarters (5.25.3), force king Lycurgus into exile (5.29.9), and feature prominently in the capture of Tarentum (8.24.10(9)ff.). In some passages, it is possible that *neaniskoi* and its cognates merely refer to soldiers without distinction of age (so Walbank 1957: 96 on 1.36.12, 1979: 93 on 21.3b.2, and elsewhere). But youth is clearly at issue in civilian contexts (e.g. of *neaniskoi* at 4.20.7, of the *neôteroi* opposed to the *presbyteroi* at 4.53.7) and in others too: when *neaniskoi* offer their general, Scipio, a girl of surpassing beauty, he declines with thanks, on the grounds (as Polybius supposes) that such diversions are a delight for *neoi* at times of leisure, but hardly proper for him (10.19.3–7). Still elsewhere, *neaniskos* is a synonym for *meirakion* (23.2.4, 3.5, 3.8 and 3.6; 31.23.5 and 24.1, 11, 12; it can describe young men as old as 30, 4.20.7; see Sacco 1979).

Polybius is persuaded that the early years of life are crucial for the establishment of sound character, or its reverse (1.32.1, 81.10, 4.20.8–10, 6.8.4, 11a.7, 10.22(25).3, 24.7.1, cf. 3.71.6, 89.5, 12.22.5); the beginning, after all, is half the whole, and even more (5.32.1–4). It is the historian's duty, therefore, to set out the upbringing and instruction of his subjects – Polybius' prior biography of Philopoemen excuses his failure to treat this theme here (10.21.5). To some extent, the need for training must stem from a belief that children have significant shortcomings. No one could expect the very young to have sense; 'common gossip' in Chaereas and Sosylus (a barbershop duet) depends on the Romans' being able to reason straight from birth – quite impossible (3.20.1–5). But even at 17, Philip is unlikely to have delivered judgement on the Spartans in his own words (4.24.1, cf. 5.4.13, 22.8). Philip, to be sure, matured fast – we have already noted his moderation as a young man. So, though the Aetolians expect to find him like a baby, *hôs paidiôi nêpiôi*, in his youth and inexperience, they themselves are exposed as easily despised and childish (*paidariôdeis*, 5.29.2). Similarly, when the Carthaginian general Bostar allows himself to be tricked into releasing young hostages, he acts more like a child than his own age (*paidikôteron ê kata tên hêlikian*, 3.99.8). These and other adjectives and adverbs formed from the root *paid-* regularly connote foolishness and naïvety (4.17.1, 42.7, 12.3.2, 25k.9, 16.12.6, 27.2.10, cf. 15.6.8; so too *meirakiôdês*, 8.11(13).2, 10.33.6, 11.14.7, 12.25i.5, 25k.2, 26d.6).

However, when Hannibal, at 9, begs to accompany his father on campaign, he does so *paidikôs*, with a boy's eagerness (3.11.7): in Polybius, as in Herodotus, children may affect the action. Here too the young Scipio is extraordinary, saving his father from death in battle at 17 (10.3.3). (Hasdrubal's daughter, a *paidiskê*, prevails on her husband Scyphax not to deport the Carthaginians at 14.7.6; we may think of Gorgo, but this girl is married, no longer a child.) It is unusual, a sign of great excitement, for less exceptional children to enter community life. When Attalus visited Athens, not only the magistrates and cavalry came to greet him, but the whole citizen body, with children and wives as well (16.25.5). Generally, Polybius disapproves. The opposition to Callicrates and Andronicus grew so great at Sicyon that even the children (*paidaria*) on the way from school called them traitors to their faces (30.29.6–7). The women of Apamea stone Hermeias' wife after his fall, and the children stone his sons (5.56.15; in Herodotus' analogous story, Lycides' wife and children are all victims of the Athenian women alone, 9.5.3). The roofs and shops of Alexandria are full of hubbub, with children and women mixed with men; indeed, *paidaria* do no less than men in such troubles at Carthage too (15.30.9–10). Significantly, Polybius is as censorious about the other side of this coin, a community's concern for the lives of children. The Rhodians should not have taken wheat from Eumenes and sold it to pay the salaries of their sons' teachers. A private person might accept such a gift from friends, in a time of temporary want, to keep his children from going untaught; but he would not beg, and still less should a state (31.31; compare the stress on children's debt of gratitude to parents, 6.6.2–5).

This sounds hard. What of sentiment? Like his classical predecessors, Polybius finds occasion to mention children held as hostages (3.98–99, 4.9.5, 8.36(2).3, 10.18.3, 34.2, 35.6, 15.18.8, 21.32.10, 28.4.7, 31.2.2, cf. 1.68.3); removed to safety (4.71.13, 21.35.3, 38.2.3); as motivations for victory (4.58.7, 6.52.7, 13.1a.3, 15.11.5); and enslaved victims of defeat (4.54.2, 9.39.3, 16.32.6). Much of this is matter of fact. Prusias routs the Gauls and puts to death nearly all their women and children, as well as allowing his men to plunder their belongings. There is nothing like pathos here; on the contrary, the exploit is 'worthy of mention', a fine demonstration for the barbarians (5.111.1–7). (Compare the brief mention of Neolaus' killing of Molon's children, 5.54.5.) Elders of Abydus are even rebuked for trying to thwart the resolve to kill their women and children rather than surrender (16.33.4, cf. Walbank 1972: 178). This is perhaps no more than we should expect from *pragmatikê historia*, the narrative of wars, of peoples and of kings, intended for the use of men of affairs like the author himself (see Sacks 1981: 72–76, 178–81);

especially when that author makes a virtue of selectivity in so large-scale a work (29.12).

But there are also traces of a more empathetic approach in the representation of children. In order to pay *eisphora* to the Achaean league, women strip the jewellery from themselves and their own children (*tôn idiôn teknôn*, 38.15.11, and cf. 15.29.13 for the phrase). Hasdrubal's wife meets Scipio holding the hands of her poorly clad children, and wraps them in her cloak (38.20.7–8). Kings die, leaving orphaned sons to succeed them (3.2.8, 7.3.6, 31.2.6–7). Enemies may take advantage, even friends. Antiochus IV treacherously attacks Ptolemy VI Philometor though he is a teenager, *paidiskon onta* (30.26.9, cf. Diodorus Siculus 30.18.2, 31.1, *meirakion*, Porphyry of Tyre *FGrH* 260 F 49a, *puer*). When Ptolemy IV Philopator dies, it is the duty of Philip and Antiochus III to help his young heir, Epiphanes; instead, they scheme to divide his kingdom. Though the boy is in fact as old as 4 or 5, he is called *paidion nêpion* as if he were an infant, and the diminutive *paidion* is again used for effect when Agathocles takes him in his arms to curry sympathy from the Macedonian troops (15.26.3, cf. 32.7).

Emotive diction is also evident later in the account of Agathocles' end. Young girls, *paidiskai*, who had been raised with Arsinoë, storm the home of her murderer, beat him to death, strangle his son, drag his wife into the public square, and kill her (15.33.12). The son is *antipais*, only just older than a boy. Agathocles' downfall is all the more interesting in that it includes a drunken henchman, naked women (one on horseback), eyes gouged out and bodies torn limb from limb – the stuff of melodrama – only to conclude with Polybius' pious comment that he has told the story with exemplary restraint and brevity (15.34). If this is sober and instructive narrative, what is sensationalism?

This swift sketch of Polybius' representations of childhood and children tends in the same direction as the quantitative data; he is very like Thucydides and Xenophon, but perhaps closer than they to Herodotus. Despite his unusual emphasis on youth and the activities of the young, children rarely play a part in the preserved portions of his history, and their attributes – simplicity, lack of sense – do not suggest more interest or a higher opinion. In this respect, in Walbank's words, 'Polybius stands for a return to the aims and methods of Thucydides; and this means that his work is in many ways somewhat traditional and even old-fashioned' (Walbank 1972: 40). But there is another side as well, since children do appear in emotive passages, and these are more frequent and more elaborate than those of Thucydides and Xenophon. Now, it is possible that these pathetic portrayals of children are a reflection of the increasing sentimentality of the Hellenistic age, so much a part of Polybius' environment that it influenced even so austere an author. If so, we should expect to find plenty of examples in other Hellenistic historians. Polybius himself provides a critical commentary on one: the capture of Mantinea according to Phylarchus, with (among other appeals to horror and pity) women clinging; their hair dishevelled and breasts bare; adults, children, and aged parents weeping and lamenting as they are led off into slavery (2.56.7 = *FGrH* 81 F 53). (Polybius thinks the Mantineans got what they deserved, and so warrant no pity. As for the women and children, presumably innocent of the treachery which provoked this verdict – well, their fate is the norm in war even for those who haven't committed such impiety: 2.58.9–10, cf. Ničev 1978: 153, n. 6.)

It turns out, however, that such purple passages are rare in the remains of Polybius' Hellenistic predecessors and contemporaries (or near contemporaries) collected by Jacoby (*FGrH*); the vivid description of the quandary of the Messenian royal fathers – destined to save their people only at the cost of the sacrifice of a *parthenos* – is an exception (Myron of Priene 106 F 10). Elsewhere, children figure (along with women again) as real or potential victims of war (Nearchus 133 F 32, Ptolemy Lagou 138 F 1, F 3, Hegesias 142 F 16, Eupolemus 724 F 1) and in brief appeals for pity (Neanthes 84 F 36, Timonides 561 F 1). Their fates, even when horrific – killed at two months because they don't meet Cathaean standards of beauty (Onesicritus 134 F 21), sacrificed at Carthage (Cleitarchus 137 F 9), swept away in a storm (Aristobulus of Cassandreia 139 F 49a), tortured, like the wives and children of the tyrants of Erythrae (Hippias 421 F 1) – are presented soberly and succinctly. Though Timaeus too recounts the tale of a school disaster, the emphasis (in Tzetzes' version anyway) is on Gelon's miraculous escape from the earthquake, not on the deaths of the one hundred or so less lucky (566 F 95 = Tzetzes, *Chiliades* 4.266ff.).

Nevertheless, it is also true that the fragments of Hellenistic historiography from the period down to about 150 BCE reveal motifs foreign to Polybius as we have him. Phylarchus himself evinces an interest in the close attachments of children and animals – elephants rock an infant's cradle (81 F 36), a boy raises an eagle 'like a lover or a younger brother' and is tended by it in turn (81 F 61a, cf. the asp, 81 F 27). (It is worth recalling here that Gelon was saved by a wolf.) Ptolemy Euergetes II writes about king Masinissa, who delighted in children and raised the many children of his sons and daughters until they were 3, then replacing them with others. Astonished by the Sybarites' passion for pets, he asked, 'Don't your women bear children (*paidia*)?' (234 F 8). Duris offers glimpses of nursery life: Timaea calling her baby 'Alcibiades' after his real father (76 F 69), Leto holding Apollo in her arms (76 F 79). His version of Eumenes' rise from poverty to power – an account Plutarch does not believe – depends on Philip's admiration of his intelligence and bravery as a boy wrestler (76 F 53 = Plutarch, *Eumenes* 1). Aristobulus says all Telmissians, children too, have the gift of divination (139 F 7a).

The implication, that Polybius is as sentimental in his portrayal of children as other historians of this period, but perhaps more narrow, is reinforced by a look at some Hellenistic lives of Plutarch (*Aemilius Paullus, Agis and Cleomenes, Aratus, Cato Maior, Demetrius, Eumenes, Fabius Maximus,*

Flamininus, Marcellus, Philopoemen, Pyrrhus). In Plutarch too we find adults, like Masinissa, who value children, at least their own. Cato showed great interest in his son right from birth, taking pains to be present when he was bathed and swaddled, and saw to his education as soon as he showed signs of understanding (*Cato Maior* 20.2–6). Aemilius Paullus, most *philoteknos* of the Romans, attended to his sons' studies unless public business prevented (*Aem.* 6.8–10), embraced his little daughter (*thygatrion*) when he found her in tears (10.6–8), and agonized at the apparent loss of his younger boy, *eti d'antipaida tên hêlikian*, after the battle of Pydna (22.2–7). The daughter, Tertia, unwittingly provides a good omen for that victory. Spartan *parthenoi* join adult women in a more conscious contribution to their city's safety, digging a defensive trench (*Pyrrhus* 27.3). The actions of other children are described for their emotive effect. Again in the life of Aemilius, Perseus tries to escape from Samothrace along with his wife and children, inexperienced as these are in wanderings and hardships (*Aem.* 26.4). After his defeat, his two boys and a girl figure in Aemilius' triumph. Barely aware of their misfortune *dia tên hêlikian*, they must be taught to make supplications, evoking so much pity from the onlookers that the pleasure of the spectacle is mixed with pain until *ta paidia* pass (33.6–8). Chilonis' children cling to her as she begs for her husband's life (*Agis* 17.1–4); tearful women and children of Sicyon embrace Aratus as a common father and saviour (*Aratus* 42.1, cf. the children who join other citizens in welcoming Philopoemen's body back to Megalopolis, *Philop.* 21.4). Aratus himself, narrowly escaping death at the hands of his father's killer at age 7, wanders frightened and helpless through the streets of Sicyon before he is taken in by a woman who sends him to safety (*Aratus* 2.2–3). At the news of Cleomenes' death, his mother Cratesicleia comforts *ta paidia*, but the older boy springs away and throws himself headlong from the roof. He survives only to die with his brother at Ptolemy's command, deaths Cratesicleia is forced to witness. 'Oh children', she cries as she too is killed, 'where have you gone?' (*Cleom.* 38.1–5).

One extended episode combines pathos and interest in ringing changes on a story we have already met in Thucydides. This concerns Pyrrhus, future king of Epirus. When faction fighting among the Molossians forced his father Aeacides to flee, Pyrrhus, still an infant (*eti nêpion onta*), was spirited away. After a stirring journey, enlivened, among other adventures, by messages written on bark and rescue by a man called Achilles, the fugitives came to the home of Glaucias, king of the Illyrians, and his wife. Pyrrhus was put on the floor before the royal couple. It was by no means certain that he had found security: Glaucias had to consider Cassander, Aeacides' enemy. As he pondered his options, Pyrrhus crept forward of his own accord, grabbed the king's robe, and pulled himself to his feet at Glaucias' knees. Glaucias laughed and then cried to see the baby seemingly supplicating him in this way, and put him in the arms of his wife, to bring him up with their own children. Plutarch provides a variant, that Pyrrhus clasped an altar, a sign Glaucias was

189

quick to see. In either case, however, the point is that the baby Pyrrhus is largely responsible for his own good fortune; furthermore, at least in the first tale, Glaucias decides as he does in response to the charm of the child's actions, and not merely (as in the similar story of Themistocles) because of the situation of supplication itself (*Pyrrhus* 2.1–3.3).

Plutarch's use of these stories is his own; that Perseus and Aemilius both have children but different fates as commanders and fathers is a thread that binds the biography together. Nor can we be sure that his sources for any one are Hellenistic or even historical (by whatever criterion); indeed, we can sometimes be certain that they are not (Tertia comes from Cicero's *De Divinatione* (*Aem.* 10.8)). Nevertheless, it seems a reasonable assumption that some of his material involving children goes back (without attribution) to the same Hellenistic historians whose work I have already discussed or to their unidentifiable contemporaries; though I would not go so far as to argue that he used everything he found or found everything there was (as Pelling 1990: 224–25). If this is so, it represents a tradition that was available to Polybius, but which he chose not to exploit. It therefore confirms the impression that we have formed: that he shared some contemporaries' predilection for the pathetic representation of children but was less willing to depict them in a positive light as objects of others' enjoyment or as subjects in their own right.

Can these data save the hypothesis regarding the discovery of real or amusing or pathetic children in the Hellenistic period or its cultural products? Indeed they can. We might suppose that Polybius' apparent low regard for children is the consequence of his conscious imitation of models like Thucydides and Xenophon, while pathos betrays the insidious influence of his own time. It is also conceivable that children appeared in more guises in Polybius' full text than they do in ours, dependent as it is after book 5 on the interests of Byzantine excerptors (see W. Thompson 1985 for an excellent discussion of the general issue). Perhaps, to put the case at its strongest, Polybius was as unwilling to admit children into his work as Thucydides and Xenophon but more prone to use them to arouse pathos (for both of which propositions we have found evidence) and more apt to present them in a variety of ways (for which we haven't). Still, no definition of the Hellenistic period is elastic enough to include Herodotus, and pathos and variety (as we have seen) play a part in his history too. Why shouldn't Hasdrubal's children, Ptolemy Epiphanes, the son of Agathocles be his progeny as well (cf. Walbank 1972: 37–38)? Once more it seems that alleged Hellenistic characteristics may be found in the classical period. An alternative hypothesis is possible, even preferable. Classical Athens' politico-military historians of interstate relations in the Greek world found a Hellenistic follower in Polybius; the more varied and receptive researches of their near contemporary, Herodotus, proved more congenial to other later writers. Perhaps the tendency to overlap grew as time went on (cf. Hutchinson 1988: 11–25). Polybius himself offers evidence that this is so. In one of his many *obiter dicta* on the historian's task,

Polybius praises vividness in the discussion of politics and warfare, as it assures the reader that the author has some experience of such things. So too those who treat everyday life, *peri biôtikôn*, ought to leave the impression that they have raised children and lived with a woman; it's essential for a writer to know both what matters most and what is commonest (12.25h.5). This sounds like a man with a private as well as a public life. If he occasionally chose to admit feelings from one into the narrative and analysis of the other, his history is the better for it. But our confidence in the usual assumption, that more interest in and different sentiments towards children are defining characteristics of the Hellenistic age, need not thereby be increased. A disappointing result, no doubt. It may seem less meagre if I draw a moral from it: Much of our sense of what is new in the Hellenistic world may be an effect of genre. We must therefore control as much as possible for genre in testing hypotheses about change in attitudes and *mentalité*. Often enough, as in this case, change will become more difficult to demonstrate.

NOTE

1 Versions of this chapter were presented to the Cambridge Philological Society and to a seminar at Corpus Christi College, Oxford in early 1995. I am grateful to members of both audiences, and to Martin Kilmer, Amy Richlin, and Mac Wallace, for encouragement and advice.

10

DID ROMAN WOMEN HAVE AN EMPIRE?

Phyllis Culham

Readers of women's history will at once recognize this question as a variant of Joan Kelly's influential 'Did women have a Renaissance?' (1984: 19–50). Castle has since asked whether women had an Enlightenment (1985: 12–13). Hallett has faulted the study of antiquity for the 'privileging of certain historical periods ... solely on the basis of evidence about men's lives' and pointed to Kelly's results (Hallett 1993: 46). It may well prove rewarding to import Kelly's type of enquiry into the history of Rome. When Kelly posed her famous question, she suggested that one of the functions of women's history was to call into question accepted schemes of periodization. Integration of women's history (often treated as a type of social history) with political history (conventionally periodized by reign and dynasty) may produce results which help us understand both women and politically defined eras better.

If one went by a number of recent books on women's history, one would have to conclude that women did not even have a Rome, let alone an empire. The immensely popular *A History of Their Own* treats Greeks and Romans as a unitary ancient blob along with Hebrews and German tribes (Anderson and Zinsser 1988). Even the more professionally sophisticated *A History of Women in the West* eschews anything so simplistic as a chronological survey within neat periods (Duby and Perrot 1992). In the case of Gerda Lerner's two volumes, *The Creation of Patriarchy* (1986) and *The Creation of Feminist Consciousness* (1993), both the republic and the empire seem to have been lost in the gap between the volumes. One can only conclude that a number of authors who varied in historiographical sophistication and in knowledge of antiquity saw no connection between the 'accomplishments' of Rome as they are generally outlined in Western civilization textbooks in chapters headed republic and empire and the history of women in the West. So much for the law codes, the Pax Romana, and the universal empire.

Historians of Rome are understandably less prone to subsume Rome into a vaguely Graeco-Roman mish-mash, but have had to counter a long estrangement, if not an actual divorce, between political history and the history of Roman women. Evans decried what he still believed to be the contemporary treatment of Roman women 'divorced from the issues of perennial concern to the broader community of political and social historians of Rome' (1991: x; I have argued elsewhere that the situation is not as dire as Evans envisions (Culham 1993)). Other recent writers have attempted to integrate women's history and political history by introducing neat periodization into the history of Roman women. Kokkinos identified a women's century – a period when women had access to power – from 44 BCE to 68 CE. Kokkinos isolates this period on the basis of the number of semi-legendary 'female figures' we hear about in that period (1992: 3). In other words, his periodization is driven by his sources' use of literary and rhetorical motifs. Bauman's *Women and Politics in Ancient Rome* (1992) explicitly periodizes all of Roman women's history through the early principate into five phases. For Bauman, women even had a distinct era defined by the triumvirs. Women's subsequent era happens to coincide neatly with the Julio-Claudian dynasty. Others have headed in the opposite direction. Dixon just as explicitly eschews periodizing women's history, describing what Richlin elsewhere in this volume calls 'the strongly felt need to find watersheds' as a 'habit' retained from early training, and not, she implies, a good one. In fact, Dixon cites Kelly's question about the Renaissance specifically to call into question whether or not it is worthwhile to distinguish republican and imperial eras in women's history (1992: 17, cf. Hallett 1993: 65).

I suspect that this periodization on the part of both modern and ancient historians of Rome is owing to the exigencies of personal history which left the first Flavians, Vespasian and Titus, without imperial consorts or daughters and thereby left us with fewer colourful anecdotes. I will concur below with many of Bauman's reasons for viewing the advent of Augustus as important to women, yet will reserve the suspicion that any truly important developments under Augustus would have had continuing social force later. Many others will agree with Kokkinos and Bauman that the ancient sources legitimately set the agenda and frame our conceptualization. Looking at the question at the top of this essay, one instantly thinks of Sir Ronald Syme, confronting again, nearly two generations after *The Roman Revolution*, the transformation of alleged republic to undoubted empire. In his *The Augustan Aristocracy* he clearly aligned himself with those who believe that ancient authors' organization of the data sets our agenda and authorizes certain questions. There he asserts, 'As always, material determines treatment', a claim partly belied by his observation that 'oligarchy is imposed as the guiding theme' (Syme 1986: 13). One can see why Galsterer, speaking of Syme on the Roman Revolution, referred to a 'typically English reluctance to pursue questions that are not explicitly dealt with and thus "legitimized" by our ancient sources', although one may suspect Galsterer meant English-speaking rather than literally English (1990: 19).

Sir Ronald was not unselfconscious in adopting this stance. His ironic comment, 'Women have their uses for the historian. They offer relief from warfare, legislation, and the history of ideas' (Syme 1986: 168), stands beside his defence of the last years of the republic against a charge of decadence. How do we measure 'vigour, innovation, enlightenment'? The answer: 'Poetry and oratory bear witness – or the position of women' (ibid.: 443). Syme was a political historian whose work rested partly upon his ability to uncover social networks. Therefore we should not take too seriously his wisecrack which identifies women's history with social history and assumes for the sake of the joke that this is lightweight subject matter compared to the traditional concerns of political history. His more serious methodological comment explicitly lifts women's history on to a level with grand cultural and intellectual history and thereby makes it a standard by which a whole culture or society may be found deficient or advanced. That is a sweeping historiographic claim which rejects older beliefs in the 'decadence' or even 'degeneracy' of Roman morals during and after the loss of allegedly austere republican mores, such decadence always understood to involve bold conduct by women.

Syme's claim for the utility of women's history responds indirectly to Kelly's reason for broaching the subject of periodization. In that essay, published originally in 1977, Kelly asserted, 'To take the emancipation of women as a vantage point is to discover that events that further the historical development of men, liberating them from natural, social, or ideological constraints, have quite different, even opposite, effects upon women' (Kelly 1984: 19). Syme's position is not the reverse or the obverse of Kelly's. It is a Romanist variation on Whig history: To examine emancipation (in this case, that of women) is to have a yardstick by which one can measure progress and therefore mark off eras. Syme's belief that 'the position of women' was considerably better in some way at the end of the republic is also at odds with Dixon's scepticism about periodization and about whether women's history needs to distinguish empire from republic.

Much older literature took for granted a process of 'emancipation' of women in the republic (see Arthur 1977 on the literature and the concept), a process to which the empire was presumably a mere afterthought. We have already noted Kokkinos' 'women's century' spanning the transitional period and Bauman's use of the usual periodization into late republic, triumvirate, and early empire as alternative ways of organizing our evidence. Still others have suggested that Augustus' creation of the empire was of significance to women, and that is the thread of reasoning I wish to follow, at first summarizing briefly arguments I have offered elsewhere on the nature of the Augustan programme (Culham 1988 and 1992).

First, as Syme himself noted, Augustus aspired to mark off a political–social élite which clearly merited respect. He especially wanted generally perceived status and publicly assigned rank to match closely. The Roman public still had a great deal of nostalgic fondness, if not respect, for the old republican élite (Levick 1985: 58–60), and Augustus needed that élite to occupy rungs on the new social ladders, openly taking their places as servitors of his regime. His new order would thereby borrow legitimacy from their acquiescence. At the same time, his creation of new offices and opportunities to display rank offered more and safer outlets for the competition for status which had, unchecked, ultimately destroyed the republic.

It is clear enough how Augustus wished to be understood publicly. From his 'restoration' of public affairs to the senate and the Roman people in 27 BCE through his establishment of senatorial officials to monitor the grain supply in 22 BCE, highways in 20 BCE, aqueducts in 12 BCE, public works in 11 BCE, oversight for the banks of the Tiber in 15 CE, and his addition of new introductory offices to a redrawn *cursus honorum* in 13 BCE, Augustus made it clear that Roman senators were to be seen assuming duties. At least some of these new officials were ceremoniously preceded by lictors, as Augustus sought explicit authorization for these innovations in *senatus consulta* and insisted that holders of the new *officia* be consistently of praetorian or even consular rank (Dio 54.8.4, Frontinus, *Aq.* 100–01). Suetonius distinguishes the new *officia* from previous *honores* or *magistratus* (*Aug.* 37: Culham 1988: 8–9). Augustus made a great display of returning many functions to the senate, consulting them, and securing their participation whenever possible.

These new posts made political rank of and among senators more manifest in publicly displayed status and function. This sequence of events might initially appear to be a series of administrative changes of limited significance even when viewed in the context of political history. In actuality, this part of Augustus' political programme had cumulative consequences for women also. Augustan marriage legislation slighted or rewarded men by enhancing or retarding (depending on their marital and reproductive choices) their ability to advance quickly within the new structure of clearly ranked jobs (modern literature is summarized in Treggiari 1991: 60–80). One consequence of this new legislative and political formalization of a senatorial status and rank hierarchy was that senators were kept from marrying freedwomen and thereby publicly compromising the special status Augustus wanted to claim for their group. As Richlin commented elsewhere, 'Augustus was trying to legislate shame into the upper class' (1981: 399; much of the evidence is in *Digest* 23.2 *De Ritu Nuptiarum* and 48.5 *Ad Legem Juliam de Adulteriis Coercendis*, but note Richlin ibid. on the difficulty of using the *Digest* to reconstruct Augustan legislation).

On the other hand, the very seriousness with which élite procreation and the birth of potential heirs was viewed meant that some men would deliberately enter liaisons with women who could not produce children in order not to cloud the status of their one or two senatorial-rank sons. Emperors were among those who could not afford to have too many potential heirs born to too many women. The example of terribly 'respectable' emperors like Vespasian and Marcus Aurelius must have done much to encourage the *de facto* and then legal development of a status of concubinage,

195

and those later developments must be counted a direct consequence of Augustus' establishment of the principate and his subsequent administrative and legislative measures which 'crystallized' status, in modern sociological terms; first, by sharpening status distinctions and rendering them visible, and second, by attempting to create a situation in which different indicators of status (wealth, noble birth, political rank) rendered more closely matching results (Landecker 1981, Lenski 1954). Hence an impact of the most boring sort of bureaucratic/administrative history upon the marital and social prospects of contemporary women and, over the *longue durée*, on the shape and nature of Roman families.

Nor was it possible for Augustus to mark off a special élite and demand respect for them without including women of the senatorial class within the bounds. The public display of senatorial rank required that women who shared a family's status also behave in a way meriting respect. Hence Augustan legislation also banned the daughters of senators from marrying freedmen, actors, or other 'disreputable' people. Syme pointed to the real effect of these measures: by including women in the strictures, Augustus effectively created a senatorial class (1986: 80). Political, even 'eventmental' exigencies of civil war had forced Augustus in his previous incarnation as the brutal triumvir Octavian to confer tribunician sacrosanctity on his wife and his sister Octavia (*Digest* 49.38.1; *histoire événementielle*, Braudel 1975: 16). One cannot claim that this event led women to claim prerogatives based on political rank, but it certainly made it more thinkable. The consequences were again only to emerge over the long term. Women eventually even forced jurists to rule on their claims to political rank. Ulpian and others certainly had to concede that women had rank; their difficulty was in deciding whether women took rank from spouse or from father (*Digest* 1.9.1, 8). A trickle-down effect was predictable. If senatorial women attempted to claim consular status and prerogatives, it is not surprising that women one social rank down from the senatorial families claimed equestrian status (*Digest* 40.10.4). Some consequences of the melding of political rank and élite social status were on display in Italian towns under the empire (as we will note below under a discussion of building for public use) in which women of both local and international élites came to recognize and visibly demonstrate their status, often in ways that had consequences for whole communities. Augustus' political and legal formalization of rank and status gave women new weapons to use in claiming status and constructing a public role.

None the less, partial integration of the most élite women into the realm of publicly displayed political rank also deepened the pitfalls awaiting publicly visible women. The republic had already stigmatized unmatronly or unmaidenly conduct in public. Hillard has described how 'visibility' was a problem *per se* and easily led to a state in which the woman was 'overexposed' and lost all respectability (1992: 46). I will suggest that more 'eventmental' exigencies of the civil war heightened the ideological and rhetorical distinctions and raised the political stakes. Delia (1991) has pointed to the sharp contrast in Augustan propaganda between the Fulvia-type (independent, notorious, taking a hand in public and even military affairs, given to brutal reprisals) and the Octavia-type (devoted to her family, matronly, involving herself in public affairs only at the behest of her family, and seeking only peace). Flory has associated the award of statues to Livia and Octavia with this Augustan propaganda (1993: 294–96). The subsequent situation of women of the imperial household was even more fraught with opportunities to misstep over the line, since their very prominence meant that they could slide all too easily from Octavia-type to Fulvia-type by being just a shade too independent or interested in public matters. Tacitus, and perhaps his sources, certainly saw many of the imperial women as examples of the Fulvia stereotype in the now-familiar rhetorical tradition.

Augustus' political stance and legislation intensified this concern for visible respectability. In order to see that we need to return for a moment to a second feature of Augustus' emphasis on élite male rank and on the regulation of sexual liaisons to protect and mark a special senatorial status. Augustus' legislation not only barred from *honores* but even degraded a man who failed to divorce and prosecute an adulterous wife within time limits. He could be prosecuted for *lenocinium*, which in turn subjected him to *infamia*, shame, the state of being without *dignitas* or even *honestas*. In such a state he was not only barred from advancement in *honores* but even less able to undertake some types of litigation. Later commentary on this legislation in the *Digest* claims that some husbands hoped to gain rank and wealth by facilitating their wives' affairs. As Gardner noted, the complaisant, rank-conscious husband certainly became a literary stereotype (1986: 132).

Clearly, legislation which punished men by slowing or halting their political careers or depriving them of their ability to participate in legal affairs was aimed not at stopping activity considered immoral but at ensuring that Augustus' political élite appeared worthy of respect. The subjection of husbands to prosecution for *lenocinium* suggests that the primary concern was with appearance or notoriety, the shock offered the observer. One need not assume active enforcement or prosecution of offenders in order to believe that the law served to reinforce respectability. Merely labelling collaboration with adultery 'pimping' insulted those who engaged in such conduct and shaped the terms of public discourse. *Digest* 47.10, on torts such as *insultum* and *iniuria*, illustrates the legal atmosphere which developed in the empire and which treated public space as a great stage on which women appeared only at their own risk and at the risk of dishonouring their families. Acts that most Western cultures would now term assault or battery were judged severe not so much according to the physical harm or pain they caused as according to the degree to which they damaged the victim's public standing or that of her family. Insult to slaves or unemancipated daughters could subject the male or female head of their household to *iniuria*.

Iniuria was considered aggravated if it was inflicted in the public view, even if no serious physical injury resulted. The jurists distinguished among injury to *dignitas* by words (*turpia verba*), injury to the body, and injury by subjecting someone to the threat of *infamia*. Women were protected from *iniuria* offered them in public to the extent to which their appearance reflected their families' respectable status. A key term, especially for women, was *palam*, 'openly'. *Digest* 23.2 is an important instance of the imperial jurists' interpretation of the Leges Juliae. A woman could become subject to *infamia* through 'openly' shameful behaviour without ever having accepted money or frequenting taverns. On the other hand, having intercourse with multiple partners after accepting money from them was not sufficient cause for declaring that a woman had engaged in prostitution *palam*. That contrast demonstrates the importance attributed to appearance as opposed to conduct. *Infamia* for adultery is contingent upon being caught in the very act of adultery or upon conviction in a public court.

Digest 48.5, on Augustus' adultery legislation, illustrates that later jurists understood that legislation too in the light of concern for respectable status. Many modern scholars have commented on how Augustus' restrictive description of circumstances under which one might kill adulterers actually reduced the rarely exercised legal options available to republican husbands and fathers. *Digest* 48.5.24 (23) on this point claims to be a direct citation of the law. Commentators have overlooked the initially bewildering provisions of the next section (25 [24]) which appears to follow on but does not explicitly claim to be a direct citation. It conditions a husband's legal prerogative to kill a man taken in adultery with his wife upon the current or former occupation as well as the legal status of the adulterer! That certainly makes it clear that the point, at least as envisioned by the drafter of that language, was to maintain the boundaries of status groups, not to achieve moral conduct *per se*. This provision also raises a point to which we will return later: the law as normative, ideological statement rather than guide for conduct meant to be easily administered or enforced. A disreputable yet famous actor might have been instantly known to any Roman, or a slave might have been branded, but few husbands could have been expected to interrogate an unfamiliar adulterer caught in the act on his employment history and perhaps invisible legal status. This stricture is surely an ideological demarcation of status in the most dramatic rhetoric of life and death, not a literal guide to conduct and litigation. That does not mean that these politically driven legal provisions had no impact on women or on society, just that they had a different sort of impact which we will discuss later.

Certainly the Augustan era attributed this concern for appearances and for status boundaries to the republic and counted it among the *mores maiorum*. There is the famous story of Lucretia, for whom the ultimate threat was not death or rape but the thought of being found dead in bed with a slave without opportunity to clear her reputation (Livy 1.58–59). Livy's tale of Verginia echoes the theme of avoiding familial shame and descent in legal status (3.44–48). Both stories criticize unrestrained lust on the part of a political élite, and the tale of Verginia explicitly threatens the élite with loss of respect and even revolution on that account. The emergence of these themes in Livy suggests that what we find in the *Digest* is not merely the extrapolation of later jurists but part and parcel of Augustan normative ideology on élite restraint and concern for reputation.

Real life on the streets of Rome contrasted strongly with the ideology of clear status boundaries. The senate's proposal that Livia be accompanied by a lictor demonstrates the extent to which women's presence in public space had been 'problematized' by this status crystallization and the degree to which Augustus had rendered some of the old lines and rules obsolete. We saw earlier how he had partially assimilated women into political ranking, and Livia's proposed lictor is a result, whether Tacitus is right in thinking that Tiberius disapproved him (*An.* 1.14.23) or Dio is correct in thinking that she got him (56.46.2). Augustus' adoption of Livia in his will (noted in the same passages) raised the difficult question of how to mark her special status. Even if the senate had been flattering Tiberius or teasing him, Augustus' own attribution of a prerogative of political rank to women, e.g. the tribunician sacrosanctity, made the lictor thinkable or suggested it as a joke.

This problem of displaying their rank must have affected all élite women in Rome and perhaps other cities. Women of all classes generally lived in close proximity. One type of house ubiquitous throughout Italy incorporated income-producing shops fronting the streets and lodgings for the shop-keepers above them. The wealthier family which owned the property shared common walls with the shopkeepers and passed the shops on their way in and out. They also shared the lack of light, air, and privacy guaranteed by the peristyle-like opening in the building. Naïvety about the lifestyles of those of different status would have been impossible. Later buildings were meant to provide what has been labelled vertical segregation, i.e. shops on the ground floor, tenement apartments above them, well-lit airy penthouses near the top. Admittedly, smaller cities and newer ones like Ostia could provide additional segregation also by having more separate residential and commercial quarters (Packer 1967, Frier 1980). But ideology and law emerged from Rome itself to have an impact on others. The fascinating vignette of Dio (58.2.4), in which Livia encountered a couple of naked men, may provide us with a brief insight into the sort of thing from which élite women could not really be protected if they ever ventured into an *insula* to visit anyone. For that matter, the élite *domus* with its intermingling of public and private sections and functions might have been the stage for some awkward encounters (Wallace-Hadrill 1988). Dio, or more likely his source, appears to be using some sort of collection of *apophthegmata* of Livia at that point, perhaps something like that posited for Julia by Richlin, but this one appealing to supporters of the regime rather than subversives (1992a: 76). The anecdote gives us no idea why or where this encounter occurred, nor does Dio express any surprise that it happened. Nor does he suggest that Livia was assaulted, nor intruded upon, nor that the encounter was other than accidental, yet the two men were to be killed, he claims. Probably legal execution was not in question; the verb is the nondescript *thanatoô*. Livia's attendants may have detained them and been about to dispatch them informally, horrified at this insult to imperial *pudor*. Livia is said to have saved them by remarking that to a chaste woman they were no more offensive than statues.

If my contextualization of the incident is accepted, it demonstrates male uneasiness about how to handle the movement of élite women outside their quarters as well as the belief of one imperial woman that some men were capable of overreacting. Livia may even have been claiming success at meeting Augustus' social aims in that she had achieved such a state of chastity that impure thoughts could not intrude upon her mind, or she could have been asserting a right to move about outside her *domus*, even if others feared for her sensibilities. The reference to statues, most of which must have been in public places, emphasized that she was accustomed to the sights of Rome. Or in the alternative, a Roman author who was not above putting words in Livia's mouth thought these plausible sentiments to attribute to the *domina* of *dominae*.

In this physical milieu, women could not have maintained their status by living in a distant, distinctive neighbourhood nor by driving a luxury car. Social distance and rank were marked by dress, and litters, and some personal distance maintained by throngs of attendants. Women who took such measures to display their status were legally protected from being followed, crowded, or addressed with the *turpia verba* mentioned above. Such behaviours were offensive precisely because they made the victim appear to be the kind of woman whom a man might accost. Women of such high status that they were surrounded by attendants received special attention in that the law attempted to protect their attendants from being accosted by strangers (*Digest* 47.10). As these women moved about surrounded by *pedisequae*, neither they nor bystanders can have been unmindful of their status for a minute. For women, the situation was double-edged. Travel in the street offered an opportunity to display their rank; on the other hand the constant presence of attendants did restrict their own conduct. Some households had a set of *lecticarii* who were assigned particularly to carrying the mistress.

This can serve to highlight the extent to which Augustus' attribution of rank to women and heightening attention to the public activities of women actually led the empire away from republican practices. The conventional culture of the republic had considered fancy transport and hordes of attendants a sign of degenerate feminine luxury. For instance, there is Plautus' *Aulularia* 477–84, Megadorus' diatribe on how uppity women from monied families want fancy carriages and flocks of maids among other outrageous luxuries, all of which drive a poor husband to distraction (on these issues of display, see Culham 1984). It is ironic that Augustus aspired to revive that sort of republican ideology of *austeritas*, but his own insistence on the display of rank produced a legal climate which rewarded the sort of women who might earlier have run afoul of the Lex Oppia.

In fact, some political steps Augustus took indirectly ensured that visual statements of women's importance would appear all over Rome and other towns. One of the greatest political problems confronting Augustus was the importance of the triumphal general in the Roman republic. Augustus undoubtedly hoped that his newly solidified rank structure, incorporating more jobs and more occasions for élite males to display their status and responsibility, would channel and tone down destructive competition. As we will see below, he eventually eliminated the potlatch-type of celebration of military victories. At the same time, Augustus wanted his stabilized élite to contribute publicly to his vision of a renewed Rome.

In 27 BCE itself, the very year of the 'restoration', Augustus called on the *triumphatores*, those senators who had been honoured with a triumph, to join him in renovating roads throughout Italy. It was an expensive proposition, and he intended to set the example by taking on repair and upgrading of the Via Flaminia, one of the longest and most difficult to maintain (Suetonius, *Aug.* 30.1, Dio 53.22.1–20). Others were not caught up in fervour for his vision; Dio describes the effort as a failure and maintains that Augustus was the only one to complete his project. Augustus had attempted to open up a new area of responsibility for the *triumphatores*, one which made a real contribution to the underpinnings of Roman society and the Roman economy, but it did not have the public visibility of building something grand right in the heart of Rome.

It must have appeared to Augustus that he was losing ground; even the republic had expected *triumphatores* to do something constructive for the state with their booty (Shatzman 1972: 204–05). Augustus' own efforts to assign more formal, visible responsibility for the fabric of social and economic life to newly bureaucratized senators undermined his efforts to get military heroes to display their *benevolentia*. There is not much honour in taking on the sort of task others are increasingly ordered to do or which the *princeps* can take on more spectacularly so that one's own effort is smaller or second rate. One may agree with that part of the famous debate on the course of the principate in which Dio presents the argument that no one volunteers to help a monarch (52.6.3–4). Eck has traced the way in which all building and major reconstruction in Augustan Rome was initially done by *triumphatores* but then came to be left to those associated with the imperial *domus* (Eck 1984: 141–42). After 19 BCE only connections of the imperial family were even awarded triumphs. Augustus had become uneasy about or had given up on his political effort to integrate an important political/military ritual of the republic into the new regime. That had consequences for women.

That which elevated the imperial *domus* at the expense of the republican-style political/military élite turned the spotlight on the whole royal family, the 'court', as it were. In his effort to highlight the special status of his own family and its contribution to Rome, Augustus was actually rather traditional. The difference was one of scale, in that Augustus and his close associates like his friend and son-in-law Agrippa were able to undertake so many projects that all members of the imperial family were honoured by some sort of public building effort. Second, Augustus' attempts to feature the concord among his extended family, as well as its descent from the gods, led him to mention specific women in an effort to establish the unique claim of the whole lineage.

We have already noted that even while he was still Octavian, he had deferred his own triumph but had his wife Livia and his sister Octavia awarded statues and that tribunician sacrosanctity (Dio 49.35–38). He used his Dalmatian spoils in particular to dedicate a portico and a library to Octavia. In this case, as in that of political prerogatives, women were accorded a rung in a previously male hierarchy: witness the senate's voting Livia an arch after her death. Dio emphasized that this was unprecedented for a woman, presumably because of the martial connotation of victory arches. The integration of women into this part of the system for according status did not meet with approval on all fronts. The socially conservative Tiberius effectively killed the project by pretending to be flattered and offering to build it from his own funds and then letting it die a quiet death (Dio 58.2.1–6). None the less, the young Caligula gave her a eulogy from the rostra, an inescapably political setting (Suetonius, *Cal.* 10.1).

It was a short step from honouring women as intrinsic members of a politically/militarily élite lineage to their dedicating public works themselves. Tiberius and Livia both dedicated the precinct of the temple of Concord and gave parallel if separate banquets for women and men upon the occasion (Dio 55.8.2). Livia's name alone was associated with the Aedes Concordiae and a statue of a grandchild in the guise of Cupid (Suetonius, *Cal.* 7.1; Flory 1984: 317). Perhaps the women of the imperial family were so associated with the renovated fabric of Rome that it explains why soldiers and urban population apparently obeyed Livia's direction when she stepped in to redirect fire-fighting efforts at the temple of Vesta (Tiberius again found such a public role unsuitable for a woman, Suetonius, *Tib.* 50.2).

Dedications by the imperial women appeared outside Rome too. An example is Livia's aqueduct for the Vicani Matrini (*CIL* 11.3322). One would not want to claim that locally élite women in the cities of Italy consciously acted on the example of imperial women, but surely the appearance of the imperial women in such a public role rendered such efforts undeniably respectable. The same integration of women into the local structure of political rank seems to occur in Italian municipal settings over time (MacMullen 1980: 217–18 notes that similar practices even reached the Greek-speaking part of the Mediterranean eventually). Forbis has collected the examples in which women are praised in the traditional public vocabulary of *munificentia*, *liberalitas*, *beneficia*, and *merita*, not in the language of womanly virtues such as *castitas*, *pietas*, *pudicitia*, and *lanificium* (Forbis 1990). This sounds much like the new application of 'traditional ideas ... based on *merita*', that Flory finds in dedications to the imperial women (1993: 297).

The subsequent use of such terms as *honesta*, *honestissima*, and *honorificentissima*, all from *honores*, 'offices', parallels the emerging custom of referring to senatorial women in explicitly political terms to emphasize how they share in the rank of their households. Cicero's sarcastic reference to a consular woman (*Att.* 2.1.5) evolved through Tacitus' more neutrally described *nobiles feminae* to the senatorial *clarissimae feminae* and *puellae* who appear almost simultaneously with *clarissimi pueri* in the final quarter of the second century CE as parallels to the senatorial *clarissimus vir*. Consular women turn up epigraphically almost at the same time as consular men at the beginning of the third century CE (Chastagnol 1979). In short, Augustus' crystallization of political rank and his ideology requiring the political élite to engage in public beneficence led to new honours for élite women. Élite women assumed this status and these roles and then had an impact on the lives of others, e.g. Marcia Aurelia Ceionia of Anagnia who not only rebuilt that local necessity, a bath, but distributed largess (*CIL* 10.5910). (Some have postulated imperial connections for this Marcia, but that is highly speculative.)

Thus, Augustus' emphasis on the importance of élite political rank, and his own benevolent display, had the impact of opening new social and economic horizons for élite women, and that in turn had some impact on the lives of men and women outside the élite (cf. MacMullen 1980: 214–16 on the visibility of priestesses and its social impact). Political changes accompanying the transition from republic to empire, in particular the crystallization of status as political rank, even changed the direction of Roman law from periodical attempts to penalize display of status or wealth by women in the republic to rewarding it in the empire. This melding of status and political rank inevitably marked some women as members of a public élite which assumed responsibilities. I have suggested above that women's resulting assertion of status and political rank had an impact both on those who served as audiences and those who were the intended beneficiaries, and I have argued elsewhere that slaves and freedmen were among the most enthusiastic consumers of Augustan assertions about respectability and attempted to use the tools he offered in order to claim a higher status for themselves (Culham 1992). This would initially appear to make a case that women's history would profit from attention to conventional political periodization in at least some cases, like the conventional separation of empire from republic at (why not?) 27 BCE.

At the end, does all this amount to an answer to the question with which we began? I am offered help by my colleague in Chinese history who tells me that the old saw is actually true. The Chinese character for 'crisis' does indeed consist of a character for 'danger' with a character for 'opportunity'. Augustus' effort to return to *mores maiorum*, which he envisioned as restraining élite conduct (particularly that of women) within the bounds of respectability, clearly threatened women with the loss of the emancipation they are often thought to have achieved by the end of the republic. Yet we have seen above how many opportunities women could seize upon in the new field opened by Augustus' efforts to mark the boundaries of rank clearly and publicly. It is not surprising that the better part of a generation later, Kelly's question would lead to a different answer than she offered for the era she studied. Our eras have a different impact on our ability to understand those of others. Women did have an empire, although they had to reassert their stake in it repeatedly, and their claims were not unquestioned. Ultimately this essay belongs in the English tradition of Whig histories of emancipation, since it explicitly assumes a framework in which freedom of action, including public action, for women is generally a Good Thing. It has served Kelly's end of calling into question historiographically prevalent concepts of progress, since it suggests that women may have been experiencing some sorts of progress, even political progress, in an era in which political liberties for the male élite were curtailed. We can allow Augustus to have the last word in the *Res Gestae*, where he claimed, in apparent reference to his social legislation, that he had handed on to posterity examples of how to conduct themselves (8.5). His may not have been the perfected Ultimate Age of Vergil's periodizing fourth *Eclogue*, but it's enough to justify a narrative structure bracketing an Augustan era or a principate.

REFERENCES

Afsmann, E. (1886) 'Zu den Schiffsbildern der Dipylonvasen', *Jahrbuch des Deutschen Archäologischen Instituts* 1: 315–16.

Alcock, S. (1994) 'Breaking up the Hellenistic world: survey and society', in I. Morris (ed.) *Classical Greece: Ancient Histories and Modern Archaeologies*, Cambridge: Cambridge University Press, 171–90.

Alcock, S. and Osborne, R. (eds) (1994) *Placing the Gods*, Oxford: Oxford University Press.

Allsebrook, Mary (1992) *Born to Rebel: The Life of Harriet Boyd Hawes*, Oxford: Oxbow.

Amandry, P. (1981) 'Chronique delphique (1970–1981)', *Bulletin de correspondence hellénique* 105: 673–769.

Anderson, Bonnie S. and Zinsser, Judith P. (1988) *A History of Their Own: Women in Europe from Prehistory to the Present*, vol. 1, New York: Harper & Row.

Andrewes, Antony (1967) *The Greeks*, Harmondsworth: Pelican.

Andronikos, Manolis (1954) 'Hê "Dôrikê eisbolê" kai ta archaiologika evrêmata', *Hêllinika* 13: 221–40.

Anzaldúa, Gloria and Moraga, Cherríe (eds) (1983) *This Bridge Called My Back: Writings of Radical Women of Color*, New York: Kitchen Table: Women of Color Press.

Argyros, A.J. (1991) *A Blessed Rage for Order: Deconstruction, Evolution, and Chaos*, Ann Arbor: University of Michigan Press.

Ariès, P. (1962) *Centuries of Childhood: A Social History of Family Life*, trans. R. Baldick, New York: Vintage.

Ariès, Philipe (1981) *The Hour of Our Death*, trans. Helen Weaver, New York: Knopf.

Armstrong, David (1994) 'The addressees of the *Ars Poetica*: Herculaneum, the Pisones and Epicurean protreptic', in Jenny Strauss Clay, Phillip Mitsis and Alessandro Schiesaro (eds) *Mega nepios: il ruolo del destinatario nell'epos didascalico = Materiali e Discussioni* 31: 185–230.

Arrowsmith, William (1966) 'Luxury and death in the *Satyricon*', *Arion* 5, 1: 303–31.

Arthur [Katz], Marylin B. (1977) 'Liberated women: the classical era', in R. Bridenthal and C. Koontz (eds) *Becoming Visible: Women in European History*, Boston: Houghton Mifflin, 60–89.

Badinter, E. (1981) *Mother Love: Myth and Reality*, New York: Macmillan.

Bakhtin, Mikhail (1968) *Rabelais and His World*, trans. Hélène Iswolsky, Bloomington: Indiana University Press.

Bartky, Sandra (1991) *Femininity and Domination*, New York: Routledge.

Barton, Carlin (1993) *The Sorrows of the Ancient Romans*, Princeton: Princeton University Press.

Bashar, N. (1984) 'Women and the concept of change in history', in S. Dixon and T. Munford (eds) *Pre-Industrial Women: Interdisciplinary Perspectives*, Canberra: ANU Women's History Group, 43–50.

Bauman, Richard A. (1992) *Women and Politics in Ancient Rome*, London and New York: Routledge.

Beard, Mary (1994) 'Women on the dig', *Times Literary Supplement*, 21 October 1994: 8.

Beazley, J.D. (1947) *Some Attic Vases in Cyprus*, Oxford: Clarendon Press.

Beazley, J.D. (1956) *Attic Black-Figure Vase Painters*, Oxford: Clarendon Press.

Beazley, J.D. (1971) *Paralipomena: Additions to Attic Black-figure Vase-painters and to Attic Red-figure Vase-painters*, 2nd edn, Oxford: Clarendon Press.

Beazley, J.D. and Robertson, D.S. (1926) 'Early Greek art', *Cambridge Ancient History* 4, Cambridge: Cambridge University Press, 579–610.

Beecher, D.A. and Ciavolella, M. (eds and trans.) (1990) *Jacques Ferrand: A Treatise on Lovesickness*, Syracuse NY: Syracuse University Press.

Bell, Robert R. (1981) *Worlds of Friendship*, Beverly Hills: Sage Publications.

Bennett, Judith M. (1993) 'Medievalism and feminism', *Speculum* 68: 309–31.

Benton, Sylvia (1935) 'Excavations in Ithaka, III', *Annual of the British School at Athens* 35: 45–73.

Benton, Sylvia (1939) 'Excavations in Ithaka, IV', *Annual of the British School at Athens* 39: 151.

Bernal, Martin (1987) *Black Athena I: The Fabrication of Ancient Greece 1785–1985*, New Brunswick: Rutgers University Press.

Bernal, Martin (1991) *Black Athena II: Archaeological and Documentary Evidence*, New Brunswick: Rutgers University Press.

Bertier, J. (1990) 'Enfants malades et maladies des enfants dans le *Corpus hippocratique*', in P. Potter, G. Maloney, and J. Desautels (eds) *La Maladie et les malades dans la collection hippocratique*, Québec: Editions du Sphinx, 209–20.

Bettini, Maurizio (1991) *Anthropology and Roman Culture: Kinship, Time, Images of the Soul*, trans. John Van Sickle, Baltimore: Johns Hopkins University Press.

Beye, C.R. (1982) *Epic and Romance in the Argonautica of Apollonius*, Carbondale: Southern Illinois University Press.

Bichler, R. (1983) *'Hellenismus'. Geschichte und Problematik eines Epochenbegriffs*, Darmstadt: Wissenschaftliche Buchgesellschaft.

Binford, Lewis (1972) *An Archaeological Perspective*, New York: Academic Press.

Blackie, John S. (1866) *Homer and the Iliad* I, Edinburgh: Edmonston & Douglas.

Blok, Josine (1987) 'Sexual asymmetry', in Josine Blok and Peter Mason (eds) *Sexual Asymmetry*, Amsterdam: Gieben, 1–57.

Boardman, John (1964) *The Greeks Overseas*, Harmondsworth: Pelican.

Boardman, John (1975) 'Herakles, Peisistratos and Eleusis', *Journal of Hellenic Studies* 95: 1–12.

Boardman, John (1988) 'Classical archaeology: whence and whither?', *Antiquity* 62: 795–97.

Boatwright, Mary T. (1991) 'The Imperial women of the early second century AD', *American Journal of Philology* 112: 513–40.

Bodéüs, Richard (1993) *The Political Dimensions of Aristotle's Ethics*, trans. Jan Edward Garrett, Albany: State University of New York Press.

Bolger, Diane (1994) 'Ladies of the expedition: Harriet Boyd Hawes and Edith Hall at work in the Mediterranean', in Claasen 1994: 41–50.

Bordo, Susan (1993) *Unbearable Weight: Feminism, Western Culture, and the Body*, Berkeley: University of California Press.

Borst, Arno (1993) *The Ordering of Time: From Ancient Computus to the Modern Computer*, trans. Andrew Winnard, Chicago: University of Chicago Press.

Boston Women's Health Book Collective (1992) *The New Our Bodies, Ourselves*, New York: Simon & Schuster.

Boswell, John (1990) 'Concepts, experience, and sexuality', *differences* 2, 1: 67–87.

Botsford, George W. and Sihler, E.G. (1915) *Hellenic Civilization*, New York: Columbia University Press.

Botsford, George W. (1924) *Hellenic History*, New York: Macmillan.

Boucher, Madeleine (1973) *L'Ennui: de Sénèque à Moravia*, Paris: Bordas.

Bouzek, Jan (1969) *Homerisches Griechenland*, Prague: Charles University.

Bowra, C.M. (1964) *Pindar*, Oxford: Clarendon Press.

Boyarin, Daniel (1993) *Carnal Israel: Reading Sex in Talmudic Culture*, Berkeley: University of California Press.

Boyd Hawes, Harriet (1901) 'Excavations at Kavousi, Crete', *American Journal of Archaeology* 5: 125–57.

Boyd Hawes, Harriet (1908) *Gournia, Vasilika and Other Prehistoric Sites on the Isthmus of Hierapetra, Crete*, Philadelphia: American Exploration Society.

Brain, Robert (1976) *Friends and Lovers*, New York: Basic Books.

Braudel, Fernand (1975) *The Mediterranean and the Mediterranean World in the Age of Philip II*, vol. 1, trans. Sian Reynolds, New York: Harper & Row.

Braudel, Fernand (1980). 'History and the social sciences: the *longue durée*', in *On History*, trans. Sarah Matthews, Chicago: The University of Chicago Press, 25–54.

Breitinger, Emil (1939) 'Die Skelette aus den submykenischen Grabern', in Kraiker and Kübler 1939: 233–55.

Brommer, F. (1980) 'Plemochoe', *Archäologischer Anzeiger* 1980: 544–49.

Brown, Peter (1988) *The Body and Society: Men, Women and Sexual Renunciation in Early Christianity*, New York: Columbia University Press.

Brulé, P. (1990) 'Enquête démographique sur la famille grecque antique', *Revue des études anciennes* 92: 233–58.

Brulé, P. (1992) 'Infanticide et abandon d'enfants. Pratiques grecques et comparaisons anthropologiques', *Dialogues d'histoire ancienne* 18, 2: 53–90.

Brumfield, A.C. (1981) *The Attic Festivals of Demeter and their Relation to the Agricultural Year*, Salem: Arno Press.

Burkert, W. (1972) *Lore and Science in Ancient Pythagoreanism*, trans. E.L. Minar Jr., Cambridge, MA: Harvard University Press.

Burkert, W. (1983) *Homo Necans: The Anthropology of Ancient Greek Sacrificial Ritual and Myth*, trans. P. Bing, 2nd edn, Berkeley: University of California Press.

Burkert, W. (1984) *Die orientalisierende Epoche in der griechischen Religion und Literatur*, Heidelberg: Sitzungsberichte der Heidelberger Akademie der Wissenschaften. Translated by Margaret Pinder and Walter Burkert as *The Orientalizing Revolution*, Cambridge, MA: Harvard University Press, 1992.

Burkert, W. (1987) *Ancient Mystery Cults*, Cambridge: Cambridge University Press.

Burkert, W. (1990) *Wilder Ursprung: Opferritual und Mythos bei den Griechen*, Berlin: K. Wagenbach.

Bury, J.B. (1900) *A History of Greece*, 1st edn, London: Macmillan.

Bury, J.B. (1913) *A History of Greece*, 2nd edn, London: Macmillan.

Bury, J.B. (1924) 'Homer', *Cambridge Ancient History* 2, Cambridge: Cambridge University Press, 498–517.

Bury, J.B. and Meiggs, R. (1975) *A History of Greece*, 4th edn, London: Macmillan.

Busolt, Georg (1967) [1904] *Griechische Geschichte bis zur Schlacht bei Chaeroneia* vol. III.2: *Der peloponnesische Krieg*, Hildesheim: Olms.

Butler, Judith (1990) *Gender Trouble*, New York: Routledge.

Calame, C. (1990) *Thésée et l'imaginaire athénien*, Lausanne: Payot.

Calder, W.M. and Cobet, J. (eds) (1990) *Heinrich Schliemann nach hundert Jahren*, Frankfurt: Klostermann.

Camp, J.M. (1990) *The Athenian Agora: A Guide to the Excavation and Museum*, 4th edn., Athens: The American School of Classical Studies.

Cargill, Jack (1981) *The Second Athenian League: Empire or Free Alliance?*, Berkeley: University of California Press.

Carpenter, Rhys (1946) *Folk Tale, Fiction and Saga in the Homeric Epics*, Berkeley: University of California Press.

Carpenter, T.H. (1983) 'On the dating of the Tyrrhenian Group', *Oxford Journal of Archaeology* 2: 279–93.

Carpenter, T.H. (1984) 'The Tyrrhenian Group: problems of provenance', *Oxford Journal of Archaeology* 3: 45–56.

Carpenter, T.H. (ed.) (1989) *Beazley Addenda*, 2nd edn, Oxford: Clarendon Press.

Cartledge, Paul (1987) *Agesilaos and the Crisis of Sparta*, Baltimore: Johns Hopkins University Press.

Castle, Theresa (1985) 'Sleeping beauties?', *Women's Review of Books* 2: 12–13.

Chambers, Mortimer H. (1990) 'Schliemann and America', in Calder and Cobet 1990: 397–414.

Chapkis, Wendy (1986) *Beauty Secrets*, Boston: Beacon Press.

Chastagnol, A. (1979) 'Les Femmes dans l'ordre sénatorial: titulature et rang social à Rome', *Revue historique* 103: 3–28.

Chelune, Gordon J. and associates (1979) *Self-Disclosure: Origins, Patterns, and Implications of Openness in Interpersonal Relationships*, San Francisco: Jossey Bass Publishers.

Cixous, Hélène (1980) 'The laugh of the Medusa', trans. Keith Cohen and Paula Cohen, in Elaine Marks and Isabelle de Courtivron (eds) *New French Feminisms*, Amherst: University of Massachusetts Press, 245–64. Originally published in *L'Arc* in 1975.

Claasen, Cheryl (ed.) (1994) *Women in Archaeology*, Philadelphia: University of Pennsylvania Press.

Clark, Stuart (1985) 'The *Annales* historians', in Quentin Skinner (ed.) *The Return of Grand Theory in the Human Sciences*, Cambridge: Cambridge University Press, 177–98.

Clarke, Howard (1979) *Homer's Readers*, East Brunswick: Associated University Presses.

Clavier, M. (1809) *Histoire des premiers temps de la Grèce*, Paris: Léopold Collins.

Clinton, K. (1974) *The Sacred Officials of the Eleusinian Mysteries*, Philadelphia: American Philosophical Society.

Clinton, K. (1979) '*IG* 1² 5, the Eleusinia and the Eleusinians', *American Journal of Philology* 100: 1–12.

Clinton, K. (1980) 'A Law in the City Eleusinion concerning the Mysteries', *Hesperia* 49: 258–88.

Clinton, K. (1986) 'The date of the classical Telesterion at Eleusis', *Philia Epê eis Geôrgion E. Mylônan dia ta exinta etê tou anaskaphikou tou ergou*, 2, Athens: Bibliothêkê tês en Athênais Archaiologikês Hetaireias, 254–62.

Clinton, K. (1988) 'Sacrifice at the Eleusinian Mysteries', in Hägg *et al.* 1988: 69–88.

Clinton, K. (1992) *Myth and Cult: The Iconography of the Eleusinian Mysteries*, Göteborg: Aström.

Clinton, K. (1993) 'The sanctuary of Demeter and Kore at Eleusis', in Marinatos and Hägg 1993: 110–24.

Clover, Carol J. (1992) *Men, Women, and Chain Saws: Gender in the Modern Horror Film*, Princeton: Princeton University Press.

Clover, Carol J. (1993) 'Regardless of sex: men, women, and power in Early Northern Europe', *Speculum* 68: 363–87.

Cogan, Marc (1988) *The Human Thing: The Speeches and Principles of Thucydides' History*, Chicago: University of Chicago Press.

Cohen, Colleen Ballerino and Robertson, Karen (1992) 'Historical presences, present silences: a critical analysis of *Fragments for a History of the Human Body*', *Journal of the History of Sexuality* 3: 129–40.

Cohen, David (1991) *Law, Sexuality and Society: The Enforcement of Morals in Classical Athens*, Cambridge: Cambridge University Press.

Cohen, David and Richard Saller (1994) 'Foucault on sexuality in Greco-Roman antiquity', in Jan Goldstein (ed.) *Foucault and the Writing of History*, Oxford: Basil Blackwell, 35–59.

Cohen, Robert (1939) *La Grèce et l'hellénisation du monde antique*, 2nd edn, Paris: Presses Universitaires de France.

Coldstream, J. Nicolas (1968) *Greek Geometric Pottery*, London: Methuen.

Coldstream, J. Nicolas (1977) *Geometric Greece*, London: Methuen.

Collinge, N.E. (1962) 'Medical terms and clinical attitudes in the tragedians', *Bulletin of the Institute of Classical Studies* 9: 43–55.

Collingwood, R.G. (1946) *The Idea of History*, repr. 1970, Oxford: Oxford University Press.

Collini, S. (1994) 'Escape from DWEMsville?', *Times Literary Supplement*, 27 May 3–4.

Connor, W.R. (1977) 'A post-modernist Thucydides?', *Classical Journal* 72: 289–98.

Connor, W.R. (1984) *Thucydides*, Princeton: Princeton University Press.

Corea, Gena *et al.* (1987) *Man-Made Women*, Bloomington: Indiana University Press.

Cornford, F. (1971) [1907] *Thucydides Mythistoricus*, Philadelphia: University of Pennsylvania Press.

Courbin, Paul (1966) *La Céramique géométrique de l'Argolide*, Paris: Boccard.

Cox, Jeffrey N. and Reynolds, Larry J. (eds) (1993) *New Historical Literary Study: Essays on Reproducing Texts, Representing History*, Princeton: Princeton University Press.

Creed, Barbara (1993) *The Monstrous–Feminine: Film, Feminism, Psychoanalysis*, New York and London: Routledge.

Csapo, E. (1993) Review of Nesselrath (1990), *Phoenix* 47: 354–57.

Culham, Phyllis (1982) 'The Lex Oppia', *Latomus* 41: 786–93.

Culham, Phyllis (1984) 'Again, what meaning lies in colour!', *Zeitschrift für Papyrologie und Epigraphik* 69: 235–45.

Culham, Phyllis (1988) 'Pragmatic or programmatic Augustus?: the case of the Italian highways', *Augustan Age* 7: 5–21.

Culham, Phyllis (1989) 'Chance, command, and chaos in ancient military engagements', *World Futures* 27: 191–205.

Culham, Phyllis (1991) 'Defense in depth: strategy, system, and self-similarity', in G.P. Scott (ed.) *Time, Rhythms, and Chaos in the New Dialogue with Nature*, Ames: Iowa State University Press, 161–76.

Culham, Phyllis (1992) 'Imperial ideology and perceptions of women's roles', *Conference on Feminism and the Classics*, University of Cincinnati.

Culham, Phyllis (1993) Review of Evans (1991), *American Journal of Philology* 14: 171–74.

Culham, Phyllis, Edmunds, L., and Smith, A. (eds) (1989) *Classics: A Discipline and Profession in Crisis?*, Lanham: University Press of America.

Curtius, Ernst (1857) *Griechische Geschichte* I, Berlin: Weidmann.

Darcque, P. (1981) 'Les Vestiges mycéniens découverts sous le Télésterion d'Éleusis', *Bulletin de correspondence hellénique* 105: 593–605.

Darnton, Robert (1984) 'Workers revolt: the great cat massacre of the Rue Saint-Séverin', in *The Great Cat Massacre*, New York: Basic Books, 74–104.

Davies, J.K. (1984) 'Cultural, social and economic features of the Hellenistic world', in F.W. Walbank *et al.* (eds) *The Cambridge Ancient History*, 2nd edn, vol. 7, Part I *The Hellenistic World*, Cambridge: Cambridge University Press, 257–320.

Davies, J.K. (1993) *Democracy and Classical Greece*, 2nd edn. Stanford: Stanford University Press.

Davis, Natalie Zemon (1975) 'Women on top', in *Society and Culture in Early Modern France*, Stanford: Stanford University Press, 124–51.

de Foucault, J.A. Â972) *Recherches sur la langue et le style de Polybe*, Paris: Les Belles Lettres.

de Polignac, François (1984) *La Naissance de la cité grecque*, Paris: Éditions de la découverte.

de Polignac, François (1994) 'Mediation, competition, and sovereignty: the evolution of rural sanctuaries in Geometric Greece', in Alcock and Osborne 1994: 3–18.

de Polignac, François (forthcoming) 'Entre les dieux et les morts. Status individuel et rites collectifs dans la cité archäique', in Robin Hägg (ed.) *The Role of Religion in the Early Polis*, Stockholm: Skrifter Utgivna i Svenska Institutet i Athen.

de Romilly, J. (1963) [1947] *Thucydides and Athenian Imperialism*, trans. P. Thody, Oxford: Oxford University Press.

de Ste Croix, G.E.M. (1972) *Origins of the Peloponnesian War*, Ithaca, NY: Cornell University Press.

Dean-Jones, Lesley (1992) 'The politics of pleasure: female sexual appetite in the Hippocratic Corpus', *Helios* 19: 72–91.

Dean-Jones, Lesley (1994) *Women's Bodies in Classical Greek Science*, New York: Oxford University Press.

Deger-Jalkotzy, S. (ed.) (1983) *Griechenland, die Agais und die Levante wahrend die 'Dark Ages', vom 12 bis Zum jh. v. Chr.*, Vienna: Verlag der Österreichischen Akademie der Wissenschaften.

Deger-Jalkotzy, Sigrid (1988) 'Diskontinuität und Kontinuität: Aspekte politischer und sozialer Organization in mykenischer Zeit und in der Welt der homerischen Epen', in D. Musti *et al.* (eds) 1991: 53–66.

Deissmann-Merten, M. (1984) 'Zur Sozialgeschichte des Kindes im antiken Griechen-land', in J. Martin and A. Nitschke (eds) *Zur Sozialgeschichte der Kindheit*, Freiburg and Munich: Alber, 267–316.

Delia, Diana (1991) 'Fulvia Reconsidered', in Sarah B. Pomeroy (ed.) *Women's History and Ancient History*, Chapel Hill: University of North Carolina Press, 173–217.

deMause, L. (1974) 'The evolution of childhood', in L. deMause (ed.) *The History of Childhood: The Untold Story of Child Abuse*, New York: Psychohistory Press, 1–73.

Demos, J. (1986) *Past, Present and Personal: The Family and the Life Course in American History*, Oxford: Oxford University Press.

Derrida, Jacques (1993) 'Politics of friendship', *American Imago* 50: 353–91.

Desborough, Vincent R. (1948) 'What is Protogeometric?', *Annual of the British School at Athens* 43: 260–72.

Desborough, Vincent R. (1952) *Protogeometric Pottery*, Oxford: Clarendon Press.

Desborough, Vincent R. (1964) *The Last Mycenaeans and Their Successors*, Oxford: Clarendon Press.

Desborough, Vincent R. (1972) *The Greek Dark Ages*, London: Methuen.

Deubner, Ludwig (1962) *Attische Feste*, Hildesheim: G. Olms.

Dingwall, Eric John (1925) *Male Infibulation*, London: J. Bale, Sons & Danielsson, Ltd.

Dirlmeier, Franz (1931) *'Philos' und 'Philia' in vorhellenistischer Griechentum*. Inaugural Dissertation, Ludwig-Maximilians-Universität, Munich: Druck der Salesianischen Offizin.

REFERENCES

Dixon, S. (1984) 'Infirmitas Sexus: womanly weakness in Roman law', Tijdschrift voor Rechtsgeschiedenis 52: 343–71.
Dixon, S. (1985a) 'The marriage alliance in the Roman elite', Journal of Family History 10: 353–78.
Dixon, S. (1985b) 'Breaking the law to do the right thing: the gradual erosion of the Voconian Law in ancient Rome', Adelaide Law Review 9: 519–34.
Dixon, S. (1985c) 'Polybius on Roman women and property', American Journal of Philology 106: 147–70.
Dixon, S. (1988) The Roman Mother, London: Croom Helm/Routledge.
Dixon, S. (1991) 'The sentimental ideal of the Roman family', in B. Rawson (ed.) Marriage, Divorce and Children in Ancient Rome, Oxford: Oxford University Press, 99–113.
Dixon, S. (1992) The Roman Family, Baltimore: Johns Hopkins University Press.
Dixon, S. (1994) 'Re-Writing the family. A review essay', Classical Journal 89: 395–407.
Dodds, E.R. (1985) 'The ancient concept of progress', in The Ancient Concept of Progress and Other Essays on Greek Literature and Belief, Oxford: Oxford University Press, 1–15.
Donlan, Walter (1980) The Aristocratic Ideal in Ancient Greece: Attitudes of Superiority from Homer to the End of the Fifth Century BCE, Lawrence: Coronado Press.
Donlan, Walter (1981) 'Scale, value, and function in the Homeric economy', American Journal of Ancient History 6: 101–17.
Donlan, Walter (1982) 'Reciprocities in Homer', Classical World 75: 137–75.
Donlan, Walter (1985) 'The social groups of Dark Age Greece', Classical Philology 80: 293–308.
Donlan, Walter (1989a) 'The pre-state community in Greece', Symbolae Osloenses 64: 5–29.
Donlan, Walter (1989b) 'Homeric temenos and the land economy of the Dark Age', Museum Helveticum 46: 129–45.
Donlan, Walter (1994) 'Chief and followers in Dark Age Greece', in Colin Duncan and David Tandy (eds) From Political Economy to Anthropology, Montreal: Black Rose, 34–51.
Donlan, Walter and Thomas, C. (1993) 'The village community of ancient Greece', Studi Micenei ed Egeo-Anatolici 31: 61–71.
Dougherty, Carol (1993) The Poetics of Colonization: From City to Text in Ancient Greece, Oxford: Oxford University Press.
Dougherty, Carol and Kurke, Leslie (eds) (1993) Cultural Poetics in Ancient Greece, Cambridge: Cambridge University Press.
Dover, K.J. (1989) [1978] Greek Homosexuality, revised edn., Cambridge, MA: Harvard University Press.
Dow, S. (1953–57) 'The law codes of Athens', Proceedings of the Massachusetts Historical Society 71: 3–36.
Dow, S. and Healey, R.F. (1965) A Sacred Calendar of Eleusis, Harvard Theological Studies 21, Cambridge, MA: Harvard University Press.
Drabkin, I.E. (ed. and trans.) (1950) Caelius Aurelianus: On Acute Diseases and on Chronic Diseases, Chicago: University of Chicago Press.
Drerup, H. (1969) Griechische Baukunst in geometrischer Zeit: Archaeologia Homerica Band II Kap. O, Göttingen: Vandenhoeck und Ruprecht.
Droop, J.P. (1906a) 'Some Geometric pottery from Crete', Annual of the British School at Athens 12: 24–62.
Droop, J.P. (1906b) 'Dipylon vases from the Kynosarges site', Annual of the British School at Athens 12: 80–92.
duBois, Page (1984) 'Sappho and Helen', in John Peradotto and J.P. Sullivan (eds)

Women in the Ancient World: The 'Arethusa' Papers, Albany: SUNY Press, 95–105. Originally published in *Arethusa* 11 (1978): 88–99.

duBois, Page (1988) *Sowing the Body: Psychoanalysis and Ancient Representations of Women*, Chicago: University of Chicago Press.

Duby, Georges and Perrot, Michelle (eds) (1992) *A History of Women in the West*, vol. 1, Cambridge, MA: Belknap Press.

Duck, Steven (1983) *Friends for Life: The Psychology of Close Relationships*, New York: St Martin's Press.

Durand, J.-L. (1986) *Sacrifice et labour en Grèce ancienne: Essai d'anthropologie religieuse*, Paris: Éditions de la découverte.

Duruy, Victor (1887) *Histoire des grecs*, 3 vols, Paris: Hachette. Translated by M.M. Ripley as *History of Greece*, Boston MA: Estes and Lauriant, 1890.

Dyke, C. (1988) *The Evolutionary Dynamics of Complex Systems: A Study in Biosocial Complexity*, New York: Oxford University Press.

Dyke, C. (1990) 'Strange attraction, curious liaison: Clio meets chaos', *Philosophical Forum* 21: 369–92.

Dyke, C. (forthcoming) 'Bourdieuan dynamics: the American middle class self constructs' in R. Shusterman (ed.) *Philosophical Perspectives on Pierre Bourdieu*, Oxford: Basil Blackwell.

Echols, Alice (1989) *Daring to Be Bad: Radical Feminism in America, 1967–1975*, Minneapolis: University of Minnesota Press.

Eck, Werner (1984) 'Senatorial self-representation: developments in the Augustan period', in Fergus Millar and Erich Segal (eds) *Caesar Augustus: Seven Aspects*, Oxford: Clarendon Press, 129–67.

Eckstein, A.M. (1995) *Moral Vision in the Histories of Polybius*, Berkeley and Los Angeles: University of California Press.

Edmunds, L. (1993) 'Thucydides in the act of writing', in R. Pretagostini (ed.) *Tradizione e innovazione nella cultura greca da Omero all'età ellenistica: Scritti in onore di Bruno Gentili*, vol. 2, Rome: GEI, 831–52.

Edwards, Catharine (1993) *The Politics of Immorality in Ancient Rome*, Cambridge: Cambridge University Press.

Ehrenberg, V. (1954) *Sophocles and Pericles*, Oxford: Basil Blackwell.

Ehrenreich, Barbara and English, Deirdre (1978) *For Her Own Good: 150 Years of the Experts' Advice to Women*, New York: Doubleday.

Eigenauer, J.D. (1993) 'The humanities and chaos theory: a response to Steenburg's "Chaos and the marriage of heaven and hell"', *Harvard Theological Review* 86: 455–69.

Eilberg-Schwartz, H. and Doniger, W. (eds) (1995) *Off with her Head! The Denial of Women's Identity in Myth, Religion and Culture*, Berkeley: University of California Press.

Elias, Norbert (1992) *Time: An Essay*, trans. E.A. Jephcott, Oxford: Basil Blackwell.

Engels, F. (1972) [1884] *The Origins of the Family, Private Property and the State*, New York: International.

Evans, John Karl (1991) *War, Women and Children in Ancient Rome*, London and New York: Routledge.

Evans-Pritchard, Edward E. (1933) 'Zande blood brotherhood', *Africa* 6: 369–401.

Eyben, E. (1993) *Restless Youth in Ancient Rome*, London: Routledge.

Fausto-Sterling, Anne (1992) [1985] *Myths of Gender: Biological Theories about Women and Men*, New York: Basic Books.

Feaver, D.D. (1957) 'Historical development in the priesthoods of Athens', *Yale Classical Studies* 15: 123–58.

Feher, Michel, with Ramona Naddaff and Nadia Tazi (eds) (1989) *Fragments for a History of the Human Body*, 3 vols, New York: Zone. (Feher's 'Introduction' appears on pp. 11–17 of vol. 1.)

Felsch, R. (1987) 'Kalapodi', *Archäologischer Anzeiger*: 1–99.

Felsch, R., Kienast, H.J., and Schuler, H. (1980) 'Apollon und Artemis oder Artemis und Apollon?', *Archäologischer Anzeiger*: 38–123.

Ferguson, Harvie (1995) *Melancholy and the Critique of Modernity: Søren Kierkegaard's Religious Philosophy*, London and New York: Routledge.

Feuer, Lewis S. (ed.) (1989) *Marx and Engels: Basic Writings on Politics and Philosophy*, New York: Doubleday.

Finley, J.H. (1942) *Thucydides*, Cambridge, MA: Harvard University Press.

Finley, J.H. (1967) *Three Essays on Thucydides*, Cambridge, MA: Harvard University Press.

Finley, Moses I. (1952) *Studies in Land and Credit in Ancient Athens*, New Brunswick: Rutgers University Press.

Finley, Moses I. (1954) *The World of Odysseus*, New York: Viking.

Finley, Moses I. (1970) *Early Greece: The Bronze and Archaic Ages*, London: Chatto & Windus.

Finley, Moses I. (1975) *The Use and Abuse of History*, London: Chatto & Windus.

Finley, Moses I. (1979) *The World of Odysseus*, 2nd edn, New York: Viking.

Finley, Moses I. (1980) *Ancient Slavery and Modern Ideology*, London: Chatto & Windus.

Finley, Moses I. (1981) [1964] *Economy and Society in Ancient Greece*, ed. Brent Shaw and Richard Saller, London: Chatto & Windus.

Finley, Moses I., Caskey, John L., Kirk, Geoffrey S., and Page, Denys (1964) 'The Trojan war', *Journal of Hellenic Studies* 84: 1–20.

Firestone, Shulamith (1970) *The Dialectic of Sex*, New York: William Morrow.

Fish, Stanley (1989) 'Commentary: the young and the restless', in Veeser 1989: 303–16.

Flashar, H. (1966) *Melancholie und Melancholiker in der medizinischen Theorien der Antike*, Berlin: De Gruyter.

Flory, Marlene Boudreau (1978) 'Family in familia: kinship and community in slavery', *American Journal of Ancient History* 3: 78–95.

Flory, Marlene Boudreau (1984) '*Sic exempla parantur*: Livia's shrine to Concordia and the Porticus Liviae', *Historia* 33: 309–30.

Flory, Marlene Boudreau (1993) 'Livia and the history of public honorific statues for women in Rome', *Transactions of the American Philological Association* 123: 287–308.

Foley, H.P. (ed.) (1994) *The Homeric Hymn to Demeter*, Princeton: Princeton University Press.

Forbis, Elizabeth P. (1990) 'Women's public image in Italian honorary inscriptions', *American Journal of Philology* III: 493–512.

Forrest, W.G. (1966) *The Emergence of Greek Democracy*, London: Weidenfeld & Nicholson.

Foucault, Michel (1967) *Madness and Civilization: A History of Insanity in the Age of Reason*, trans. A.M. Sheridan, London and New York: Routledge.

Foucault, Michel (1970) *The Order of Things: An Archaeology of the Human Sciences*, trans. A.M. Sheridan, London and New York: Routledge.

Foucault, Michel (1972) *The Archaeology of Knowledge*, trans. A.M. Sheridan Smith, London and New York: Routledge.

Foucault, Michel (1973) *The Birth of the Clinic: The Archaeology of Medical Perception*, trans. A.M. Sheridan, London and New York: Routledge.

Foucault, Michel (1977) *Discipline and Punish: The Birth of the Prison*, trans. A.M. Sheridan, Harmondsworth: Penguin Books.

Foucault, Michel (1978) *The History of Sexuality, Vol. I: An Introduction*, trans. Robert Hurley, New York: Vintage.

Foucault, Michel (1985) *The Use of Pleasure: History of Sexuality, Vol. 2*, trans. Robert Hurley, New York: Vintage.

Foucault, Michel (1986) *The Care of the Self: History of Sexuality, Vol. 3*, trans. Robert Hurley, New York: Vintage.

Foucault, Michel (1987) *Mental Illness and Psychology*, trans. A.M. Sheridan, foreword Hubert Dreyfus, Berkeley: University of California Press.

Fowler, B.H. (1989) *The Hellenistic Aesthetic*, Madison: University of Wisconsin Press.

Fraisse, Jean Claude (1974) *Philia: La notion d'amitié dans la philosophie antique*, Paris: Vrin.

Francotte, Henri (1907) *La polis grecque*, Paderborn: Schoningh.

Francotte, Henri (1922) *Histoire politique de la Grèce ancienne*, Brussels: Albert Dewit.

Fränkel, Hermann (1975) *Early Greek Poetry and Philosophy*, trans. M. Hadas and J. Willis, Oxford: Basil Blackwell.

Freeman, Edward A. (1880) *Historical Essays: Second Series*, 2nd edn, London: Macmillan.

French, V. (1991) 'Children in antiquity', in J.M. Hawes and N.R. Hiner (eds) *Children in Historical and Comparative Perspective*, New York: Greenwood, 13–29.

Frier, Bruce (1980) *Landlords and Tenants in Imperial Rome*, Princeton: Princeton University Press.

Furtwängler, Adolf (1879) 'Die Bronzefunde aus Olympia und deren kunst-geschichtliche Stellung', *Abhandlungen der Preussischen Akademie der Wissenschaft*: 3–106.

Fustel de Coulanges, Numa Denis (1980) [1864] *The Ancient City*, Arnaldo Momigliano and S.C. Humphreys (eds) Baltimore: Johns Hopkins University Press.

Gallagher, Catherine and Laqueur, Thomas (eds) (1987) *The Making of the Modern Body: Sexuality and Society in the Nineteenth Century*, Berkeley: University of California Press. (Based on 'Sexuality and the social body in the nineteenth century', special issue, *Representations* 14 [Spring 1986].)

Gallet de Santerre, H. (1958) *Délos primitive et archaïque*, Paris: Boccard.

Galsterer, H (1990) 'A man, a book, and a method: Sir Ronald Syme's *Roman Revolution* after fifty years', in Kurt A. Raaflaub and Mark Toher (eds) *Between Republic and Empire: Interpretations of Augustus and His Principate*, Berkeley: University of California Press, 1–20.

García Márquez, Gabriel (1988) *Love in the Time of Cholera*, trans. Edith Grossman, Harmondsworth: Penguin Books.

Gardiner, Patrick (1961) *The Nature of Historical Explanation*, Oxford: Oxford University Press.

Gardner, Jane (1986) *Women in Roman Law and Society*, Bloomington: Indiana University Press.

Gardner, P. (1882) 'The palaces of Homer', *Journal of Hellenic Studies* 3: 264–82.

Garland, R. (1992) *Introducing New Gods: The Politics of Athenian Religion*, Ithaca: Cornell University Press.

Garnsey, P. (1970) *Social Status and Legal Privilege in the Roman Empire*, Oxford: Clarendon Press.

Garnsey, P. and Saller, R. (1987) *The Roman Empire: Economy, Society and Culture*, Berkeley and Los Angeles: University of California Press.

Geddes, William (1878) *The Problem of the Homeric Poems*, London: Macmillan.

Gero, Joan (1983) 'Gender bias in archaeology', in Joan Gero, D. Lacy, and M.L.

Blakey (eds) *The Socio-Politics of Archaeology*, Amherst: University of Massachusetts Department of Anthropology Research Report 23, 51–57.

Gero, Joan (1985) 'Socio-politics of archaeology and the woman-at-home ideology', *American Antiquity* 50: 342–50.

Gibbs, James L., Jr. (1962) 'Compensatory blood-brotherhood: a comparative analysis of institutionalized friendship in two African societies', *Proceedings of the Minnesota Academy of Sciences* 30: 67–74.

Gill, Christopher (1994) 'Peace of mind and being yourself: Panaetius to Plutarch', *Aufstieg und Niedergang der römischen Welt* II.36.7: 4599–4640.

Gill, Christopher, Postlethwaite, Norman, and Seaford, Richard (eds) (forthcoming) *Reciprocity in Ancient Greece*, Oxford: Oxford University Press.

Gilman, Sander (1991) *The Jew's Body*, New York: Routledge.

Gilmore, David D. (1990) *Manhood in the Making*, New Haven: Yale University Press.

Gladstone, William (1857) 'On the place of Homer in classical education and in historical inquiry', in *Oxford Essays*, Oxford: Oxford University Press, 1–56.

Gladstone, William (1878) 'Preface', in Heinrich Schliemann, *Mycenae*, London: Macmillan, v–xl.

Gleason, Maud (1995) *Making Men: Sophists and Self-Presentation in Ancient Rome*, Princeton: Princeton University Press.

Glotz, Gustave (1929) *The Greek City and Its Institutions*, trans. N. Mallinson [1950], London: Routledge & Kegan Paul.

Golden, Mark (1985) '"Pais", "child" and "slave"', *Antiquité classique* 54: 91–104.

Golden, Mark (1988) 'Did the ancients care when their children died?', *Greece & Rome* 35: 152–63.

Golden, Mark (1990) *Children and Childhood in Classical Athens*, Baltimore: Johns Hopkins University Press.

Golden, Mark (1992) 'Continuity, change and the study of ancient childhood', *Échos du monde classique/classical Views* 36: 7–18.

Golden, Mark (1995) 'Baby talk and child language in ancient Greece', in F. De Martino and A.H. Sommerstein (eds) *Lo spettacolo delle voci*, Bari: Levante, 2.11–34.

Goldhill, Simon (1995) *Foucault's Virginity: Ancient Erotic Fiction and the History of Sexuality*, Cambridge: Cambridge University Press.

Goldsmith, Victor (1979) *Le Système stoïcien et l'idée du temps*, 4th edn, Paris: Vrin.

Goldstein, Jan (ed.) (1994) *Foucault and the Writing of History*, Oxford: Basil Blackwell.

Gomme, A.W., Andrewes, A., and Dover, K.J. (1970) *A Historical Commentary on Thucydides*, vol. 4, *Books V 25 – VII*, Oxford: Clarendon Press.

Goody, J. (1990) *The Oriental, the Ancient and the Primitive: Systems of Marriage and the Family in the Pre-Industrial Societies of Eurasia*, Cambridge: Cambridge University Press.

Gordon, Pamela (forthcoming) 'Sappho in Rome: Or, why is Sappho a man?', in Hallett and Skinner (forthcoming).

Graef, B. (1896) 'Bild von einer Dipylonvase', *Mitteilungen des Deutschen Archäologischen Instituts: Athenische Abteilung* 21: 448–49.

Graf, F. (1974) *Eleusis und die orphische Dichtung Athens in vorhellenistischer Zeit*, Berlin and New York: de Gruyter.

Graf, F. (1985) *Nordionische Kulte. Religionsgeschichtliche und epigraphische Untersuchungen zu den Kulten von Chios, Erythrai, Klazomenai und Phokaia*, Rome: Schweizerischer Institut.

Grafton, A., Most, G., and Zetzel, J. (1985) 'Introduction', in Wolf 1985, 3–35.

Grant, V.J. and Martin, J.F. (1995) 'On sex ratio and coital rate: a hypothesis without foundation/reply', *Current Anthropology* 36: 295–98.

Gray, Dorothea (1954) 'Homer and the archaeologists', in Maurice Platnauer (ed.) *Fifty Years of Classical Scholarship*, Oxford: Basil Blackwell, 24–31.

Green, P. (1990) *Alexander to Actium. The Historical Evolution of the Hellenistic Age*, Berkeley and Los Angeles: University of California Press.

Greenblatt, Stephen (1989) 'Towards a poetics of culture', in Veeser 1989: 1–14.

Greenblatt, Stephen (1993) 'Kindly visions', *The New Yorker*, 11 October: 112–20.

Greenidge, A.J.H. (1884) *'Infamia': Its Place in Roman Public and Private Law*, Oxford: Clarendon Press.

Grote, George (1826) 'Fasti Hellenici', *Westminster Review* 5: 269–331.

Grote, George (1843) 'Grecian legends and early history', *Westminster Review* 39: 285–328.

Grote, George (1846a) *History of Greece* I, London: Murray.

Grote, George (1846b) *History of Greece* II, London: Murray.

Gruen, E.S. (1993) 'The polis in the Hellenistic world', in R.M. Rosen and J. Farrell (eds) *Nomodeiktes: Greek Studies in Honor of Martin Ostwald*, Ann Arbor: University of Michigan Press, 339–54.

Gutting, Gary (ed.) (1994) *The Cambridge Companion to Foucault*, Cambridge: Cambridge University Press.

Hacking, I. (1986) 'The archaeology of Foucault', in D.C. Hoy (ed.) *Foucault: A Critical Reader*, Oxford: Blackwell, 27–40.

Hacking, I. (1995) *Rewriting the Soul: Multiple Personality and the Sciences of Memory*, Princeton: Princeton University Press.

Hägg, Robin, ed. (1983) *The Greek Renaissance of the Eighth Century BC*, Stockholm: Skrifter Utgivna i Svenska Institutet i Athen.

Hägg, Robin, Marinatos, N., and G.C. Nordquist (eds) (1988) *Early Greek Cult Practice*, Stockholm: Skrifter Utgivna i Svenska Institutet i Athen.

Hall, Edith (1914) 'Excavations in Eastern Crete, Vrokastro', University of Pennsylvania, The Museum Anthropological Publications 3, part 3, 79–185.

Hallett, Judith P. (1977) *'Perusinae glandes* and the changing image of Augustus', *American Journal of Ancient History* 2: 151–71.

Hallett, Judith P. (1989) 'Female homoeroticism and the denial of Roman reality in Latin literature', *Yale Journal of Criticism* 3: 209–27.

Hallett, Judith P. (1993) 'Feminist theory, historical periods, literary canons, and the study of Greco-Roman antiquity', in Rabinowitz and Richlin 1993: 44–72.

Hallett, Judith P. and Skinner, Marilyn (eds) (forthcoming) *Roman Sexualities*, Princeton University Press.

Halperin, David M. (1990) *One Hundred Years of Homosexuality*, New York: Routledge.

Halperin, David M. (1995) *Saint Foucault: Towards a Gay Hagiography*, New York: Oxford University Press.

Halperin, David M., Winkler, John J., and Zeitlin, Froma I. (eds) (1990) *Before Sexuality: The Construction of Erotic Experience in the Ancient Greek World*, Princeton: Princeton University Press.

Hansen, Mogens H. (ed.) (1993) *The Ancient Greek City-State*, Copenhagen: Historisk-Filosofiske Meddelelser det Kongelike Danske Videnskabernes 67.

Hanson, Ann Ellis (1975) 'Hippocrates: diseases of women 1', *Signs* 1: 567–84.

Hanson, Ann Ellis (1990) 'The medical writers' woman', in Halperin *et al.* 1990: 309–38.

Hanson, Ann Ellis (1992) 'Conception, gestation, and the origin of female nature in the *Corpus Hippocraticum*', *Helios* 19: 31–71.

Harris, W.V. (1982) 'The theoretical possibility of extensive infanticide in the Graeco-Roman world', *Classical Quarterly* 32: 114–16.

Harris, W.V. (1989) *Ancient Literacy*, Cambridge, MA: Harvard University Press.

Harvey, D. (1985) 'Women in Thucydides', *Arethusa* 18: 67–90.

Hayles, K. (1989) 'Chaos as orderly disorder: shifting ground in contemporary literature and science', *New Literary History* 20: 305–22.

Heath, Malcolm (1987) *The Poetics of Tragedy*, London: Duckworth.

Henderson, B.W. (1973) [1927] *The Great War between Athens and Sparta: A Companion to the Military History of Thucydides*, New York: Arno Press.

Henderson, Jeffrey (1972) 'Aristophanes obscenus: sexual and scatological language in Aristophanes', PhD thesis, Harvard University.

Henderson, Jeffrey (1975) *The Maculate Muse: Obscene Language in Attic Comedy*, 2nd edn 1991, New York: Oxford University Press.

Henderson, Jeffrey (1987) 'Older women in Attic Old Comedy', *Transactions of the American Philological Association* 117: 105–29.

Herman, Gabriel (1987) *Ritualised Friendship and the Greek City*, Cambridge: Cambridge University Press.

Herter, H. (1927) 'Das Kind im Zeitalter des Hellenismus', *Bonner Jahrbücher* 132: 250–58.

Herter, H. (1993) 'Kind', in H.H. Schmitt and E. Vogt (eds) *Kleines Lexikon des Hellenismus*, 2nd edn, Wiesbaden: Otto Harrassowitz, 371–75.

Heurtley, W.A., and Lorimer, H. (1933) 'Excavations in Ithaca, I', *Annual of the British School at Athens* 33: 22–65.

Heurtley, W.A., and Skeat, T.C. (1931) 'The tholos tombs of Marmariane', *Annual of the British School at Athens* 31: 1–55.

Hexter, J.H. (1961) 'Storm over the gentry', in *Reappraisals in History: New Views on History and Society in Early Modern Europe*, London: Longmans, 117–62.

Heyck, T.W. (1982) *The Transformation of Intellectual Life in Victorian England*, New York: St Martin's Press.

Heylbut, Gustavus (ed.) (1889) *Aspasii in Ethica nicomachea commentaria*, Berlin: Georg Reimer.

Hillard, T. (1992) 'On the stage, behind the curtain: images of politically active women in the late Roman Republic', in B. Garlick, S. Dixon, and P. Allen (eds) *Stereotypes of Women in Power: Historical Perspectives and Revisionist Views*, New York: Greenwood Press, 37–64.

Himmelfarb, Gertrude (1992) 'Telling it as you like it: post-modernist history and the flight from fact', *Times Literary Supplement*, 16 October: 12–15.

Hodder, Ian (1991) *Reading the Past*, 2nd edn, Cambridge: Cambridge University Press.

Hodder, Ian (1993) *Method and Theory in Archaeology*, London: Routledge.

Hooker, James (1989) 'Homer, Patroclus, Achilles', *Symbolae Osloenses* 64: 30–35.

Hornblower, Simon (1987) *Thucydides*, Baltimore: Johns Hopkins University Press.

Hornblower, Simon (1991) *A Commentary on Thucydides*, vol. 1: *Books I–III*, Oxford: Clarendon Press.

How, W.W. and Wells, J. (1912) *A Commentary on Herodotus*, vol. 1, Oxford: Clarendon Press.

Humphreys, S.C. (1993) *The Family, Women and Death*, 2nd edn, Ann Arbor: University of Michigan Press.

Hunt, L. (ed.) (1989) *The New Cultural History*, Berkeley: University of California Press.

Hunt, L. (1992a) *The Family Romance of the French Revolution*, Berkeley and Los Angeles: University of California Press.

Hunt, L. (1992b) 'Foucault's subject in *The History of Sexuality*', in Stanton 1992b: 78–93.

Hunt, L. (ed.) (1993) *The Invention of Pornography. Obscenity and the Origins of Modernity, 1500–1800*, New York: Zone Books.

Hunter, R.L. (1985) 'Horace on friendship and free speech (*Epistles* 1.18 and *Satires* 1.4)', *Hermes* 113: 480–90.

Hunter, V. (1973) *Thucydides the Artful Reporter*, Toronto: Hakkert.

Hupperts, C.A.M. (1988) 'Greek love: homosexuality or paederasty? Greek love in black figure vase-painting', in J. Christiansen and T. Melander (eds) *Proceedings of the 3rd Symposium on Ancient Greek and Related Pottery*, Copenhagen: Nationalmuseet, Ny Carlsberg Glyptothek and Thoraldsens Museum, 255–68.

Hutchinson, G.O. (1988) *Hellenistic Poetry*, Oxford: Clarendon Press.

Immerwahr, H. (1990) *Attic Script*, Oxford: Clarendon Press.

Isham, N.M. (1898) *The Homeric Palace*, Baltimore: Johns Hopkins University Press.

Jackson, Stanley W. (1986) *Melancholia and Depression: From Hippocratic Times to Modern Times*, New Haven: Yale University Press.

Jacoby, F. (1957g) *Die Fragmente der Griechischen Historiker: Dritter Teil b (Supplement)*, vol. 1 Text, vol. 2 Notes, Leiden: Brill.

Jaeger, Werner (1945) *Paideia: the Ideals of Greek Culture*, trans. G. Highet, 3 vols, New York: Oxford University Press.

James, P., Thorpe, I.J., Kokkinos, N., Morkot, R., and Frankish, J. (1991) *Centuries of Darkness*, London: Jonathan Cape.

Jameson, M.H. (1951) 'The hero Echetlaeus', *Transactions of the American Philological Association* 82: 48–61.

Jebb, Richard C. (1881) 'Homeric and Hellenic Ilium', *Journal of Hellenic Studies* 2: 7–43.

Jebb, Richard C. (1882) 'The ruins at Hissarlik; their relation to the *Iliad*', *Journal of Hellenic Studies* 3: 185–217.

Jebb, Richard C. (1886) 'The Homeric house, in relation to the remains at Tiryns', *Journal of Hellenic Studies* 7: 170–88.

Jebb, Richard C. (1887) *Homer: An Introduction to the 'Iliad' and 'Odyssey'*, Boston MA: Ginn & Co.

Jebb, Richard C. (1907) *Essays and Addresses*, Cambridge: Cambridge University Press.

Jeffery, L.H. (1948) 'The boustrophedon sacral inscriptions from the Agora', *Hesperia* 17: 86–111.

Jeffery, L.H. (1976) *Archaic Greece*, London: E. Benn.

Johansson, S.R. (1991) 'Welfare, mortality and gender. Continuity and change in explanations for male/female mortality differences over three centuries', *Continuity and Change* 6: 135–77.

Joshel, Sandra R. (1992) *Work, Identity, and Legal Status at Rome*, Norman: University of Oklahoma Press.

Jourard, S.M. (1971) *Self Disclosure*, New York: Wiley.

Kagan, Donald (1974) *The Archidamian War*, Ithaca: Cornell University Press.

Kagan, Donald (1987) *The Fall of the Athenian Empire*, Ithaca: Cornell University Press.

Kagan, Donald (1991) *Pericles of Athens and the Birth of Democracy*, New York: Free Press.

Kakutani, Michiko (1993) Review of Hunt (1993) *The New York Times*, 17 August: C18.

Kanta, A. (1991) 'Cult, continuity and the evidence of pottery at the sanctuary of Syme Viannou, Crete', in Musti *et al.* 1991: 479–505.

Kassel, R. (1987) *Die Abgrenzung des Hellenismus in der griechischen Literaturgeschichte*, Berlin and New York: De Gruyter.

Kearns, E. (1989) *The Heroes of Attica, Bulletin of the Institute for Classical Studies* Supplement 57, London: Institute of Classical Studies.

Keller, Albert (1902) *Homeric Society: A Sociological Study of the Iliad and Odyssey*, London: Longman.

Kelly, Joan (1984) [1977] 'Did women have a Renaissance?', in *Women, History and Theory: The Essays of Joan Kelly*, Chicago: University Of Chicago Press, 19–50.

Kertzer, D.I. and Saller, R.P. (eds) (1991) *The Family in Italy: From Antiquity to the Present*, New Haven: Yale University Press.

Keuls, Eva (1985) *The Reign of the Phallus* (2nd edn 1993) Berkeley: University of California Press.

Kilmer, M.F. (1993) *Greek Erotica on Attic Red-Figure Vases*, London: Duckworth.

King, Helen (1983) 'Bound to bleed: Artemis and Greek women', in Averil Cameron and Amélie Kuhrt (eds) *Images of Women in Antiquity*, Detroit: Wayne State University Press, 109–27.

King, Helen (1986) 'Sacrificial Blood: the role of the *amnion* in ancient gynecology', *Helios* 13, 2: 117–26.

Kirk, Geoffrey S. (1975) [1964] 'The Homeric poems as history', *Cambridge Ancient History* 2 part 2, 2nd edn, Cambridge: Cambridge University Press, 820–50.

Klibansky, R., Panofsky, E., and Saxl, F. (1964) *Saturn and Melancholy: Studies in the History of Natural Philosophy, Religion, and Art*, London: Nelson.

Knox, B. (1957) *Oedipus at Thebes: Sophocles' Tragic Hero and His Time*, New Haven: Yale University Press.

Kokkinos, Nikos (1992) *Antonia Augusta: Portrait of a Great Roman Lady*, London and New York: Routledge.

Kokkou-Vyridi, K. (1991) 'Proïmes pyres thysion sto Telesterion tes Eleusinas', PhD thesis, University of Athens.

Konstan, David (1994a) 'Friendship and the state: the context of Cicero's *De amicitia*', *Hyperboreus* 1, 2: 1–16.

Konstan, David (1994b) *Sexual Symmetry: Love in the Ancient Novel and Related Genres*, Princeton: Princeton University Press.

Konstan, David (forthcoming) 'Reciprocity and friendship', in Gill, Postlethwaite and Seaford (forthcoming).

Kopcke, G. and Tokumaru, I. (eds) (1992) *Greece between East and West: 10th–8th Centuries BC*, Mainz: Franz Steiner.

Kourouniotis, K. (1931–32) 'Anaskaphê Eleusinos kata to 1933', *Archaiologikon Deltion* 14, Supplement: 1–30.

Kraiker, W. (1939) 'Nordische Einwanderung in Griechenland', *Die Antike* 15: 195–230.

Kraiker, W. and Kübler, K. (1939) *Kerameikos* I, Berlin: De Gruyter.

Kroker, E. (1886) 'Die Dipylonvasen', *Jahrbuch des Deutschen Archäologischen Instituts* 1: 95–125.

Kron, U. (1976) *Die zehn attischen Phylenheroen. Geschichte, Mythos, Kult und Darstellungen*, *MDAI(A)* Beiheft 5, Berlin: Mann.

Kübler, Karl (1943) *Kerameikos* IV, Berlin: De Gruyter.

Kudlien, F. (1989) 'Kindesaussetzung im antiken Roma: ein Thema zwischen Fiktionalität und Lebenswirklichkeit', in H. Hofmann (ed.) *Groningen Colloquia on the Novel* 2, Groningen: Egbert Forsten, 25–44.

Kuhn, Reinhold (1976) *The Demon of Noontide: Ennui in Western Literature*, Princeton: Princeton University Press.

Kuhn, Thomas (1970) *The Structure of Scientific Revolutions*, 2nd edn, Chicago: University of Chicago Press.

Lambrechts, P. (1957) 'L'Importance de l'enfant dans les religions à mystères', in *Hommages à W. Déonna*, Brussels: Collection Latomus, 322–33.

Landecker, Werner S. (1981) *Class Crystalization*, New Brunswick: Rutgers University Press.

Landry, Donna and MacLean, Gerald (1993) *Materialist Feminisms*, Oxford: Basil Blackwell.

Lane Fox, R. (1986) 'Hellenistic culture and literature', in J. Boardman, J. Griffin, and O. Murray (eds) *The Oxford History of the Classical World: Greece and the Hellenistic World*, Oxford: Oxford University Press, 338–64.

Lang, Andrew (1893) *Homer and the Epic*, London: Longman.

Lang, Andrew (1906) *Homer and His Age*, London: Longman.

Lang, Andrew (1910) *The World of Homer*, London: Longman.

Laqueur, Thomas (1990) *Making Sex: Body and Gender from the Greeks to Freud*, Cambridge, MA: Harvard University Press.

Lateiner, D. (1989) *The Historical Method of Herodotus*, Toronto: University of Toronto Press.

Lattimore, Richmond (1951) *The Iliad of Homer*, Chicago: University of Chicago Press.

Le Gall, J. (1970) 'Un critère de différenciation sociale: la situation de la femme', in *Recherches sur les structures sociales dans l'antiquité classique*, Paris: Éditions du CRNS, 275–86.

Le Roy, C. (1984) 'Mémoire et tradition: réflexions sur la continuité', *Aux origines de l'hellénisme: La Crète et la Grèce: Hommage à Henri Van Effenterre*, Paris 1984: Université de Paris I Panthéon-Sorbonne, 163–72.

Leaf, Walter (1883a) 'Some questions concerning the armour of Homeric heroes', *Journal of Hellenic Studies* 4: 73–85.

Leaf, Walter (1883b) 'Notes on Homeric armour', *Journal of Hellenic Studies* 4: 281–304.

Leaf, Walter (1884) 'The Homeric chariot', *Journal of Hellenic Studies* 5: 185–94.

Leaf, Walter (1915) *Homer and History*, London: Longman.

Lebow, R.N. and Strauss, B.S. (eds) (1991) *Hegemonic Rivalry from Thucydides to the Nuclear Age*, Boulder: Westview Press.

Lenski, Gerhard (1954) 'Status crystalization: a non-vertical dimension of social studies', *American Sociological Review* 19: 405–13.

Lerner, Gerda (1986) *The Creation of Patriarchy*, New York: Oxford University Press.

Lerner, Gerda (1993) *The Creation of Feminist Consciousness*, New York: Oxford University Press.

Levick, Barbara (1985) 'The politics of the early principate', in T.P. Wiseman (ed.) *Roman Political Life 90 BC–AD 69*, Exeter: University of Exeter.

Lewis, N. (1970) '"Greco-Roman Egypt": fact or fiction?', in D.H. Samuel (ed.) *Proceedings of the XIIth International Congress of Papyrology*, American Studies in Papyrology 7, Toronto and Amsterdam: Hakkert, 3–14.

Lewis, N. (1984) 'The Romanity of Roman Egypt: a growing consensus', in *Atti del XVII Congresso internazionale di papirologia*, Naples: Centro internazionale per lo studio dei papiri ercolanesi, 1077–84.

Lloyd, G.E.R. (1990) *Demystifying Mentalities*, Cambridge: Cambridge University Press.

Lloyd-Jones, H. (1967) 'Heracles at Eleusis: P.Oxy. 2622 and P.S.I. 1391', *Maia* 19: 206–29.

Loraux, N. (1986) 'Thucydide a écrit la guerre du Péloponnèse', *METIS: Revue d'anthropologie du monde grec ancien* 1: 139–61.

Lord, Albert B. (1948) 'Homer and Huso III', *Transactions of the American Philological Association* 79: 113–24.

Lord, Albert B. (1953) 'Homer's originality: oral dictated texts', *Transactions of the American Philological Association* 84: 124–33.

Lord, Albert B. (1960) *The Singer of Tales*, Cambridge, MA: Harvard University Press.

Lorimer, H.L. (1947) 'The hoplite phalanx', *Annual of the British School at Athens* 42: 76–138.

Lorimer, H.L. (1950) *Homer and the Monuments*, London: Macmillan.

Lovejoy, Arthur O. and Boas, George (1965) *Primitivism and Related Ideas in Antiquity*, New York: Octagon Books.

MacDonald, W. and Thomas, C. (1990) *Progress into the Past*, 2nd edn, Bloomington: Indiana University Press.

McGregor, M.F. (1956) 'The politics of the historian Thucydides', *Phoenix* 10: 93–102.

McGuire, Brian Patrick (1988) *Friendship and Community: The Monastic Experience*, Cistercian Studies 95, Kalamazoo: Cistercian Publications.

MacKinnon, Catharine A. (1992) 'Does sexuality have a history?', in Stanton 1992b: 117–36.

Macmillan, G.A. (1911) 'A short history of the British School at Athens, 1886–1911', *Annual of the British School at Athens* 17: ix–xxxviii.

MacMullen, Ramsay (1980) 'Women in public life in the Roman Empire', *Historia* 29: 208–18.

MacMullen, Ramsay (1982) 'The epigraphic habit in the Roman Empire', *American Journal of Philology* 103: 233–46.

Mahaffy, J.P. (1882) 'The site and antiquity of the Hellenic Ilion', *Journal of Hellenic Studies* 3: 69–80.

Mahaffy, J.P. (1890) 'A critical introduction', in Victor Duruy, *History of Greece*, trans. M.M. Ripley, Boston MA: Estes and Lauriant, 1–119.

Manson, M. (1983) 'The emergence of the small child in Rome (third century BC–first century AD)', *History of Education* 12: 149–59.

Marinatos, N. and Hägg, R. (eds) (1993) *Greek Sanctuaries: New Approaches*, London: Routledge.

Martin, Emily (1987) *The Woman in the Body: A Cultural Analysis of Reproduction* (revised edn 1992), Boston: Beacon Press.

Martin, J.F. (1994) 'Changing sex ratios: the history of Havasupai fertility and its implications for human sex ratio variation', *Current Anthropology* 35: 255–80.

Martin, L. (1994) 'The anti-individualistic ideology of Hellenistic culture', *Numen* 41: 117–40.

Matz, F. (1960) Review of Nilsson (1957), *Gnomon* 32: 540–52.

Meiggs, R. and Lewis, D. (eds) (1988) *A Selection of Greek Historical Inscriptions. To the End of the Fifth Century BC*, 2nd edn, Oxford: Clarendon Press.

Meyer, E.A. (1990), 'Explaining the epigraphic habit in the Roman empire: the evidence of epitaphs', *Journal of Roman Studies* 80: 74–96.

Millett, Paul (1991) *Lending and Borrowing in Classical Athens*, Cambridge: Cambridge University Press.

Milns, R.D. (1986) 'Attitudes to mental illness in antiquity', *Australian and New Zealand Journal of Psychiatry* 20: 458–62.

Milojčić, V. (1948–49) 'Die dorische Wanderung im Lichte der vorgeschichtlichen Funde', *Archäologischer Anzeiger*: 12–36.

Miltner, Franz (1934) 'Die dorische Wanderung', *Klio* 27: 54–68.

Mitford, William (1784) *The History of Greece* I, London: Cadell.

Momigliano, Arnaldo (1952) *George Grote and the Study of Greek History*, London: University College London.

Momigliano, Arnaldo (1970) 'J.G. Droysen between Greeks and Jews', *History and Theory* 9: 139–53.

Momigliano, Arnaldo (1977) *Essays in Ancient and Modern Historiography*, Oxford: Basil Blackwell.

Momigliano, A. and Humphreys, S.C. (1980) 'Foreword', in Fustel de Coulanges 1980: ix–xxiii.

Morgan, Catherine (1990) *Athletes and Oracles*, Cambridge: Cambridge University Press.

Morris, Ian (1986) 'The use and abuse of Homer', *Classical Antiquity* 5: 81–138.

Morris, Ian (1987) *Burial and Ancient Society*, Cambridge: Cambridge University Press.

Morris, Ian (1992) *Death-ritual and Social Structure in Classical Antiquity*, Cambridge: Cambridge University Press.

Morris, Ian (1994) 'Archaeologies of Greece', in Ian Morris (ed.) *Classical Greece: Ancient Histories and Modern Archaeologies*, Cambridge: Cambridge University Press, 8–47.

Morris, Sarah P. (1989a) 'A tale of two cities', *American Journal of Archaeology* 93: 511–35.

Morris, Sarah P. (1989b) 'Daidalos and Kadmos: classicism and orientalism', in John Peradotto and Molly Levine (eds), *The Challenge of Black Athena*, *Arethusa* special edition, Buffalo: Dept. of Classics, State University of New York at Buffalo, 39–54.

Morris, Sarah P. (1990) 'Greece and the Levant', *Journal of Mediterranean Archaeology* 3: 57–66.

Morris, Sarah P. (1992a) 'Introduction', in Kopcke and Tokumaru 1992: xiii–xviii.

Morris, Sarah P. (1992b) *Daidalos and the Origins of Greek Art*, Princeton: Princeton University Press.

Mulder, M.B. (1995) 'On polygyny and sex ratio at birth: an evaluation of Whiting's study', *Current Antropology* 36: 625–27.

Munn, N.D. (1992) 'The cultural anthropology of time', *Annual Review of Anthropology* 21: 92–123.

Murray, Gilbert (1907) *The Rise of the Greek Epic*, Oxford: Clarendon Press.

Murray, Oswyn (1980) *Early Greece*, Glasgow: Fontana.

Musgrave, J. (1990) 'Dust and damn'd Oblivion: a study of cremation in ancient Greece', *Annual of the British School at Athens* 85: 271–99.

Musti, D., Sacconi, A., Rocchetti, L., Rocchi, M., Scafa, E., Sportiello, L., and Giannotta, M.E. (eds) (1991) *La transizione dal miceneo all' alto arcaismo*, Rome: Consiglio nazionale delle ricerche.

Mylonas, G. (1961) *Eleusis and the Eleusinian Mysteries*, Princeton: Princeton University Press.

Mylonas, G. and Travlos, J. (1952) 'Anaskapha en Eleusini', *Praktika tês en Athênais Archaiologikês Hetaireias*, 53–72.

Myres, J.L. and Gray, D. (1958) *Homer and His Critics*, London: Routledge & Kegan Paul.

Nagy, Gregory (1979) *The Best of the Achaeans*, Baltimore: Johns Hopkins University Press.

Narducci, Emanuele (1985) 'L'archeologia del desiderio: Michel Foucault sulla sessualità degli antichi', *Quaderni di storia* 22: 185–214.

Negri, A.M. (1988) 'La fortuna letteraria dell'*inertia*', *Paideia* 43: 177–88.

Nesselrath, H.-G. (1990) *Die attische Mittlere Komödie: Ihre Stellung in der antiken Literaturkritik und Literaturgeschichte*, Berlin and New York: de Gruyter.

Newton, Charles (1880) *Essays on Art and Archaeology*, London: Longman.

Ničev, A. (1978) 'Questions éthiques et esthétiques chez Polybe', *Revue des études grecques* 91: 149–57.

Nilsson, M.P. (1933) *Homer and Mycenae*, London: Methuen.

Nilsson, M.P. (1957) *The Dionysiac Mysteries of the Hellenistic and Roman Age*, Lund: Gleerup.

Nottbohm, G (1943) 'Der Meister der grossen Dipylon-Amphora in Athen', *Jahrbuch des Deutschen Archäologischen Instituts* 58: 1–31.

Ohly-Dumm, M. (1985) 'Tripod-pyxis from the Sanctuary of Aphaia on Aigina', in von Bothmer (1985): 236–38.

Ohnuki-Tierney, Emiko (1990) 'Introduction: the historicization of anthropology', in Ohnuki-Tierney (ed.) *Culture through Time*, Stanford: Stanford University Press, 1–25.

Orwin, C. (1994) *The Humanity of Thucydides*, Princeton: Princeton University Press.

Osborne, R.G. (1985) *Demos: The Discovery of Classical Attika*, Cambridge: Cambridge University Press.

Packer, J.E. (1967) 'Housing and population in imperial Ostia and Rome', *Journal of Roman Studies* 57: 80–95.

Padel, R. (1992) *In and Out of the Mind: Greek Images of the Tragic Self*, Princeton: Princeton University Press.

Page, Denys (1959) *History and the Homeric Iliad*, Berkeley: University of California Press.

Paley, Frederic A. (1866) *The 'Iliad' of Homer*, London: Whitaker & Co.

Papadopoulos, John (1993) 'To kill a cemetery: the Athenian Kerameikos and the Early Iron Age in the Aegean', *Journal of Mediterranean Archaeology* 6: 175–206.

Parke, H.W. (1977) *Festivals of the Athenians*, Ithaca: Cornell University Press.

Parker, Andrew, Russo, Mary, Sommer, Doris, and Yaeger, Patricia (eds) (1992) *Nationalisms and Sexualities*, New York: Routledge.

Parker, Holt (1992) 'Love's body anatomized: the ancient erotic handbooks and the rhetoric of sexuality', in Richlin 1992b: 90–111.

Parker, Holt (forthcoming) 'The teratogenic grid', in Hallett and Skinner (forthcoming).

Parker, R. (1983) *Miasma. Pollution and Purification in Early Greek Religion*, Oxford: Clarendon Press.

Parker, R. (1987a) 'Festivals of the Attic demes', in T. Linders and G. Nordquist (eds) *Gifts to the Gods*, Proceedings of the Uppsala Symposium 1985, Uppsala: Acta Universitatis Upsaliensis BOREAS, 137–47.

Parker, R. (1987b) 'Myths of early Athens', in J. Bremmer (ed.) *Interpretations of Greek Mythology*, London and Sydney: Croom Helm, 187–214.

Parker, R. (1991) 'The *Hymn to Demeter* and the *Homeric Hymns*', *Greece and Rome* 38: 1–17.

Parry, Milman (1971) *The Making of Homeric Verse*, ed. Adam Parry, Oxford: Clarendon Press.

Patterson, C.B. (1985) '"Not worth the rearing": the causes of infant exposure in ancient Greece', *Transactions of the American Philological Association* 115: 103–23.

Payne, Humfry (1929) 'Early Greek vases from Knossos', *Annual of the British School at Athens* 29: 224–98.

Pelling, C. (1990) 'Childhood and personality in Greek biography', in Pelling (ed.) *Characterization and Individuality in Greek Literature*, Oxford: Clarendon Press, 213–44.

Peppe, L. (1984) *Posizione giuridica e ruolo sociale della donna romana in età repubblicana*, Milan: Giuffrè.

Percival, Geoffrey (1940) *Aristotle on Friendship: Being an Expanded Translation of* the *Nicomachean Ethics Books VIII and IX*, Cambridge: Cambridge University Press.

Perkin, Harold (1972) [1969] *The Origins of Modern English Society, 1780–1880*, Toronto: University of Toronto Press.

Pernice, E. (1892) 'Über die Schiffsbilder auf den Dipylonvasen', *Mitteilungen des Deutsches Archäologischen Instituts: Athenische Abteilung* 17: 285–306.

Pernice, E. (1900) 'Geometrische Vase mit Schiffsdarstellung', *Jahrbuch des Deutschen Archäologischen Instituts* 15: 92–96.

Pflaum, H.G. (1970) 'Titulature et rang social sous le Haut empire', in *Recherches sur les structures sociales dans l'antiquité classique*, Paris: Éditions du CRNS, 159–85.

Piercy, Marge (1976) *Woman on the Edge of Time*, New York: Knopf.

Pigeaud, J. (1987) *Folie et cures de la folie chez les médecins de l'antiquité gréco-romaine: la manie*, Paris: Les Belles Lettres.

Pitt-Rivers, Julian A. (1954) 'Ritual kinship in Spain', *Transactions of the New York Academy of Science* 2nd series 20: 424–31.

Plassart, A. (1973) 'Un siècle de fouilles à Délos', in *Études déliennes, Bulletin de correspondance hellénique* supp. vol. 1, Paris: Boccard, 5–16.

Pollitt, J.J. (1986) *Art in the Hellenistic Age*, Cambridge: Cambridge University Press.

Pollitt, J.J. (1993) 'Response', in P. Green (ed.) *Hellenistic History and Culture*, Berkeley and Los Angeles: University of California Press, 90–103.

Pollock, L. (1983) *Forgotten Children: Parent–Child Relations from 1500 to 1900*, Cambridge: Cambridge University Press.

Pollock, L. (1987) '"An action like a stratagem." Courtship and marriage from the Middle Ages to the twentieth century', *Historical Journal* 30: 483–98.

Pomeroy, S.B. (1976) 'The relationship of the married woman to her blood relatives in Rome', *Ancient Society* 7: 215–27.

Pomeroy, S.B. (1983) 'Infanticide in Hellenistic Greece', in A. Cameron and A. Kuhrt (eds) *Images of Women in Antiquity*, London and Canberra: Croom Helm, 207–22.

Pomeroy, S.B. (1986) 'Copronyms and the exposure of infants in Egypt', in R.S. Bagnall and W.V. Harris (eds) *Studies in Roman Law in Memory of A. Arthur Schiller*, Leiden: Brill, 147–62.

Popham, Mervyn (1990) 'Reflections on "An Archaeology of Greece"', *Oxford Journal of Archaeology* 9: 29–35.

Popham, Mervyn, Calligas, P., and Sackett, L.H. (1993) *Lefkandi* II.2, London: *Annual of the British School at Athens* supp. vol. 23.

Porter, Roy (1987) *Mind Forg'd Manacles*, London: Athlone Press.

Poulsen, Friedrich (1905) *Die Dipylongräber und die Dipylonvasen*, Leipzig: Teubner.

Powell, J.E. (1960) *A Lexicon to Herodotus*, 2nd edn, Hildesheim: Olms.

Puglia, Enzo (ed.) (1988) *Demetrio Lacone: Aporie testuali ed esegetiche in Epicuro*, Naples: Bibliopolis.

Purcell, N. (1986) 'Livia and the womanhood of Rome', *Proceedings of the Cambridge Philological Society* 32: 78–105.

Quinlan, D.C. and Shackelford, J.A. (1994) 'Economy and English families, 1500–1850', *Journal of Interdisciplinary History* 24: 431–63.

Qviller, Bjørn (1981) 'Dynamics of the Homeric society', *Symbolae Osloenses* 56: 109–55.

Raaflaub, Kurt (1993) 'Homer to Solon: the rise of the polis. The written sources', in Hansen 1993: 41–105.

Rabinowitz, Nancy Sorkin and Richlin, Amy (eds) (1993) *Feminist Theory and the Classics*, New York: Routledge.

Radin, Paul (1949) *The Culture of the Winnebago*, Chicago: University of Chicago Press.

Raepsaet-Charlier, M.T. (1981) 'Clarissima femina', *Revue internationale des droits de l'antiquité* 28: 189–212.

Raepsaet-Charlier, M.T. (1987) *Prosopographie des femmes de l'ordre sénatorial (Ier-IIe siècles)*, Louvain: Peeter.

Rahe, Paul A. (1992) *Republics Ancient and Modern: Classical Republicanism and the American Revolution*, Chapel Hill: University of North Carolina Press.

Rasmussen, T. and Spivey, N. (eds) (1991) *Looking at Greek Vases*, Cambridge: Cambridge University Press.

Ravi, Z. (1993) 'The myth of the immutable English family', *Past and Present* 140: 3–44.

Rawlings, Hunter R. III (1981) *The Structure of Thucydides' History*, Princeton: Princeton University Press.

Rayet, O. and Collignon, M. (1888) *Histoire de la céramique grecque*, Paris: G. Decaux.

Redfield, James (1983) 'The economic man', in Carl Rubino and Cynthia Shelmerdine (eds) *Approaches to Homer*, Austin: University of Texas Press, 218–47.

Redfield, James (1986) 'The growth of markets in Archaic Greece', in B.L. Anderson and A.J.M. Latham (eds) *The Market in History*, London: Routledge, 29–58.

Rémy, B. (1976/77) '*Ornatu et ornamenta quaestoria praetoria et consularia* sous le Haut Empire romain', *Révue des études anciennes* 78/79: 160–98.

Rennell, Lord (1933) 'The Ithaca of the *Odyssey*', *Annual of the British School at Athens* 33: 1–21.

Rhodes, P.J. (1981) *A Commentary on the Aristotelian 'Athenaion Politeia'*, Oxford: Clarendon Press.

Richardson N.J. (1974) *The Homeric Hymn to Demeter*, Oxford: Clarendon Press.

Richlin, Amy (1978) 'Sexual terms and themes in Roman satire and related genres', PhD thesis, Yale University.

Richlin, Amy (1981) 'Approaches to the sources on adultery at Rome', in Helene P. Foley (ed.) *Reflections of Women in Antiquity*, New York: Gordon and Breach, 379–404.

Richlin, Amy (1984) 'Invective against women in Roman satire', *Arethusa* 17: 67–80.

Richlin, Amy (1990) 'Hijacking the Palladion', *Helios* 17: 175–85.

Richlin, Amy (1991) 'Zeus and Metis: Foucault, feminism, classics', *Helios* 18: 160–80.

Richlin, Amy (1992a) 'Julia's jokes, Galla Placidia, and the Roman use of women as political icons', in B. Garlick, S. Dixon, and P. Allen (eds) *Stereotypes of Women in Power: Historical Perspectives and Revisionist Views*, New York: Greenwood Press, 65–91.

Richlin, Amy (ed.) (1992b) *Pornography and Representation in Greece and Rome*, New York: Oxford University Press.

Richlin, Amy (1992c) [1983] *The Garden of Priapus: Sexuality and Aggression in Roman Humor*, 2nd edn, New York: Oxford University Press.

Richlin, Amy (1993a) 'Not before homosexuality: the materiality of the *Cinaedus* and the Roman law against love between men', *Journal of the History of Sexuality* 3: 523–73.

Richlin, Amy (1993b) 'The ethnographer's dilemma and the dream of a lost Golden Age', in Rabinowitz and Richlin 1993: 272–303.

Richlin, Amy (1995) 'Making up a woman: the face of Roman gender', in Eilberg-Schwartz and Doniger 1995.

Richlin, Amy (forthcoming a) 'Foucault's *History of Sexuality*: a useful theory for women?', in *Foucault, Sexuality and Classics*, eds David Larmour and Paul Allen Miller.

Richlin, Amy (forthcoming b) 'Pliny's brassiere', in Hallett and Skinner (forthcoming).

Richlin, Amy (forthcoming c) 'Carrying water in a sieve: class and the body in Roman women's religion', in Karen King and Karen Jo Torjesen (eds) *Women and Goddess Traditions*, Minneapolis: Fortress.

Roberts, Jennifer T. (1994) *Athens on Trial*, Princeton: Princeton University Press.

Rose, P.W. (1992) *Sons of the Gods, Children of Earth: Ideology and Literary Form in Ancient Greece*, Ithaca, NY: Cornell University Press.

Rosen, G. (1968) *Madness in Society: Chapters in the History of Mental Illness*, Chicago: University of Chicago Press.

Rousselle, Aline (1988) *Porneia: On Desire and the Body in Antiquity*, trans. Felicia Pheasant, Oxford: Basil Blackwell.

Ruggles, S. (1994) 'The transformation of American family structure', *American Historical Review* 99: 103–28.

Rühfel, H. (1984) *Das Kind in der griechischen Kunst. Von der minoisch-mykenischen Zeit bis zum Hellenismus*, Mainz am Rhein: Philipp von Zabern.

Russo, Mary (1986) 'Female grotesques: carnival and theory', in Teresa de Lauretis (ed.) *Feminist Studies/Critical Studies*, Bloomington: Indiana University Press, 213–29.

Rütten, T. (1992) *Demokrit, lachender Philosoph und sanguinischer Melancholiker: eine pseudohippokratische Geschichte*, *Mnemosyne* Supplement 118, Leiden: E.J. Brill.

Sacco, G. (1979) 'Sui *neaniskoi* dell'età ellenistica', *Rivista di filologia e di istruzione classica* 107: 39–49.

Sacks, K. (1981) *Polybius on the Writing of History*, Berkeley and Los Angeles: University of California Press.

Sallares, R. (1991) *The Ecology of the Ancient Greek World*, London: Duckworth.

Saller, R.P. (1988a) '*Pietas*, obligation and authority in the Roman family', in P. von Kneissl and V. Losemann (eds) *Alte Geschichte und Wissenschaftsgeschichte: Festschrift für Karl Christ zum 65. Geburtstag*, Darmstadt: Wissenschaftliche Buchgesellschaft, 392–410.

Saller, R.P. (1988b) Review of Gardner (1986), *Classical Philology* 83: 263–69.

Saller, R.P. (1989) 'Patronage and friendship in early imperial Rome: drawing the distinction', in Andrew Wallace-Hadrill (ed.) *Patronage in Ancient Society*, London: Routledge, 49–62.

Saller, R.P. (1994) *Patriarchy, Property and Death in the Roman Family*, Cambridge: Cambridge University Press.

Saul, John Ralston (1992) *Voltaire's Bastards: The Dictatorship of Reason in the West*, New York: Free Press.

Sayce, A.H., and Jebb, R.C. (1883) 'The ruins at Hissarlik', *Journal of Hellenic Studies* 4: 142–55.

Scarpat, Giuseppe (1964) *Parrhesia: Storia del termine e delle sue traduzioni in latino*, Brescia: Paideia.

Schiebinger, Londa (1989) *The Mind Has No Sex? Women in the Origins of Modern Science*, Cambridge, MA: Harvard University Press.

Schiebinger, Londa (1990) 'The anatomy of difference: race and sex in eighteenth-century science', *Eighteenth-Century Studies* 23: 387–405.

Schliemann, Heinrich (1881) *Ilios*, London: Macmillan.

Schliemann, Heinrich (1884) *Troia*, London: Macmillan.

Schmitt-Pantel, P. (1980) 'Les repas au prytanée et à la tholos dans l'Athènes classique. *Sitesis, trophé, misthos*: réflexions sur le mode de nourriture démocratique', *Annali dell'istituto universitario orientale di Napoli. Sezione di archeologia e storia antica* 2: 55–68.

Schollmeier, Paul (1994) *Other Selves: Aristotle on Personal and Political Friendship*, Albany, NY: State University of New York Press.

Schuchhardt, Carl (1891) *Schliemann's Excavations: An Archaeological and Historical*

226

Study, London: Macmillan, reprinted as *Schliemann's Discoveries of the Ancient World*, New York, 1979.

Schulz, F. (1951) *Classical Roman Law*, Oxford: Clarendon Press.

Schur, Edwin M. (1983) *Labeling Women Deviant: Gender Stigma and Social Control*, Philadelphia: Temple University Press.

Schweitzer, A. (1917) 'Untersuchungen zur Chronologie und Geschichte der geometrischen Stile in Griechenland I', *Mitteilungen des Deutschen Archäologischen Instituts: Athenische Abteilung* 43: 1–152.

Seaford, R. (1994) *Reciprocity and Ritual: Homer and Tragedy in the Developing City-State*, Oxford: Clarendon Press.

Sealey, R. (1990) *Women and Law in Classical Greece*, Chapel Hill and London: University of North Carolina Press.

Seccombe, W. (1992) *A Millennium of Family Change: Feudalism to Capitalism in Northwestern Europe*, London and New York: Verso.

Segal, Lore (1989) 'The reverse bug', *The New Yorker*, 1 May: 34–40.

Seymour, T.D. (1908) *Life in the Homeric Age*, New York: Macmillan.

Shanks, Michael (1992) 'Artifact design and pottery from Archaic Korinth (c. 720–640 BCE). An archaeological interpretation', PhD thesis, Cambridge Univerity.

Shapiro, H.A. (1981) 'Courtship scenes in Attic vase-painting', *American Journal of Archaeology* 85: 133–43.

Shapiro, H.A. (1989) *Art and Cult under the Tyrants in Athens*, Mainz: Philipp von Zabern.

Shatzman, I. (1972) 'The Roman general's authority over booty', *Historia* 21: 177–205.

Shaw, B. and Saller, R. (1981) 'Editors' introduction', in Finley 1981: ix–xxvi.

Shaw, Joseph (1989) 'Phoenicians in southern Crete', *American Journal of Archaeology* 93: 165–83.

Shear, T.L. Jr. (1982) 'The demolished temple at Eleusis', *Studies in Athenian Architecture, Sculpture and Topography Presented to Homer A. Thompson*, *Hesperia* Supplement 20, Princeton: Princeton University Press, 128–40.

Sherratt, S. and Sherratt, A. (1991) 'From luxuries to commodities: the nature of Mediterranean Bronze Age trading systems', in N.H. Gale (ed.) *Bronze Age Trade in the Mediterranean*, Jonsered: *Studies in Mediterranean Archaeology* 90, 351–86.

Sherratt, S. and Sherratt, A. (1993) 'The growth of the Mediterranean economy in the early first millennium BC', *World Archaeology* 24: 361–78.

Shorter, E. (1977) *The Making of the Modern Family*, London: Fontana.

Sieff, D.A. (1990) 'Explaining biased sex ratios in human populations: a critique of recent studies', *Current Anthropology* 31: 25–48.

Siegel, Rudolph E. (1976) *Galen: On the Affected Parts*, Basle, New York: Karger.

Silver, Allan (1989) 'Friendship and trust as moral ideals: an historical approach', *European Journal of Sociology* 30: 274–97.

Silver, Allan (1990) 'Friendship in commercial society: eighteenth-century social theory and modern sociology', *American Journal of Sociology* 95: 1474–1504.

Simon, B. (1978) *Mind and Madness in Ancient Greece: The Classical Roots of Modern Psychiatry*, Ithaca, NY: Cornell University Press.

Simonsuuri, Kirsti (1979) *Homer's Original Genius: Eighteenth-Century Notions of the Early Greek Epic (1688–1798)*, Cambridge: Cambridge University Press.

Skeat, Theodore C. (1932) *The Dorians in Archaeology*, London: A. Moring.

Skinner, Marilyn B. (1979) 'Parasites and strange bedfellows: a study in Catullus' political imagery', *Ramus* 8: 137–52.

Skinner, Marilyn B. (1993) '*Ego mulier*: the construction of male sexuality in Catullus', *Helios* 20: 107–30.

Skinner, Quentin (1985) 'Introduction: the return of grand theory', in Skinner (ed.)

The Return of Grand Theory in the Social Sciences, Cambridge: Cambridge University Press, 3–20.

Slater, Niall W. (1990) *Reading Petronius*, Baltimore: Johns Hopkins University Press.

Smith, E.A. and Smith, S.A. (1995) 'Inuit sex-ratio variation. Population control, ethnographic error, or parental manipulation?', *Current Anthropology* 36: 595–624.

Smith, Martin S. (ed.) (1975) *Petronii Arbitri Cena Trimalchionis*, Oxford: Clarendon Press.

Smith, R.D. (1995) 'The inapplicability principle: what chaos means for social science', *Behavioral Science* 40: 22–40.

Smith, R.R.R. (1991) *Hellenistic Sculpture: A Handbook*, London: Thames & Hudson.

Snell, Bruno (1953) *The Discovery of the Mind*, trans. T.G. Rosenmeyer, Oxford: Basil Blackwell.

Snodgrass, Anthony M. (1964) *Early Greek Armour and Weapons*, Edinburgh: Edinburgh University Press.

Snodgrass, Anthony M. (1965a) 'The hoplite reform and history', *Journal of Hellenic Studies* 85: 110–22.

Snodgrass, Anthony M. (1965b) 'Barbarian Europe and early Iron Age Greece', *Proceedings of the Prehistoric Society* 31: 229–40.

Snodgrass, Anthony M. (1971) *The Dark Age of Greece*, Edinburgh: Edinburgh University Press.

Snodgrass, Anthony M. (1974) 'An historical Homeric society?', *Journal of Hellenic Studies* 94: 114–25.

Snodgrass, Anthony M. (1977) *Archaeology and the Rise of the Greek State*, Cambridge: Cambridge University Press.

Snodgrass, Anthony M. (1980) *Archaic Greece*, London: Dent.

Snodgrass, Anthony M. (1982) 'La prospection archéologique en Grèce et dans le monde méditerranéen', *Annales: économies, sociétés, civilisations* 37: 800–12.

Snodgrass, Anthony M. (1986) 'Interaction by design: the Greek city-state', in Colin Renfrew and John Cherry (eds) *Peer Polity Interaction and the Development of Sociocultural Complexity*, Cambridge: Cambridge University Press, 47–58.

Snodgrass, Anthony M. (1987) *An Archaeology of Greece*, Berkeley: University of California Press.

Snodgrass, Anthony M. (1990) 'Survey archaeology and the rural landscape of the Greek city', in Oswyn Murray and Simon Price (eds) *The Greek City from Homer to Alexander*, Oxford: Oxford University Press, 113–36.

Snodgrass, Anthony M. (1991) 'Archaeology and the study of the Greek city', in John Rich and Andrew Wallace-Hadrill (eds) *City and Country in the Ancient World*, London: Routledge, 1–24.

Snodgrass, Anthony M. (1993) 'The rise of the polis: the archaeological evidence', in Hansen 1993: 30–40.

Snodgrass, Anthony M. (1994) 'The growth and standing of the early western colonies', in Gocha Tsetskhladze and Franco de Angelis (eds) *The Archaeology of Greek Colonisation*, Oxford: Oxford University Committee for Archaeology, Monograph 10, 1–10.

Sokolowski, F. (1962) *Lois sacrées des cités grecques, Supplément*, Paris: de Boccard.

Sokolowski, F. (1969) *Lois sacrées des cités grecques*, Paris: de Boccard.

Sourvinou-Inwood, C. (1981) 'To die and enter the house of Hades: Homer, before and after', in J. Whaley (ed.), *Mirrors of Mortality. Studies in the Social History of Death*, New York: St Martin's Press, 15–39.

Sourvinou-Inwood, C. (1983) 'A trauma in flux: death in the 8th century and after', in Hägg 1983: 33–48.

Sourvinou-Inwood, C. (1988a) 'Further aspects of polis religion', *Annali dell' istituto universitario orientale di Napoli: Sezione di archeologia e storia antica* 10: 259–74.

Sourvinou-Inwood, C. (1988b) *Studies in Girls' Transitions: Aspects of the Arkteia and Age Representation in Attic Iconography*, Athens: Kardamitsa.

Sourvinou-Inwood, C. (1990) 'What is polis religion?', in O. Murray and S. Price (eds) *The Greek City from Homer to Alexander*, Oxford: Clarendon Press, 297–322.

Sourvinou-Inwood, C. (1991) *'Reading' Greek Culture: Texts and Images, Rituals and Myths*, Oxford: Clarendon Press.

Sourvinou-Inwood, C. (1993) 'Early sanctuaries, the eighth century and ritual space: fragments of a discourse', in Marinatos and Hägg 1993: 1–17.

Sourvinou-Inwood, C. (1994) *'Reading' Greek Death. To the End of the Classical Period*, Oxford: Clarendon Press.

Spacks, Patricia Meyer (1995) *Boredom: A Literary History of a State of Mind*, Chicago: University of Chicago Press.

Spencer, Nigel (1995) *Time, Tradition, and Society in Greek Archaeology*, London and New York: Routledge.

Spencer, W.G. (trans.) (1948–53) *Celsus: De Medicina*, 3 vols, London: Heinemann.

Spivey, N. (1991) 'Greek vases in Etruria', in Rasmussen and Spivey (1991): 131–50.

Stallybrass, Peter and White, Allon (1986) *The Politics and Poetics of Transgression*, Ithaca, NY: Cornell University Press.

Stanton, Domna C. (1992a) 'Introduction: the subject of sexuality', in Stanton 1992b: 1–46.

Stanton, Domna C. (ed.) (1992b) *Discourses of Sexuality: From Aristotle to AIDS*, Ann Arbor: University of Michigan Press.

Stanton, G.R. (1988) *'Teknon, pais*, and related words in Koine Greek', in B.G. Mandilaras (ed.) *Proceedings of the XVIIIth International Congress of Papyrology, Athens, 25–31 May 1986* 1, Athens: Greek Papyrological Society, 463–80.

Stanyan, Temple (1739) *The Grecian History*, London: J. Temple and R. Tonson.

Starobinski, J. (1962) *History of the Treatment of Melancholy from the Earliest Times to 1900*, Basle: J.R. Geigy.

Starr, Chester G. (1961) *The Origins of Greek Civilization*, New York: Knopf.

Starr, Chester G. (1974) Review of Desborough (1972), *American Journal of Philology* 95: 114–16.

Starr, Chester G. (1977) *Economic and Social Growth of Early Greece, 800–500 BC*, Oxford: Oxford University Press.

Starr, Chester G. (1992) 'History and archaeology in the early first millennium BC', in Kopcke and Tokumaru 1992: 1–6.

Stearns, C.Z. and Stearns, P.N. (1988) 'Introduction' in Stearns and Stearns (eds) *Emotion and Social Change: Toward a New Psychohistory*, New York and London: Holmes and Meier, 1–21.

Steenburg, D. (1991) 'Chaos and the marriage of heaven and hell', *Harvard Theological Review* 84: 447–66.

Stone, L. (1977) *The Family, Sex and Marriage in England, 1500–1800*, London: Weidenfeld & Nicholson.

Stone, M.A. (1989) 'Chaos, prediction, and LaPlacean determinism', *American Philosophical Quarterly* 26: 123–31.

Strauss, Barry S. (1991) 'Athenian exile and diaspora in the Peloponnesian war', in John M. Fossey (ed.) *Proceedings of the First International Congress on the Hellenic Diaspora from Antiquity to Modern Times*, vol. 1: *From Antiquity to 1453*, Amsterdam: J.C. Gieben, 61–71.

Strauss, Barry S. (1993a) Review of Golden (1990), *Classical Philology* 88: 90–94.

Strauss, Barry S. (1993b) *Fathers and Sons in Athens: Ideology and Society in the Era of the Peloponnesian War*, Princeton University Press.

Stubbings, Frank (1962) 'Editorial preface', in Wace and Stubbings 1962: v–viii.

Suleiman, Susan Rubin (ed.) (1986) *The Female Body in Western Culture*, Cambridge, MA: Harvard University Press.

Syme, Ronald (1986) *The Augustan Aristocracy*, Oxford: Clarendon Press.

Tandy, D. and Neale, W.C. (1994) 'Karl Polanyi's distinctive approach to social analysis and the case of ancient Greece', in Colin Duncan and David Tandy (eds) *From Political Economy to Anthropology*, Montreal: Black Rose, 9–33.

Taylor, Charles (1989) *Sources of the Self: The Making of the Modern Identity*, Cambridge, MA: Harvard University Press.

Telfer, Elizabeth (1991) 'Friendship', in Michael Pakaluk (ed.) *Other Selves: Philosophers on Friendship*, Indianapolis: Hackett, 250–67.

Themelis, P.G. (1983) 'Delphoi kai periochê ton 8° kai 7° p.Ch. aiôna', *Annuario della scuola archeologica di Atene e delle missioni italiane in oriente* 45: 213–55.

Thirlwall, Connop (1835) *History of Greece* I, London: Longman.

Thomas, Brook (1991) *The New Historicism and Other Old Fashioned Topics*, Princeton: Princeton University Press.

Thomas, Elizabeth Marshall (1993) *The Hidden Life of Dogs*, Boston: Houghton Mifflin.

Thomas, Julian (1995) *Time, Culture, and Identity*, London and New York: Routledge.

Thompson, H.A. and Wycherley, R.E. (1972) *The Athenian Agora* vol. xiv. *The Agora of Athens. The History, Shape and Uses of an Ancient City Centre*, Princeton: Princeton University Press.

Thompson, W.E. (1985) 'Fragments of the preserved historians – especially Polybius', in *The Greek Historians: Literature and History. Papers Presented to A.E. Raubitschek*, Stanford: Department of Classics, Stanford University, 119–39.

Thury, E.M. (1988) 'A study of words relating to youth and old age in the plays of Euripides and its special implications for Euripides' *Suppliant Women*', *Computers and the Humanities* 22: 293–306.

Toepffer, A. (1889) *Attische Genealogie*, Berlin: Weidmann.

Toohey, Peter (1987) 'Plutarch, *Pyrrh.* 13: *alys nautiôdês*', *Glotta* 65: 199–202.

Toohey, Peter (1988) 'Some ancient notions of boredom', *Illinois Classical Studies* 13: 151–64.

Toohey, Peter (1990) 'Some ancient histories of literary melancholia', *Illinois Classical Studies* 15: 143–63.

Toohey, Peter (1992) 'Love, lovesickness, and melancholia', *Illinois Classical Studies* 17: 265–86.

Travlos, J. (1971) *Pictorial Dictionary of Ancient Athens*, New York: Praeger.

Travlos, J. (1983) 'Hê Athêna kai hê Eleusina ston 8° kai 7° p.Ch. aiôna', *Annuario della scuola archeologica di Atene e delle missioni italiane in oriente* 45: 323–38.

Travlos, J. (1988) *Bildlexikon zur Topographie des Antiken Attika*, Tübingen: Wasmuth.

Treggiari, Susan (1991) *Roman Marriage: Iusti Coniuges from the Time of Cicero to the Time of Ulpian*, Oxford: Clarendon Press.

Trigger, Bruce (1989) *A History of Archaeological Thought*, Cambridge: Cambridge University Press.

Trumbach, Randolf (1978) *The Rise of the Egalitarian Family: Aristocratic Kinship and Domestic Relations in Eighteenth Century England*, New York: Academic Press.

Tsountas, C. and Manatt, J. (1897) *Mycenae and Mycenaean Civilisation*, New York: Houghton, Mifflin and Company.

Turner, Frank M. (1981) *The Greek Heritage in Victorian Britain*, New Haven: Yale University Press.

Turner, James Grantham (ed.) (1993) *Sexuality and Gender in Early Modern Europe*, Cambridge: Cambridge University Press.

Vaio, John (1990) 'Gladstone and the early reception of Schliemann in England', in Calder and Cobet 1990: 415–30.

van Hook, L.R. (1920) 'The exposure of infants at Athens', *Transactions of the American Philological Association* 51: 134–45.

van Wees, Hans (1992) *Status Warriors*, Amsterdam: Gieben.

Veeser, H. Aram (ed.) (1989) *The New Historicism*, New York: Routledge.

Verdelis, N.M. (1958) *Ho Prôtogeômetrikos Rythmos en Thessalia*, Athens: Bibliothêkê tês en Athênais Archaiologikês Hetaireias.

Vérilhac, A.-M. (1982) *PAIDES AÔROI. Poésie funéraire 2, Pragmateiai tês Akadêmias Athênôn* 41, Athens: *Grapheion Demosieumatôn tês Akadêmias Athênôn*.

Vernant, Jean-Paul (1965) *Mythe et pensée chez les Grecs*, Paris: François Maspéro.

Vernant, Jean-Paul (1983) *Myth and Thought among the Greeks*, trans. J. Lloyd, London: Routledge & Kegan Paul.

Vestergaard, T., Hansen, M.H., Rubinstein, L., Bjertrup, L., and Nielsen, T.H. (1992) 'The age-structure of Athenian citizens commemorated in sepulchral inscriptions', *Classica et Mediaevalia* 43: 5–21.

Veyne, P. (1978) 'La famille et l'amour sous le haut-empire romain', *Annales: économies, sociétés, civilisations* 33: 345–63.

Victor, K. and Beaudry, M. (1992) 'Women's participation in American prehistoric and historic archaeology', in Cheryl Claasen (ed.) *Exploring Gender through Archaeology*, Madison: Prehistory Press, 11–21.

von Bothmer, D. (ed.) (1985) *The Amasis Painter and His World*, Malibu: J. Paul Getty Museum.

Wace, A. and Stubbings, F. (eds) (1962) *A Companion to Homer*, London: Macmillan.

Wace, A. and Thompson, M. (1912) 'Excavations at Halos', *Annual of the British School at Athens* 18: 1–29.

Wack, M.F. (1990) *Lovesickness in the Middle Ages: The 'Viaticum' and its Commentaries*, Philadelphia: University of Pennsylvania Press.

Walbank, F.W. (1957) *A Historical Commentary on Polybius* 1, Oxford: Clarendon Press.

Walbank, F.W. (1972) *Polybius*, Berkeley and Los Angeles: University of California Press.

Walbank, F.W. (1979) *A Historical Commentary on Polybius* 3, Oxford: Clarendon Press.

Walbank, F.W. (1991/92) 'The Hellenistic world: new trends and directions', *Scripta Classica Israelica* 11: 90–113.

Walde, D. and Willows, N. (eds) (1991) *The Archaeology of Gender*, Calgary: University of Calgary Archaeological Association.

Waldstein, Charles (1900) 'The earliest Hellenic art and civilization and the Argive Heraeum', *American Journal of Archaeology* 4: 40–73.

Wallace-Hadrill, Andrew (1987) 'Time for Augustus', in Michael Whitby, Philip Hardie, and Mary Whitby (eds) *Homo Viator: Critical Essays for John Bramble*, Bristol: Bristol University Press.

Wallace-Hadrill, Andrew (1988) 'The social structure of the Roman house', *Papers of the British School at Rome* 56: 43–97.

Ward, W.A., and Joukowsky, M.S. (eds) (1992) *The Crisis Years: The Twelfth Century BC*, Dubuque: Kendall-Hunt.

Watson, A. (1965) 'The divorce of Carvilius Ruga', *Tijdschrift voor Rechtsgeschiedenis* 33: 38–50.

Watson, A. (1975) *Rome of the Twelve Tables – Persons and Property*, Princeton: Princeton University Press.

Wayne, Don E. (1991) 'New Historicism' in Martin Coyle, Peter Garside, Malcolm Kelsall, and John Peck (eds) *Encyclopedia of Literature and Criticism*, London: Routledge.

Wemelsfelder, F. (1985) 'Animal boredom: is a scientific study of the subjective experiences of animals possible?', in M.W. Fox and L.S. Mickley (eds) *Advances in Animal Welfare Since 1984*, Boston: Martinus Nijhoff, 115–54.

Wemelsfelder, F. (1989) 'Boredom and laboratory animal welfare', in B.E. Rollin (ed.) *The Experimental Animal in Biomedical Research*, Boca Raton: CRC Press, 1–48.

West, M.L. (1983) *The Orphic Poems*, Oxford: Clarendon Press.

Westlake, H.D. (1968) *Individuals in Thucydides*, Cambridge, MA: Harvard University Press.

Wheatley, H.B. (ed.) (1962) *The Diary of Samuel Pepys*, London: G. Bell & Sons.

White, Luise (1994) 'Blood brotherhood revisited: kinship, relationship, and the body in East and Central Africa', *Africa* 64: 359–72.

White, Peter (1993) *Promised Verse: Poets in the Society of Augustan Rome*, Cambridge, MA: Harvard University Press.

Whitehouse, Helen (1986) *The British School at Athens: The First Hundred Years*, London: Thames and Hudson.

Whitley, James (1987) 'Art history, archaeology and idealism: the German tradition', in Ian Hodder (ed.) *Archaeology as Long-Term History*, Cambridge: Cambridge University Press, 9–15.

Whitley, James (1991) *Style and Society in Dark Age Greece*, Cambridge: Cambridge University Press.

Wiedemann, T.E.J. (1983) '*Elachiston ... en tois arsesi kleos*: Thucydides, women and the limits of rational analysis', *Greece & Rome* 30: 163–70.

Wilamowitz-Moellendorff, Ulrich von (1922) *Pindaros*, Berlin: Weidmann.

Wilamowitz-Moellendorff, Ulrich von (ed.) (1959) *Euripides Herakles*, vol. 3, 2nd edn, reprinted Darmstadt: Wissenschaftliche Buchgesellschaft.

Williams, B. (1993) *Shame and Necessity*, Berkeley and Los Angeles: University of California Press.

Winkler, John J. (1990a) 'Introduction', in Halperin *et al.* 1990: 3–20.

Winkler, John J. (1990b) *The Constraints of Desire*, New York: Routledge.

Wirth, Friedrich (1938) 'Der nordische Charakter des Griechentums', *Mannus* 30: 222–46.

Wittig, Monique (1981) 'One is not born a woman', *Feminist Issues* 1, 2: 47–54.

Wojcik, M.R. (1989) *Museo Claudio Faina di Orvieto: Ceramica attica a figure nere*, Perugia: 'Curatela scientifica di Francesco Roncalli'.

Wolf, Eric R. (1966) 'Kinship, friendship, and patron–client relations in complex societies', in Michael Banton (ed.) *The Social Anthropology of Complex Societies*, New York: Frederick A. Praeger, 1–22.

Wolf, Friedrich Augustus (1985) [1795] *Prolegomena to Homer*, Anthony Grafton, Glenn Most, and James Zetzel (eds), Princeton: Princeton University Press.

Wood, Gordon S. (1992) *The Radicalism of the American Revolution*, New York: Alfred A. Knopf.

Wood, I.N. (1992) 'Continuity or calamity? The constraints of literary models', in J. Drinkwater and H. Elton (eds) *Fifth-century Gaul: A Crisis of Identity?*, Cambridge: Cambridge University Press, 9–18.

Young, David C. (1964) 'Pindaric criticism', *Minnesota Review* 4: 584–641.

Zahn, R. (1970) 'Das Kind in der antiken Kunst', *Forschungen und Berichte*, Berlin: Berlin Museum, 12: 21–31 (a lecture first delivered in 1926).

Zanker, Paul (1988) *The Power of Images in the Age of Augustus*, trans. H.A. Shapiro, Ann Arbor: University of Michigan Press.

Ziro, D.G. (1991) *Eleusis: hê kyria eisodos tou hierou tês Eleusinos*, Athens: Bibliothêkê tês en Athênais archaiologikês Hetaireias.

Zweig, Bella (1993) 'The primal mind: using Native American models for the study of women in ancient Greece', in Rabinowitz and Richlin 1993: 145–80.

INDEX